Accelerating Climate Action in Israel

REFOCUSING MITIGATION POLICIES FOR THE ELECTRICITY, RESIDENTIAL AND TRANSPORT SECTORS

OECD
BETTER POLICIES FOR BETTER LIVES

Please cite this publication as:
OECD (2020), *Accelerating Climate Action in Israel: Refocusing Mitigation Policies for the Electricity, Residential and Transport Sectors*, OECD Publishing, Paris, *https://doi.org/10.1787/fb32aabd-en*.

ISBN 978-92-64-68251-1 (print)
ISBN 978-92-64-42029-8 (pdf)

Photo credits: Cover © vvvita/Shutterstock.

Corrigenda to publications may be found on line at: *www.oecd.org/about/publishing/corrigenda.htm*.

Foreword

Israel, along with the rest of the world, is confronting an immediate health and economic crisis due to COVID-19, which is adding greater complexity to the low-carbon transition. The development of Israel's long-term low emissions development strategy (LT-LEDS) has constituted an opportunity to align government action around the pursuit of a low-emissions future. This instrument is today, more than ever; key to support the alignment of near-term action with long-term goals. An integrated approach that addresses climate and well-being as part of a cohesive and coherent strategy is indispensable for making climate action more feasible, acceptable and cost effective as well as to avoiding further lock-in of emissions and inequalities. Developing sectoral policy packages in line with this approach – especially for sectors that are difficult or key to decarbonise - will be necessary. This will allow Israel to transform the economy, benefit from its capacity for technological innovation, and reach multiple well-being priorities while building its resilience towards future shocks, such as heat waves, droughts or other diseases.

This report is part of a collaboration project between Israel's Ministry of Environmental Protection and the OECD Environment Directorate to support the development of Israel's LT-LEDS. The report is an input to governmental discussions in Israel to develop a roadmap that will back the implementation of Israel's LT-LEDS. It analyses needed actions in the next five to ten years to align three sectors – electricity, residential and transport – with long-term climate objectives and broader well-being goals such as incomes, jobs, good and affordable housing, access to services and opportunities, health, and equity. Whilst written before the COVID-19 crisis, this report can inform decisions for Israel's economic recovery, helping to ensure that stimulus packages do not risk locking the country into carbon intensive infrastructure and activities, but instead advance and catalyse long-term aims for well-being in the country, of which climate change mitigation is a pillar.

This report can also serve as a resource for other governments, particularly as countries form stimulus packages to recover from COVID-19 and continue to work on longer-term instruments (such as revised Nationally Appropriate Mitigation Actions – NDCs or LT-LEDs). There are examples of national and sub-national governments who are using the recovery from COVID-19, as an opportunity to advance both climate and wider well-being goals, but this is far from ubiquitous. This OECD report provides an application of the well-being approach to climate change mitigation, which governments can use to increase viability and acceptance of climate action, while ensuring consistency across actions planned for different timeframes.

Rodolfo Lacy

OECD Environment Director

Acknowledgments

This working paper is an output of the Climate, Biodiversity, and Water Division of the OECD Environment Directorate. It has been prepared under item 2.3.2.2.1 in the Programme of Work and Budget for 2019-2020 of the Environmental Policy Committee (EPOC).

The report was authored by Aimée Aguilar-Jaber, Brilé Anderson, Hélène Blake, Daniel Nachtigall and Fatoumata Ngom from the Climate Change Mitigation team of the OECD Environment Directorate (ENV). All authors contributed to the analysis and drafting of this report. Simon Buckle (ENV), Nicolina Lamhauge (ENV), and Aimée Aguilar-Jaber (ENV) supervised the preparation of the report.

The authors would like to thank OECD colleagues for the input and comments on earlier versions of the report: Nils Axel Braathen (ENV), Gérard Bonnis (ENV), Lisa Danielson (ENV), Alexander Dobrinevski (ENV), Jane Ellis (ENV), Chiara Falduto (ENV), Florens Flues (CTP), Federico Giovannelli (ECO), Daniela Glocker (ECO), Andrés Fuentes Hutfilter (CFE), Katia Karousakis (ENV), Mireille Martini (ENV), Rokas Markunas (BIAC), Dimitrios Papaioannou (ITF), Stephen Perkins (ITF), Edward Perry (ENV), Marissa Plouen (CFE), Oliver Roehn (ECO), Dirk Röttgers (ENV), Will Symes (TAD), Aayush Tandon (ENV), Jonas Teusch (CTP), and Kurt Van Dender (CTP). In addition, the authors would like to thank Israeli colleagues for their contributions to earlier versions: Avital Eshet (Ministry of Environmental Protection), Yuval Laster (Ministry of Environmental Protection), Gil Proaktor (Ministry of Environmental Protection), and Ron Kamara (Eco Traders). The authors are also grateful for the oversight, review and comments by the Working Party on Climate, Investment, and Development (WPCID) and the Environment Policy Committee (EPOC). The final report benefited greatly from the assistance of Sama Al Taher Cucci (ENV) and Elodie Prata-Leal (ENV).

Financial support from Ministry of Environmental Protection in Israel is gratefully acknowledged.

Table of contents

FIGURES

TABLES

Follow OECD Publications on:

http://twitter.com/OECD_Pubs

http://www.facebook.com/OECDPublications

http://www.linkedin.com/groups/OECD-Publications-4645871

http://www.youtube.com/oecdilibrary

OECD Alerts http://www.oecd.org/oecddirect/

This book has...

StatLinks
A service that delivers Excel® files from the printed page!

Look for the *StatLinks* at the bottom of the tables or graphs in this book. To download the matching Excel® spreadsheet, just type the link into your Internet browser, starting with the ***https://doi.org*** prefix, or click on the link from the e-book edition.

Abbreviations and acronyms

AMB	Àrea Metropolitana de Barcelona
BAU	Business as Usual
BER	Building Emissions Rate
BID	Business Improvement Districts
BRT	Bus Rapid Transit
CCUS	Carbon capture, utilisation and storage
CIL	Community Infrastructure Levy
CNG	Compressed Natural Gas
CO_2	Carbon dioxide
CO_2e	Carbon dioxide equivalent
CV	Contribución de Valorización
DEFRA	Department for Environment, Food and Rural Affairs
DER	Dwelling Emissions Rate
DfT	Department for Transport
DG	Distributed Generation
DR	Demand response
EDS	Economic Development Strategy
ENTSO-E	European Network of Transmission System Operators
EV	Electric Vehicles
FiP	Feed-in premiums
FIT	Feed-in-Tarrifs
GBD	Green Business District
GBP	British pound
GHG	Greenhouse gases
GIVAT	green infrastructure valuation toolkit
GSF	Green Space Factor
IEC	Israel Electric Corporation
IMF	International Monetary Fund
IPA	Israeli Planning Administration
IPP	Independent power producers
IPPC	Intergovernmental Panel on Climate Change
JTMT	Jerusalem Transportation Masterplan Team
KfW	Kreditanstalt für Wiederaufbau
kWh	kilowatt hour
LCOE	Levelised cost of electricity
LEED	Leadership in Energy and Environmental Design
LEZ	Low Emission Zones
LIHCS	low-income high-cost share
LNG	Liquid Natural Gas
LT-LEDS	Long-term low emission development strategies

LVC	Land Value Capture
MaaS	Mobility as a Service
Mayoral CIL	Mayoral CIL
Mbi	Market-based instruments
MEAT	Most Economically Advantageous Tender
MEP	Minimum energy performance standards
MOT	Ministry of Transport
MRDH	Metropole Region Rotterdam The Hague
Mt	Megatonnes
MTA	Metropolitan Transport Authorities
MTS	Mayor's Transport Strategy
MWh	Megawatt hours
NDC	Nationally Determined Contribution
NGSF	Network for Greening the Financial System
NIS	Israeli Dollar
NO_x	Nitrous oxides
OAPF	Opportunity Area Planning Framework
p.a.	per annum
PDU	Plan de Déplacements Urbains
PDUIF	Plan de Développement Urbain Île-de-France
PM	Particulate Matter
PPP	Public-Private Partnerships
PTAL	Public Transport Accessibility Level
PV	Photovolaic
REIPPP	Renewable Energy Independent Power Procurement Program
SCoT	Schéma de cohérence territoriale
SEK	Swedish Krona
SO_x	Sulphur oxides
SRQ	Sustainable Residential Quality
t	tonnes
TER	Target carbon dioxide Emission Rate
TfL	Transport for London
TIF	Tax Increment Finance
TWh	terawatt hours
UNFCCC	United Nations Framework Convention on Climate Change
USD	US Dollars
VRE	variable renewable energy
WebTAG	Web-based Transport analysis Guidance

Executive Summary

The development of Israel's long-term low emissions development strategy (LT-LEDS), a process led by the Ministry of Environmental Protection in Israel and supported by the OECD's Environment Directorate, provides a unique opportunity to align efforts across the government to create a low-emissions future. So far, 17 countries have submitted LT-LEDS to the UNFCCC. Even though, Israel's greenhouse gas (GHG) emissions are small in global terms; *emissions have been rising in recent years.* If Israel continues on this trajectory, emissions would rise about 23.6% by 2030 (from 80.18 $MtCO_2e$ in 2015 to nearly 99.1 $MtCO_2e$ by 2030).[1] Putting in place policy packages in the near-term is essential to achieve the deep emission reductions needed in the longer-term.

This report is one input to whole of government discussions for the development of a roadmap to support Israel's LT-LEDS. It offers policy recommendations based on in-depth analysis for next five to ten years in the electricity, residential and transport sectors that will not only reduce emissions now, but will also kick-start the systemic transformations needed beyond that. The report takes a well-being approach, recognising that climate change is just one of Israel's policy priorities and climate action must be fully integrated into other societal agendas – income, jobs, affordable housing, reliable energy, improved accessibility, good air quality, health, life quality in cities, and biodiversity. While written before the COVID-19 crisis, this report can also inform decisions on Israel's recovery from this crisis, helping to ensure that recovery measures integrate climate action and avoid lock-in to "inferior" carbon-intensive paradigms that may also entrench inequalities and reduce life quality more broadly.

Prioritising renewable energy over fossil fuel generation in the electricity sector ensures a pathway to low-carbon future, whilst safeguarding well-being. The use of the recently discovered natural gas resources in Israel can reduce GHG emissions (compared to coal), but creating an electricity system based predominantly on natural gas will jeopardise deep decarbonisation goals due to the lock-in of carbon intensive infrastructure and will not fully resolve air pollution problems. Solar PV, in contrast, is cheaper than gas *and* its use would reduce air pollution and improve health, create jobs as well as provide other benefits. Pricing fossil fuels according to their carbon content - and other external damages from extraction and use - will discourage the use of natural gas. In the meantime, Israel can scale up renewable electricity deployment by removing administrative barriers, upgrading the transmission network, and promoting energy efficiency to reduce future strain on the grid (e.g., strengthening energy performance standards). In parallel, pursuing demand-side responsiveness (i.e. managing when consumers use electricity) can facilitate flexibility in the grid and better accommodate the expansion of renewables.

The residential sector is undergoing a rapid transformation in Israel, since the government is in the process of building 1.5 million new homes by 2040. Ensuring that these new homes use state-of-the-art designs to minimise energy usage to the greatest extent possible during the building's life is pertinent to avoid locking-in carbon-intensive housing, for example, by establishing emission limits on buildings (since none presently exist for new or existing buildings). Likewise, minimising embodied carbon (from construction, retrofits, and demolition of buildings), for example, by using green public procurement will help to reduce emissions across the lifecycle of a building. Managing and planning for rapid growth in housing in cities, e.g. via minimum densities, urban infill, or redeveloping brownfield sites, is also key to create cities that are more compact and sustainable. Nevertheless, careful attention needs to be paid to ensuring the continued liveability of cities as they become denser, for example, by upgrading infrastructure, planning for green spaces to curb heat island effects and contribute to physical and mental health, and guaranteeing that newly built homes are accessible to opportunities and services. Devolving responsibility to municipalities and increasing their financial capacity will help to better guide this growth in light of local circumstances.

In transport, focusing policies on accessibility (the ease of reaching opportunities) rather than mobility (physical movement) can unlock greater emission reductions. Mainstreaming accessibility criteria into appraisal methodologies of projects is a means to steer investment towards public transport (buses, trams, and so on) and active modes (e.g., walking or cycling). Reallocating and re-designing road space in Israel as to prioritise public and active transport modes will help ease the transition away from private vehicles. In addition, tools such as congestion charging and parking policies will enable a more efficient use of space. Better aligning fuel taxation with the carbon content of fuels, for example, by phasing out tax benefits for diesel consumption, will also help to limit environmental and social damage. Accessibility-focused policy could be facilitated by shifting funding and responsibility towards local levels, for example, via Metropolitan Transport Authorities in order to enhance responsiveness whilst avoiding over-fragmentation of responsibilities.

Notes

[1] Ministry of Environmental Protection (2018): Israel's third national communication on climate change

1 Introduction

This chapter argues that by approaching climate change mitigation through a well-being lens, Israel can not only reduce its emissions, avoid locking in carbon-intensive technologies, but also improve the well-being of its citizens, both, now and in the future. A well-being lens can also help build the social and political support amongst stakeholders to accelerate action on climate. The chapter also brings a summary of the main findings and recommendations that result from following this approach in Israel's electricity, residential and transport sectors.

1.1. How to accelerate climate action in Israel

Urgent, accelerated and concerted action is needed to limit global warming to well-below 2°C, let alone 1.5°C (IPCC, 2018[1]). At whatever temperature target, anthropogenic net emissions of (long-lived) carbon dioxide to the atmosphere must fall to zero or below globally. This means that while major emitters have to accelerate their actions to reduce greenhouse gas (GHG) emissions, even smaller countries contributing only a fraction of global emissions like Israel, also need to move to pathways consistent with net-zero carbon dioxide emissions by around the middle of this century or shortly thereafter. Limiting climate change necessitates a systemic transformational change across sectors (IPCC, 2018[1]). Nevertheless, the evolution of this change – and the policies used to catalyse decarbonisation – will have to be adjusted to national circumstances, priorities and challenges (OECD, 2019[2]).

Collective failure to achieve a balance in GHG emissions from sources and removal by sinks in the second half of this century will have severe consequences. The recent Intergovernmental Panel on Climate Change (IPCC) Special Report on Global Warming of 1.5°C warns that climate-related risks to health, livelihoods, food security, water supply, human security and the economy will all increase with the extent of climatic change. Israel along with other Mediterranean countries is expected to suffer major impacts. In particular, increasing severity as well as frequency of extreme heat, droughts and wildfires (OECD, 2019[2]; Ministry of Environmental Protection, 2018[3]), increasing pressure on ecosystems, health, food production, as well as exacerbating the already existing problem of water scarcity in the country (Cramer et al., 2018[4]). Even in a moderate climate change scenario (Representative Concentration Pathway 4.5), winter temperatures could increase by 1.5°C to 3°C while summer temperatures by 1.5°C to 4°C by 2100 relative to 1986-2005 (Ministry of Environmental Protection, 2018[3]).[1] Israel is well-placed to use its advanced technological expertise, for example in the water sector, to help it and other countries to adapt. However, still poorly understood future climate extremes and potential tipping points in the climate system mean that effective adaptation action and societal resilience requires strong mitigation action globally to limit climate risks.

Israel's GHG emissions have been rising in recent years. In 2015, GHG emissions increased by 40% above their level in 2000, reaching 80.18 $MtCO_2e$ or 9.38 tCO_2e per capita (Ministry of Environmental Protection, 2018[3]). This places Israel's *per capita* emissions in the midrange of those of OECD countries, lower than countries like Australia (22 tCO_2e per capita) and the US (20 tCO_2e per capita), but higher than countries with comparable climate conditions, including Greece (8.6 tCO_2e per capita), Italy (7.1 tCO_2e per capita) and Spain (7 tCO_2e per capita) (OECD, 2018[5]). If Israel continues down its present path, emissions would rise to nearly 99.1 $MtCO_2e$ by 2030 or 9.3 tCO_2e per capita (Ministry of Environmental Protection, 2018[3]). Energy and transport would be the biggest contributors, accounting for 53% and 21% of these emissions, respectively (Ministry of Environmental Protection, 2018[3]).

Israel is starting to change its course towards a lower carbon trajectory but only to a modest extent. In September 2015, Israel set a target of reducing GHG emissions to 7.7 tCO_2e per capita by 2030 in Decision 542, also contained in its Nationally Determined Contribution (NDC) submitted to the UNFCCC (Ministry of Environmental Protection, 2018[3]). The only other countries to have set per capita emission targets include Malawi, Albania, Armenia and Zimbabwe; the bulk of OECD countries set absolute emission reduction targets for 2030, typically, compared to 1990 or 2005 levels of GHG emissions. Under business as usual (BAU) assumptions, Israel's per capita target translates into an absolute emissions target of 76.3 $MtCO_2e$ as projected by the Ministry of Environmental Protection (2015[6]). This is only slightly lower than emissions in 2015 and almost 5% higher than emissions in 2005 (72.4 $MtCO_2e$). This pales in comparison to other OECD countries with similar GDP levels like Norway, which has committed to a 40% reduction in absolute emissions below 1990 levels by 2030, or facing similar climate conditions such as Spain and Portugal that committed to a reduction of 26 % and 17 % respectively, both relative to 2005 levels. Other small countries, albeit with lower population growth rates, are stepping up to the challenge with even greater ambition. For example, Denmark, who is aiming for 70% below 1990 levels by 2030 (UNFCCC, 2019[7]).

In addition to the economy-wide target, Decision 542 also includes specific targets in sectors included in the NDC (regarding energy efficiency, renewable energy and public transport), but the NDC itself does not include sector-specific targets (Ministry of Environmental Protection, 2018[3]). For example, Decision 542 aims to increase the share of renewables in electricity generation to 17% by 2030 and to reduce electricity consumption by at least 17% by 2030 and private car mileage by at least 20%, both relative to BAU. In addition, the Israeli government passed Decision 1403 in April 2016, which set up an advisory team to the Finance Minister, providing grants for energy efficiency.[2]

Israel is now confronted with the challenge of putting in place the policy packages that will catalyse deep emission reductions and ambitious sector-specific targets. Formulating an effective *policy package becomes complex given the realities on the ground.* For a range of reasons, Israel is an energy island to a large extent, cut off from sharing electricity with its neighbours. Energy security is paramount and has been reinforced by newly found natural gas reserves. Meanwhile, Israel faces a rapidly growing population (around a 2% increase each year) posing challenges for the availability and affordability of housing. In addition, it suffers high levels of congestion on its roads in comparison with other OECD countries (the societal costs of this are around 2% of GDP,[3] according to the Israeli Tax Authority) and an overall limited accessibility to opportunities for its population (in particular through active and public transport modes). The exposure of Israel's population to air pollution – $PM_{2.5}$ and PM_{10} - is one of the highest in OECD countries, causing 2,500 premature deaths per year (OECD, 2019[2]).

Attaining these broader wellbeing goals – whether affordable housing, reliable energy, improved accessibility, good health, life quality in cities, or biodiversity - depends on Israel's ability to limit climate risks. And the way in which these challenges are tackled will have major implications for Israel's future GHG emissions and its resilience to increasingly severe and frequent climate impacts. While climate change is just one of Israel's priorities, it must be fully integrated into these other agendas. These different objectives cannot be pursued separately, either financially or substantively (OECD, 2019[2]).

Climate actions will also be easier to implement politically, economically and socially – and more cost-effective – when there is ***two-way alignment*** between climate action and broader societal priorities (OECD, 2019[2]). Non-climate policies and action should support rather than undermine the pursuit of climate change mitigation goals (OECD, 2015[8]). Likewise, climate change mitigation should also meet other important societal goals, or in the least, identify and manage any trade-offs with such goals, in order to enhance the attractiveness and feasibility of such actions. Applying a well-being lens to these simultaneous challenges helps identify policy options that better capture the synergies between mitigation and other priorities (OECD, 2019[2]).[4] It can also help manage trade-offs, opening up the potential for more coherent policy packages that can yield significant benefits across different goals and sectors. A full definition of well-being is given in Box 1.1 below.

Moreover, the well-being benefits that can be achieved from well-designed GHG emissions reduction policies will accrue far earlier than the benefits from the reduction of climate risks. Improvements in well-being, as a by-product of mitigation, could therefore help counter the short-termism pervasive in decision-making at all levels, from individuals to governments (OECD, 2019[2]). For example, switching from coal to gas in Israel's electricity generation not only reduces electricity-related GHG emissions,[5] but also reduces emissions of nitrous oxides (NO_x) and sulphur oxides (SO_x)[6] that have damaging health effects (OECD, 2019[9]). This change brought important short-term health benefits - reductions in cardiovascular events and lower mortality in major cities (Ministry of Health, 2017[10]).

Conversely, any potentially negative well-being impacts are likely to inhibit, or even roll back, action on climate change mitigation. These potential negative impacts therefore need to be identified in advance of policy action, carefully analysed and managed in a targeted and cost-effective way. While some negative impacts may be unavoidable (e.g. some regressive impacts of pricing changes), they can be managed through complementary policies such as income transfers or energy efficiency improvements targeted at energy-poor households that can help vulnerable households cope with desired policy changes.

The objective of this report is to support the Ministry of Environmental Protection in Israel to identify climate actions that will be necessary in the near-term to reduce GHG emissions in three sectors – electricity, residential and transport, serving as input to whole of government discussions for the development of the roadmap to support Israel's Long-term Low Emissions Development Strategy (LT-LEDS). The report analyses the opportunities and challenges in each of these sectors and makes recommendations for how mitigation interventions can be better designed to integrate both climate and broader well-being objectives, i.e. to achieve greater two-way alignment. Wherever possible, the benefits and costs of these actions are quantified. While it was written before the current COVID-19 crisis, the report can also inform decisions about Israel's recovery from the crisis; ensuring that these foster transformation in the three sectors rather than lock them into "inferior" carbon-intensive paradigms that also entrench inequalities and reduce the quality of life more broadly.

Box 1.1. OECD and Israeli Well-being Frameworks

In broad terms, a state of well-being "requires meeting various human needs, some of which are essential (e.g. being in good health), as well as the ability to pursue one's goals, to thrive and feel satisfied with [one's] life" (OECD, 2011[11]). Throughout this report, the term "well-being" refers to present and future well-being.

The OECD Well-being Framework and the closely-related Israeli Framework on Well-being, Resilience, and Sustainability are analytical tools to examine well-being beyond its purely economic aspects. The OECD framework enables the analysis of the distribution of well-being across the population by analysing both current and future well-being, an important feature for climate change mitigation policies. Current well-being – in the OECD Framework- is broken into two domains, (1) material conditions and (2) quality of life. Each of these is disaggregated further into: income and wealth, jobs and earnings, housing conditions, health status, work and life balance, education and skills, social connections, civic engagement and governance, environmental quality, personal security and subjective well-being. These dimensions coincide with the Israeli Well-being Framework, with one addition in the Israeli framework of Information Technology (2016[12]). Future well-being in the OECD Framework captures the availability of the natural, economic, human and social capital stocks necessary to maintain well-being for future generations. This aspect was excluded from the Israeli framework, but is a critical element of well-being and sustainability.

Figure 1.1. OECD Well-being Framework

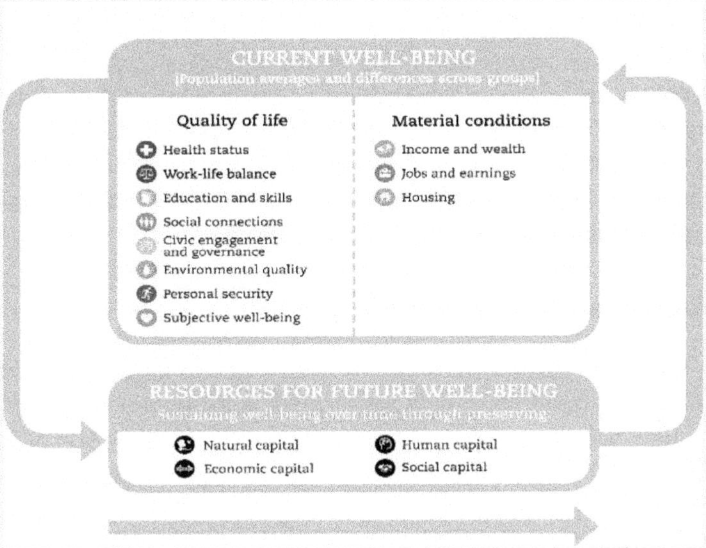

Source: (OECD, 2011[11])

OECD (2016[12]) finds that Israel is a top performer in comparison with other OECD countries, with respect to educational attainment, life satisfaction and health status in each of the two frameworks. However, it is one of the worst performing countries in terms of income poverty, housing and air pollution, when compared with other OECD countries (OECD, 2016[12]). Mitigation is an opportunity for Israel to improve its performance on these poorer performing dimensions as well as to ensure that it takes adequate account of the conditions under which future well-being can be better assured.

1.2. Aligning short-term actions with a low-carbon trajectory

The Ministry of Environmental Protection is in the process of developing Israel's LT-LEDS, as invited by the Paris Agreement (UNFCCC, 2015[13]). So far, 17 countries have submitted LT-LEDS to the UNFCCC. While there is no definition of what a LT-LEDS should be in the Paris Agreement, it typically envisions pathways for low emissions economic development taking into the account national, institutional, economic, technological and social circumstances (Aguilar Jaber et al., 2020[14]).One key recommendation, informed by an earlier OECD analysis of LT-LEDS in three major economies (Aguilar Jaber et al., 2020[14]), is the critical importance of broad political and societal commitment for these challenging, transformative pathways. One element of this commitment could be to enshrine the vision and targets of its LT-LEDS in national legislation to provide confidence to and set the expectations of different societal and economic actors about the long-term direction of change. ***This is the first recommendation of this report: that Israel should give appropriate legislative effect to the vision and goals of its LT-LEDS, once these have been developed and agreed***.

As Israel articulates a long-term vision until mid- century, simultaneous consideration also needs to be given to the near-term actions required to move the country towards this longer-term goal. Particular attention needs to be given to choices that might lock-in unsustainable development pathways that would impede the achievement of net-zero carbon dioxide emissions in the second half of the century. The objective of this report is to analyse what these near-term actions should be in the electricity (Chapter 2), residential (Chapter 3) and transport sectors (Chapter 4). The report also includes an Annex, which is focuses on how to align finance with the low-carbon transition.

As illustrated in the recent report, *Accelerating Climate Action: Refocusing policies through a well-being lens,* starting points matter (OECD, 2019[15]). Each sector is starting with existing infrastructure, policy and investment frameworks, political economy barriers and opportunities, in addition to the future challenges from climatic changes. This report analyses the starting points in each of these sectors to determine what near-term actions are feasible – indeed essential – to ensure a sustainable development pathway towards mid-century that avoids locking-in emissions-intensive infrastructure. The analysis also points to cross-sectoral actions to facilitate this, such as placing greater responsibility in the hands of municipalities. The rest of this section provides a brief overview of each of the chapters.

1.2.1. Electricity: Prioritise solar over natural gas (Chapter 2)

Electricity is the largest source of GHG emissions in Israel, accounting for almost 50% of emissions in 2016. A by-product of electricity generation with fossil fuels is air pollution, which takes its toll on public health reducing current well-being; it produced 85% and 58% of Israel's SO_x and NO_x emissions, respectively, in 2016 (OECD, 2018[16]). Over the last decade, natural gas has steadily replaced coal in electricity generation, rising from a share of 39% in 2010 to 66% in 2018, driven chiefly by the discovery of off-shore natural gas reserves. This discovery offers enhanced energy security, but still contributes to GHG emissions and other forms of pollution, albeit at a lower level than coal. A rising population and the electrification of end-use sectors means the increasing future electricity demand. This in turn will only lead to increasing emissions and pollution if unabated natural gas generation continues to dominate the generation mix. Despite a vast potential for solar generation, a key impediment is land availability close to demand centres.

Chapter 2 starts from these long-term trends and existing policy frameworks, charting a path forward for the electricity sector in Israel. It argues that predominantly relying on natural gas in the longer-term jeopardises deep decarbonisation and calls for urgent action to scale up solar generation. Accelerating the pace of renewables deployment would also enhance public health, spur economic development in rural areas (e.g. the Negev desert) and create high-tech jobs as well as export opportunities related to smart-grid technologies, all of which improve current and future well-being. Natural gas reserves could be used predominantly for industrial sectors where emissions are hard to abate or exported to countries with less abundant renewable resources. Revenues from royalties could feed a sovereign wealth fund that should adopt strong sustainability criteria for its investments.

Chapter 2 outlines how to accelerate the deployment of renewables, for example, by aligning energy taxes with the social costs of electricity generation, so that more polluting plants face higher costs than less polluting plants. Highlighting the role of continuing support for renewables, the chapter also emphasises the priority of exploiting the potential of distributed generation (DG), which would deliver electricity close to demand centres while increasing the resilience of the power system. As solar PV generation is variable, the chapter also outlines key strategies to improve the flexibility of the power system (e.g. by incentivising participation in demand response and investments in storage), facilitating the integration of higher levels of renewables. In the very short-term, improving the energy efficiency of end-use sectors can deliver emission reductions, but this will be insufficient to bring about the deep emission reductions needed and the effects may be offset by rebound effects.[7]

1.2.2. Residential: Creating affordable and sustainable homes (Chapter 3)

Rapid population growth (2% p.a.) and associated housing needs are a major and urgent challenge. So too are the climate implications of how this challenge is tackled. The housing shortage is driving increases in housing costs throughout Israel impacting Israelis' well-being. The government plans for a total of 1.5

million new dwellings to be built by 2040. Emissions from energy use in the residential sector, which plateaued over the last decade, could consequently increase dramatically. If Israel does not take this near-term opportunity to integrate better its housing and climate mitigation goals, it runs the risk of creating an emission-intensive building stock that will lock-in GHG emissions for the decades to come.

Chapter 3 dives into the links between the spatial scales of housing – dwelling, neighbourhood and city level - with mitigation. At the dwelling-level, the chapter outlines the rationale for retrofitting existing dwellings and how to establish and enforce best practices in the construction of new homes. It then reviews supply-side instruments as means to reduce emissions from housing, e.g. emission limits on buildings, as well as demand-side measures such as green public procurement. In addition, the chapter estimates the total financing needed to retrofit the existing building stock. High upfront costs and long payback periods make retrofits fairly unattractive for property owners. The chapter therefore proposes alternative financial instruments for Israel to consider that could alleviate these problems.

Beyond the dwelling level, rapid housing developments can lead to sprawl and low-density cities if badly managed; Israel will need to guide this growth. On the one hand minimum densities and policies that can incentivise the development of vacant land, in addition to the use of land value capture mechanisms can help to re-develop and densify the urban cores. However, anticipating and planning for the inevitable growth that will occur in less– or non- urbanized zones due to projected population growth will also be paramount for ensuring urban areas expand in a sustainable way. Overall, with greater densities comes the need for infrastructure that can sustain it, including transport infrastructure but also the green infrastructure needed to avoid urban heat islands, which could inadvertently increase emissions from higher electricity demand when cooling homes. The chapter also explores how Israel needs to integrate infrastructure with newly built dwellings such as green areas, transport, energy and water.

As cities become more compact and attractive, ensuring that low-income people still have access to affordable housing will be key. Local governments can better adapt approaches to local circumstances than central government ministries. Providing municipalities with greater autonomy could be an opportunity for Israel to manage these coming decades of growing cities in a more responsive and locally-appropriate way that fosters well-being and climate goals. Israel could build on international experience by embedding this process in a framework that allows for metropolitan bodies, which can help integrate and coordinate actions of different municipalities (in many cases urban and rural) that are part of the same economic unit. The chapter ends with options for financing sustainable development, such as urban renewal and eco-districts.

1.2.3. Transport: Enhancing accessibility by prioritising public and active transport (Chapter 4)

Transport is the second largest contributor to emissions after electricity (23% of Israel's emissions); emissions rose by 24% from 2006 to 2016. Car dependency is high in Israel, because of the limited public transport available and the mismatch between low active and public transport infrastructure investment and a rapidly expanding residential sector. The by-product of this is not only emissions, but also air pollution, congestion and severe accessibility gaps, all of which worsens Israelis' well-being now and in the future.

Chapter 4 analyses ways forward to transform the transport system in Israel in order to bring mitigation and wider well-being benefits. It finds that taxation of private car use needs to be better aligned with environmental damage and external costs (air pollution, congestion, noise, road wear). Allowing for a regular update of the car purchase tax in the short term will allow to maintain its environmental benefits and limit erosion of the tax base. A further step would be to replace the fuel tax by a tax proportional to the distance driven, varying with a vehicle's characteristics. This could enhance economic efficiency, appears technically feasible and would also automatically deliver the benefits of a more limited measure like a congestion charge (which could still be a good option in the short term). The chapter also brings attention to the need to manage road space (both through re-allocation and pricing) under the principle of prioritising public and active transport modes, and with the aim to improve safety and accessibility. It puts forward a number of tools to do so.

This chapter highlights the overall need to adopt accessibility-based planning and investment frameworks, and sets out ways in which these can be developed. This can help Israel seize the significant opportunity to create or reshape neighbourhoods and cities in ways that improve the population's access to services and opportunities through more sustainable modes.[8] The chapter then discusses how to ensure transport budgets are sustainable. Improving methodologies to set public transport fares and enlarging funding sources for transport (e.g. by using land-value capture) to go beyond fare box revenues and transfers from the central government will be essential to covering expansion, upgrade and regulatory costs, as well operation and maintenance.

The chapter closes with a discussion of the governance of the transport sector. It highlights the important role that Metropolitan Transport Authorities (MTAs) could play in improving mobility systems in cities in Israel. This type of institutional arrangement has proven successful in numerous cities around the world in delivering sustainable long-term improvements in accessibility and quality of life. Their development in Israel would facilitate a process of decentralising transport responsibilities while ensuring continued coordination and coherence in decisions across entities that are part of a same economic unit. It would also help to develop planning and regulatory capacity inside the public sector, which is an important limitation of the current model.[9] At the same time, the central government will need to develop a national policy for metropolitan and urban transport to guide local policy decisions and investments, to standardise local planning tools to make sure they follow good practice and bridge technical capacity gaps across territories.

1.2.4. Aligning finance with the low-carbon transition (Annex)

The Annex at the end of this report contains suggestions on how to align finance with the transition towards a sustainable economy. It notes the chronic underinvestment of Israel in infrastructure over the last decade compared to other OECD countries in infrastructure in terms of roads, homes, schools, and so on. It highlights that aligning financial flows with the low-carbon transition will need to make strategic use of public finance to mobilise private investment. It also points out the need for project pipelines to specify needed low-carbon infrastructure projects, so that private investors know where to invest funds. Likewise, Israel could try to classify whether different economic activities are green, such as being undertaken by the European Union's Sustainable Finance Taxonomy, or classify whether financial instruments aide, rather than impede the transition, such as the Climate Bonds Initiatives. Finally, it reviews how institutional actors like the Central Bank can mobilise and direct finance towards sustainable activities.

References

Aguilar Jaber, A. et al. (2020), "Long-term low emissions development strategies: Cross-country experience", *OECD Environment Working Papers*, No. 160, OECD Publishing, Paris, https://dx.doi.org/10.1787/1c1d8005-en. [14]

Cramer, W. et al. (2018), "Climate change and interconnected risks to sustainable development in the Mediterranean", *Nature Climate Change*, Vol. 8/11, pp. 972-980, http://dx.doi.org/10.1038/s41558-018-0299-2. [4]

IPCC (2018), *Global Warming of 1.5°C. An IPCC Special Report on the impacts of global warming of 1.5°C above pre-industrial levels and related global greenhouse gas emission pathways, in the context of strengthening the global response to the threat of climate change, sustainable development, and efforts to eradicate poverty*, IPCC, http://dx.doi.org/ipcc-2018-1.5-5062019. [1]

Ministry of Environmental Protection (2018), *ISRAEL'S THIRD NATIONAL COMMUNICATION ON CLIMATE CHANGE*, State of Israel, https://www4.unfccc.int/sites/SubmissionsStaging/NationalReports/Documents/386415_Israel-NC3-1-UNFCCC%20National%20Communication%202018.pdf. [3]

Ministry of Environmental Protection, Eco Traders Ltd. and Ricardo Energy and Environment (2015), *Assessment Of Greenhouse Gas Emission Reduction Potential And Recommended National Target For Israel*, Inter-ministerial Committee for the Formulation of the National Greenhouse Gas Reduction Target. [6]

Ministry of Health (2017), *Environmental Health in Israel | 2017*, http://www.ehf.org.il/en (accessed on 4 November 2019). [10]

OECD (2019), *Accelerating Climate Action: Refocusing Policies through a Well-being Lens*, OECD Publishing, Paris, https://dx.doi.org/10.1787/2f4c8c9a-en. [2]

OECD (2019), "Air and climate: Air and greenhouse gas emissions by industry - OECD Estimates", *OECD Environment Statistics* (database), https://dx.doi.org/10.1787/68a25273-en (accessed on 15 November 2019). [9]

OECD (2019), *Taxing Energy Use 2019: Using Taxes for Climate Action*, OECD Publishing, Paris, https://dx.doi.org/10.1787/058ca239-en. [15]

OECD (2018), "Air and climate: Air emissions by source (Edition 2018)", *OECD Environment Statistics* (database), https://dx.doi.org/10.1787/33987876-en (accessed on 15 November 2019). [16]

OECD (2018), "Air and climate: Greenhouse gas emissions by source (Edition 2018)", *OECD Environment Statistics* (database), https://dx.doi.org/10.1787/cf2ec84e-en (accessed on 18 December 2019). [5]

OECD (2016), *Measuring and Assessing Well-being in Israel*, OECD , Paris, https://www.oecd.org/sdd/measuring-and-assessing-well-being-in-Israel.pdf. [12]

OECD (2015), *Aligning Policies for a Low-carbon Economy*, OECD Publishing, Paris, https://dx.doi.org/10.1787/9789264233294-en. [8]

OECD (2011), *How's Life?: Measuring Well-being*, OECD Publishing, Paris, https://dx.doi.org/10.1787/9789264121164-en. [11]

Sorrell, S., J. Dimitropoulos and M. Sommerville (2009), "Empirical estimates of the direct rebound effect: A review", *Energy Policy*, Vol. 37/4, pp. 1356-1371, http://dx.doi.org/10.1016/j.enpol.2008.11.026. [17]

UNFCCC (2019), *NDC Registry*, https://www4.unfccc.int/sites/NDCStaging/Pages/All.aspx. [7]

UNFCCC (2015), *ADOPTION OF THE PARIS AGREEMENT - Paris Agreement text English*, United Nations, https://unfccc.int/sites/default/files/english_paris_agreement.pdf (accessed on 25 June 2018). [13]

Notes

[1] Prior experience with heat waves of 1°C above average in the summer increased mortality in Tel Aviv by 3.7% and increased emergency hospital visits by 1.47% (Ministry of Environmental Protection, 2018[3]).

[2] http://www.sviva.gov.il/English/env_topics/climatechange/NatlEmissionsReductionPlan/Documents/Govt-Decision-1403-National-GHG-Reduction-Plan-April-2016.pdf

[3] Including the extra gasoline lost in traffic jams and the value of time lost due to congestion.

[4] The concept of well-being goes beyond economic welfare: it incorporates such aspects as political and social rights, health, education, security and environmental quality (OECD, 2011[11]).

[5] From 42.3 Mt CO_2e in 2010 to 40.2 Mt CO_2e in 2016.

[6] By 38% and 33%, respectively between 2010 and 2016.

[7] See for example, (Sorrell, Dimitropoulos and Sommerville, 2009[17]).

[8] For example, public transport, cycling and walking.

[9] This is particularly needed in the context of fast evolving transport services and the need to adopt a Mobility as a Service (MaaS) approach.

2 Towards A Sustainable Electricity Sector for Israel

This chapter discusses electricity-related policies for Israel to accelerate climate mitigation and deliver on broader well-being goals. The chapter first compares natural gas with renewable energy sources. It concludes that a larger focus on renewables avoids the risk of jeopardising deep decarbonisation in the long term while contributing to broader well-being goals, including better public health, jobs and economic development. Second, the chapter sets out a number of policies and recommendations to accelerate renewables uptake: pricing carbon and other externalities; supporting utility-scale renewables and distributed generation; enhancing power system flexibility to integrate renewables; improving energy efficiency.

In Brief

Key findings and recommendations for Israel's electricity sector

Prioritise renewable energy over fossil fuel generation

- Natural gas can reduce GHG emissions in the near term, but risks jeopardising deep decarbonisation and broader well-being goals in the long term. Natural gas power plants are cleaner than coal, but have a number of other issues, including the emission of GHGs (including fugitive emissions), NOx and other air pollutants along the gas supply chain.
- Electricity from solar photovoltaic (PV) on a Levelised Cost of Electricity (LCOE) basis is cheaper than that from gas and delivers multiple other benefits, including improvements in public health, rural development, creation of high-tech jobs and export opportunities related to smart grid technologies.
- Natural gas resources can be used in some industrial sectors or for export to countries with fewer renewable resources.

Align the energy tax system with the social costs and address energy poverty

- Price fossil fuels according to the external costs, including greenhouse gases and air pollution
- Measure and monitor fugitive emissions in the gas supply chain to allow these to be priced.
- Adjust the (residential) electricity price to reflect all costs (social costs of generation and network costs) to improve incentives for energy efficiency and rooftop solar PV deployment.
- Address the impacts of energy price reform on energy-poor households and energy-intensive firms, for example through targeted income transfers or dedicated programmes to deploy rooftop solar PV (e.g. on social housing units) and enhance energy efficiency.

Scale-up renewable electricity deployment

- Support distributed solar PV cost-effectively (e.g. through tenders and incentives for self-consumption of solar generation).
- Remove administrative barriers (e.g. streamlining the permit procedure) and integrate other well-being objectives (e.g. development of industrial clusters) into competitive tenders for utility-scale solar PV.
- Foster integrated long-term planning of the power system to identify appropriate sites for solar PV and investment needs in the transmission network.

Improve power system flexibility to support grid integration of renewables

- Create electricity markets to improve operational efficiency and to enable business models for providing power system flexibility (storage and demand response).
- Reinitiate voluntary dynamic or time-of-use pricing in the residential sector to tap the potential of demand response, e.g. from air conditioners, refrigerators or heat pumps.
- Modulate remuneration of solar PV to incentivise renewable energy developers to provide electricity at times when it is most valuable, e.g. by investing in on-site storage.

Improve energy efficiency

- Promote electrification and map electrification pathways to estimate power infrastructure needs (generation as well as network assets).
- Implement and strengthen minimum energy performance standards, energy labels and market-based instruments, including obligations for the Israel Electric Corporation (IEC).
- Strengthen energy efficiency policies targeted to energy-poor households (e.g. to replace old and inefficient appliances).

2.1. Introduction

The electricity sector is the largest source of greenhouse gas (GHG) emissions in Israel, accounting for almost 50% of total GHG emissions in 2016 (OECD, 2019[1]). Between 2010 and 2016, GHG emissions from electricity generation declined by 3.5%, as a result of the ongoing fuel switch from coal to natural gas. Yet, in 2017, Israel's electricity-related carbon intensity amounted to 560g/kWh (EcoTraders, 2019[2]), one of the highest values among OECD countries (IEA, 2018[3]).

In the near term, natural gas will continue to play an important role in phasing out coal, reducing GHG emissions while bringing important immediate benefits in terms of improved public health through lower levels of air pollution, notably sulphur oxides (SO_x) and particulate matter (PM) (IPCC, 2014[4]). However, predominantly relying on natural gas for the longer-term, in the absence of options for capturing and storing or using carbon dioxide (CO_2) emissions, will jeopardise deep decarbonisation in line with international commitments. Natural gas power plants, even when equipped with carbon capture, utilisation and storage (CCUS), will still emit some GHG emissions, including fugitive emissions from the gas supply chain (IPCC, 2014[4]). Gas power plants are a major contributor to nitrous oxides (NO_x) emissions with adverse health and biodiversity effects (OECD, 2018[5]), while gas extraction is responsible for a number of substances that are known to be carcinogenic (IEA, 2016[6]). Electricity from gas is already more expensive than that from utility-scale solar photovoltaic (PV) (Ministry of Energy, 2019[7]) and the cost difference is expected to widen, posing long-term economic risks to investments in gas. All this calls for a greater focus on renewables, notably solar energy.

The objective of this chapter is twofold. First, it takes a holistic view of Israel's electricity sector, drawing on the OECD's well-being framework applied to climate mitigation (OECD, 2019[8]). Looking at the sector in a holistic way reveals many synergies and trade-offs between transitioning to a low-carbon electricity sector and broader societal goals, including improved public health through lower levels of air pollution, the creation of jobs and the development of economically less developed areas. Exploiting these synergies can importantly accelerate climate action in Israel's electricity sector.

Second, this chapter provides concrete good-practice policy examples that Israel can draw on in its planning for the next 5 to 10 years to enable a transition towards a sustainable electricity sector with high shares of solar energy. Besides discussing the effectiveness of the policies proposed, the chapter provides, where applicable, evidence of their effect on broader well-being dimensions, including health, affordability and equity. This chapter discusses three building blocks for decarbonising the electricity sector: i) pricing carbon and other externalities; ii) supporting solar PV (both utility-scale and distributed) and facilitating integration; iii) improving energy efficiency.

There are three major challenges for Israel in decarbonising the electricity sector while delivering other well-being benefits. First, despite improvements in energy efficiency, electricity demand is expected to grow by 2.1% per year to 2030 (Electricity Authority, 2018[9]). Growth in electricity demand is primarily due to population growth, increased electrification of end-uses (e.g. electric vehicles in transport) and further need for desalination from increased water stress linked to climate change (Electricity Authority, 2018[9]). Electrifying end-uses increases energy efficiency and is a major strategy to decarbonise some end-uses that are hard to abate otherwise (IEA, 2018[10]). Second, due to its geopolitical situation, Israel is an energy island without electricity interconnection to neighbouring countries. Third, despite having excellent solar resources, land availability next to major consumption centres is a barrier to scaling up low-cost utility-scale solar PV (Vardimon, 2011[11]).

2.2. State of play and Israel's electricity sector through a well-being lens

Using electricity is fundamental for well-being as it supports a wide range of basic services as well as economic infrastructure and activities. Electricity consumption has been rising at an annual rate of 2.5% from 54.6 terawatt hours (TWh) in 2000 to 69.6 TWh in 2018 (Electricity Authority, 2018[9]). In 2016, the residential sector accounted for 29%, the commercial and public sector for 28%, the industry sector for 25%, water desalination for 5% and other uses for the remainder (Ministry of Environmental Protection, 2018[12]). Israel aims to reduce electricity consumption by 17% by 2030, relative to Business as Usual (BAU), amounting to an absolute target of 80 TWh in 2030 (EcoTraders, 2019[2]).

Electricity generation, however, is not only the major contributor to GHG emissions, it also accounted for 85% and 58% of SO_x and NO_x emissions respectively in 2016 (OECD, 2018[13]) with serious impacts on public health and ecosystems. The power sector is the main source of some important air pollutants, accounting, e.g. for 34% and 40% of PM2.5 and PM10 emissions in the Haifa region (Ministry of Environmental Protection, 2019[14]). Air pollution is associated with adverse health effects, causing almost 2,500 premature deaths per year in Israel (Ministry of Health, 2017[15]). Vulnerable population groups, including children, pregnant women and the elderly are affected most, even at low concentrations. Pollution is also detrimental to Israeli students' performance and subsequent labour market outcomes (Lavy, Ebenstein and Roth, 2014[16]), reducing labour productivity (e.g. due to increased sickness absences) and lowering economic output (Dechezleprêtre, Rivers and Stadler, 2019[17]).

Israel has been increasingly switching power supply from coal to gas and this trend is expected to continue. In 2018, coal accounted for 30% of total power generation, half the share of 2010 (Electricity Authority, 2018[9]). The share of natural gas has increased from 39% in 2010 to 66% in 2018, primarily driven by the availability of domestic natural gas discovered off the coast of Israel. Since 2016, the Ministry of Energy implemented an environmental load order, meaning that coal plants are mandated to operate at the minimum load possible and are increasingly used as back-up to maintain reliability and provide flexibility (EcoTraders, 2019[2]). The Minister of Energy announced his intention to phase out coal completely by 2025, but a final government decision is still pending (EcoTraders, 2019[2]). Israel joined the Power Past Coal Alliance end of 2018 (Ministry of Energy, 2018[18]). In December 2019, the Energy Minister Yuval Steinitz announced that the coal phase out could be as early as 2025.

The switch from coal to gas has reduced CO_2 emissions somewhat and air pollutants substantially while contributing to energy security. According to OECD data, between 2010 and 2016, electricity related CO_2 emissions have decreased from 42.3 $MtCO_2e$ to 40.2 $MtCO_2e$ whereas NO_x and SO_x emissions attributable to the electricity sector decreased by 38 and 33% respectively (OECD, 2019[1]).[1] The transition from coal to gas also reduced the SO_x and $PM_{2.5}$ concentrations in major population centres, including Haifa, Tel Aviv and Ashdod with statistically significant reductions in cardiovascular events (-13.3%) and in total mortality (-19%) (Ministry of Health, 2017[15]).

Royalties from gas extraction has increased government revenues and may feed into a sovereign wealth fund to share the wealth with future generations. Royalty revenue amounted to NIS 542 million in 2013, but is expected to rise to NIS 2.1 billion by 2020 (Ministry of Energy, 2017[19]), accounting for around 0.5% of Israel's central government budget in 2020.[2] In addition to royalty income, Israel is planning to set up a sovereign wealth fund, fed by a special levy of 20 – 50% on gas extractors' profits over normal returns on investment (OECD, 2018[20]). By 2040, this fund could accumulate up to USD 40 billion, representing more than 10% of Israel's current GDP. (OECD, 2018[20]). This fund could be set up in a similar way as Norway's Government Pension Fund Global (Box 2.1).

Box 2.1. Investment Strategy, governance and ethical standards of Norway's Government Pension Fund Global

Norway's Government Pension Fund Global, previously the Petroleum Fund of Norway, was established in 1990 to sustain the wealth from Norway's oil revenue for future generations. As of 2019, the fund manages more than USD 1 trillion, making it one of the largest funds in the world (Norges Bank, 2019[21]). The fund invests in international financial markets, including bonds, real estate and private equity with stakes in more than 9,000 companies across 73 countries.

The Ministry of Finance has tasked Norway's central bank, Norges Bank, with the management of the fund based on the Government Pension Fund Act, enacted by the Norwegian Parliament. The Ministry has the overall responsibility of the Fund and provides clear guidelines for the management, including guidelines for the observation and exclusion of companies that violate specific ethical standards. Based on the guidelines the Council of Ethics, appointed by the Ministry, proposes a list of firms to be excluded from investment. As of November 2019, the list included 154 companies that had been excluded for reasons such as violations of human rights, corruption as well as production of tobacco, weapons and coal or coal-based energy. As of 2014, the guidelines explicitly stipulate to exclude all companies whose revenue from thermal coal exceeds 30% (Ministry of Finance, 2014[22]). In addition, the updated 2019 guidelines force the fund to divest from companies that produce more than 20 million tonnes of coal annually and recommend the exclusion of companies involved in oil and gas exploration (Ministry of Finance, 2019[23]).

Source: Authors based on (Norges Bank, 2019[21])

Natural gas power plants have improved the environmental performance of Israel's electricity sector, but relying on large contribution of natural gas to electricity generation in the longer-term and in the absence of CCUS or similar technologies will jeopardise the achievement of deep decarbonisation in line with Israel's international commitments under the Paris Agreement. Assuming a share of natural gas of 70% and renewables of 30%, annual carbon emissions could still be as high as 37.2 Mt CO_2 in 2050, similar to electricity-related carbon emissions in 2018.[3] In addition, relying on natural gas is detrimental for achieving broader well-being objectives for the following reasons:

1. The extraction and combustion of natural gas still emits large amounts of GHG emissions, albeit half the amount of coal on average (IPCC, 2014[4]). Lifecycle GHG emissions of gas power plants are around half of coal power plants, ranging from 410 to 650gCO_2e/kWh (IPCC, 2014[4]).[4] Fugitive emissions through leaks in the extraction, transmission and distribution of natural gas can cause the GHG emission intensity of gas to be even higher than that of coal if leakage rates exceed 3% (OECD, 2017[24]). In addition, methane emissions also contribute to the production of tropospheric ozone, which has detrimental impacts on both human health and ecosystems (Shindell et al., 2012[25]). Measuring, monitoring and minimising fugitive emissions in the gas supply chain is therefore a key priority. Even equipping natural gas power plants with CCUS would not entirely exclude CO_2 emissions, but could reduce them by approximately 88% (Ministry of Environmental Protection, 2018[26]), still requiring carbon removal technologies to achieve net-zero emissions. CCUS with current technologies would raise estimated capital costs for natural gas-fired plants by between 55 – 100%, translating into a 26 – 40% increase of levelised cost of electricity (LCOE) - the unit costs of electricity over the lifetime of the plant (IPCC, 2014[4]). This estimate does not

include transport and storage, which would add USD 10/tCO_2 on average (IPCC, 2014[4]). Increasingly blending natural gas with green hydrogen – hydrogen produced with electrolysers, using renewable electricity – may be a lower cost strategy to reduce GHG intensity of the electricity sector. For example, a 5% blend of green hydrogen would reduce CO_2 emissions from gas combustion by 2% (IEA, 2019[27]).[5] It would also improve system flexibility through providing a long-term storage option for a dispatchable fuel (IEA, 2019[28]). As the typical lifetime of gas power plants is 36 years (IPCC, 2014[29]), equipping new gas power plants with turbines that accommodate high shares of hydrogen would reduce the risk of stranded assets.

2. While gas power plants emit hardly any direct SO_x and PM, they are still significant contributors to NO_x emissions, albeit to a lesser extent than coal (IEA, 2016[6]). Gas power plants account for 20% of global power-related NO_x emissions (IEA, 2016[6]). NO_x emissions contribute to the acidification of fresh water and soils as well as to the eutrophication of water, all of which threaten biodiversity (OECD, 2018[5]). NO_x emissions have direct negative impacts on public health and are responsible for the creation of summer smog, aggravating the negative health impacts (IPCC, 2014[29]). In addition, gas extraction is a major contributor to air pollutants known or suspected to be carcinogenic. However, the implementation of abatement measures for existing gas extraction and stricter environmental planning and permitting for gas extraction coming online can reduce the negative effects of gas operation on air quality (Ministry of Environmental Protection, 2019[30]).
3. The LCOE of natural gas is higher than that of solar PV, even at current fuel tax levels that do not include the full social costs (Gallo and Porath, 2017[31]). The latest clearing prices of Israel's utility-scale solar auctions (USD 55/MWh) is lower than the generation costs of fossil fuels (80 USD/MWh) (EcoTraders, 2019[2]).[6] The cost of solar PV has fallen sharply over the last years and this trend is expected to continue with expected cost reductions between 15 – 35% in the next 5 years (IEA, 2019[32]). The cost for distributed solar PV (USD 150/MWh), however, is still above that of fossil fuels (Ministry of Energy, 2019).

> The long-term risks related to natural gas call for a greater focus on renewable energy sources in the generation of electricity.

The long-term risks related to natural gas call for a greater focus on renewable energy sources in the generation of electricity. Israel could use its natural gas resources in some industrial sectors that are hard to decarbonise otherwise or for export to other countries with fewer renewable resources. Exports to Egypt and Jordan are expected to start in 2020 and there are also longer-term plans to export gas to Europe via the EastMed pipeline. However, exporting gas requires substantial investments in gas transport infrastructure, amounting to as much as EUR 6 billion for the EastMed pipeline project (Eastmed, 2017[33]) and gas demand in Europe is expected to decline (IEA, 2019[27]). Similarly, liquefied natural gas terminals enabling exports to growing Asian economies face key uncertainties as gas exports to those countries may not be cost-competitive (IEA, 2019[27]). The investment risks would be further exacerbated as and when gas-importing countries increased their own climate ambition, e.g. through higher taxes on gas. If Israel's gas extraction and transport costs were too high to be internationally competitive, some reserves might not be economic to extract.

The transition to an electricity sector with higher shares of renewables likely will result in a modest increase in employment in the sector, but power plants relying on fossil fuels are expected to experience employment losses (OECD, 2017[34]). In 2018, almost 17,000 people or 0.5% of Israel's total workforce were directly employed in the electricity sector (OECD, 2019[35]). The Israel Electric Corporation (IEC) – the state-owned electricity supplier and owner of the transmission and distribution network - alone employed 11,139 persons, but this number is expected to decline to 9,300 by 2026 in accordance with the latest electricity sector reform that foresees privatisation and prevents the IEC from investing in new capacities (Electricity Authority, 2018[9]).

At the same time, renewables, notably solar PV, can create new jobs and business opportunities, including for small and medium enterprises, while boosting productivity through innovation (OECD, 2012[36]). For example, a 50 megawatt (MW) solar plant can create between 60 and 80 permanent full-time jobs (IRENA, 2018[37]), notably in Israel's rural areas that are economically less developed. For example, renewables expansion in the Negev desert could significantly spur economic development and diversify the local economy while reducing unemployment and poverty, notably for the Bedouin minority (Potter et al., 2012[38]).[7] Rooftop solar is even more labour intensive and creates higher shares of high-skilled jobs (IEA and CEEW, 2019[39]). Integrating solar PV into the grid also requires smart technologies that enable new business models and can provide highly skilled IT jobs as well as export opportunities.

In 2018, renewables accounted for approximately 4% of total electricity generation with solar power accounting for the biggest share (3.6%) (EcoTraders, 2019[2]). This share is low compared to other OECD countries (Figure 2.1). Israel aims to achieve a renewable share of at least 10% by 2020, 13% by 2025 and 17% by 2030 (Ministry of Environmental Protection, 2018[12]). In 2018, total renewables capacity amounted to 1,450 MW with solar PV accounting for 1,358 MW, most of which was distributed solar (Electricity Authority, 2018[9]). To achieve the stated 2030 target of 17% generation from renewables, the expected installed capacity of renewables would have to increase to 8,600 MW, with 7,500 MW from solar PV. The Ministry of Energy's 2030 Targets for the Energy Sector will review the 2030 goals in the coming years and has already announced a preliminary decision to raise the target to 25% to 30% (EcoTraders, 2019[2]). Based on the stated target (17%), extrapolating the speed of renewable energy deployment between 2020 and 2030 would result in a renewables share of 31% by 2050. Conversely, reaching a renewables share of 70% by 2050 would require raising the 2030 target to 30%. A 30% target by 2030 would translate into a renewable capacity of more than 15,200 MW in 2030. This would require annual capacity additions of around 1,140 MW after 2020, which is actually lower than the expected capacity addition in the year 2020.[8]

Israel has excellent solar resources, but limited resources for other renewables. Israel is currently re-assessing the technical long-term potential of renewables (EcoTraders, 2019[2]). Past assessments revealed that Israel has no potential for hydro or geothermal power (Solomon, Bogdanov and Breyer, 2018[40]) and only limited potential for wind and biomass (Ministry of National Infrastructures, 2010[41]). However, Israel's annual solar radiation is between 1,900 and 2,200 kWh/m^2 (Vardimon, 2011[11]), up to 50% higher than in Greece where solar radiation ranges between 1,450 and 1,800kWh/m^2 (Fantidis et al., 2012[42]). The maximum total ground area available for solar PV is reported to be 6% of the total land area, equivalent to 1,324 km^2 (Solomon, Bogdanov and Breyer, 2018[40]). If this area was entirely devoted to utility-scale solar PV, this could generate, with current technologies, at least 280 TWh electricity, more than four times the electricity consumption in 2018 and more than three times the expected consumption in 2030.

Israel is currently focusing on distributed solar PV to achieve its renewable energy targets as transmission grid constraints have slowed down deployment of utility-scale solar (Gallo and Porath, 2017[31]). An early study estimated the nation-wide technical potential for rooftop solar PV (based on 75 km^2 available rooftop area) to be 15.9 TWh, almost one quarter of Israel's electricity consumption in 2018 (Vardimon, 2011[11]).[9] A more recent study from 2020 conducted by the Ministry of Environmental Protection and EcoTraders estimated the potential of solar PV in urban built areas in 2030 to be 38 TWh with more than a third from rooftop solar PV, 7% from building-applied PV on facades, and the remainder from utilising water reservoirs as well as additional built-areas, including highways and parking lots.

Table 2.1. Estimates of the technical solar PV potential in Israel

Potential	Type of area	Source
280 TWh	Land area	(Solomon, Bogdanov and Breyer, 2018[40])
38 TWh	Urban built area	Ministry of Environmental Protection and EcoTraders (2020)
15.9 TWh	Rooftop area	(Vardimon, 2011[11])

Source: (Solomon, Bogdanov and Breyer, 2018[40]); (Vardimon, 2011[11]); Ministry of Environmental Protection and EcoTraders (2020).

Realising the full potential of distributed PV is key as distributed solar PV has a number of advantages. Relative to utility-scale PV located far away from consumption centres, a power system with high shares of distributed PV would reduce losses due to electricity transmission and voltage conversion. Distributed PV, though more expensive on an LCOE basis, would not require investments in transmission capacity and would also increase the resilience of the power system while reducing the risks of wild fires, which are frequently caused by electric faults in the transmission system in dry regions, as in California (RFF, 2019[43]).

Figure 2.1. Renewables and solar share of electricity generation across OECD countries in 2018

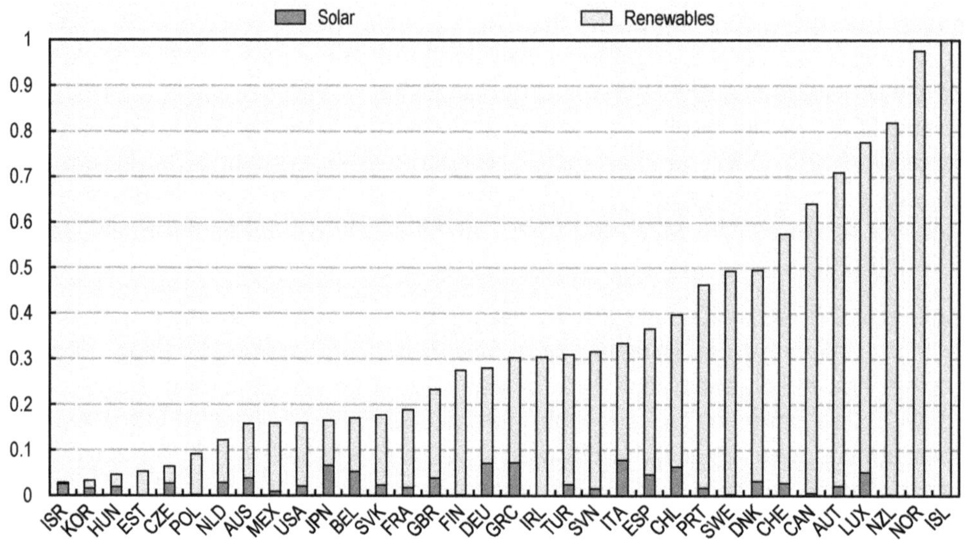

Source: (IEA, 2019[44]).

StatLink https://doi.org/10.1787/888934156048

Deployment of solar PV faces challenges and barriers related to the intermittency of generation and land availability, but these challenges can be addressed:

1. Solar PV is a variable renewable energy (VRE) source that generates energy only during the day. With rising shares of solar PV, the need for power system flexibility – flexible power plants, storage and demand response - increase to ensure that supply meets demand at every hour of the day (IEA, 2019[27]). The existing stock of gas power plants is well suited for integrating solar PV due to their ability to quickly ramp generation up and down. Additional flexibility needs can be delivered by pumped hydro storage and battery storage with battery costs expected to decline rapidly (IEA, 2019[27]). Demand response (DR), e.g. shifting load from peak demand hours to hours of the day where solar power is abundant, can provide flexibility at a low cost. Developing smart technologies

to manage flexible loads could also strengthen Israel's technological leadership and create new high-skill jobs.

2. The sparsely populated Negev desert seems suitable for utility-scale solar PV deployment, but other competing users exist. The Negev covers more than 55% of Israel's land area equivalent to 13,000km^2. However, much land is currently occupied by other uses: Israeli military (55%), nature reserves and national parks (90% of the Negev desert is classified as preserved land) as well as agriculture (8%) (Fischhendler, Nathan and Boymel, 2015[45]). Reassessing land uses in the Negev is key for further deployment of utility-scale solar PV. This becomes even more important in view of rising electricity demand due to electrification and – potentially – to the use of electrolysers to produce hydrogen. Yet, deploying utility-scale solar PV along with transmission lines would most likely affect sensitive ecosystems, calling for a robust full environmental assessment of all generating technologies along their lifecycle. Accounting for the most relevant external costs and benefits of generating technologies implies that Israel should seek to limit its need for additional large-scale generating capacity to the extent possible. There should therefore be a stronger focus on energy efficiency, on smart grid and storage solutions (including through sector-coupling) as well as on realising the potential of distributed solar in built-areas, water reservoirs and brownfield sites (e.g. decommissioned industrial areas). Solar PV on water reservoirs would in addition save up to 80% of evaporating water (Taboada et al., 2017[46]) and reduce algae growth while improving the solar panels' power conversion efficiency due to lower ambient air temperatures underneath the panels (Spencer et al., 2018[47]).

2.3. Policies for a sustainable electricity sector

The previous section has argued that the shift from coal to natural gas has important benefits in terms of reducing both GHG and air pollution in the near term, but that a predominant focus on natural gas will constrain the ambition of future GHG emission reduction targets and broader well-being goals in the long-term. Instead, more emphasis should be given to renewables, notably solar PV. This section discusses three building blocks for decarbonising the electricity sector. First, section 2.3.1 presents pricing instruments to address externalities as well as how these instruments need to be designed to avoid a too high burden on lower-income groups. Second, this part discusses support measures for both utility-scale (Section 2.3.2) and distributed solar PV (Section 2.3.3) as well as solutions to better integrate solar PV through enabling policies, including electricity market regulation (Section 2.3.4). Third, Section 2.3.5 provides insights on policies promoting energy efficiency.

2.3.1. Pricing carbon and other externalities correctly and removing subsidies

Pricing carbon and other externalities (notably air pollution) according to its social costs, aligns the incentives of emitters with those of society and reduces emissions in a cost-effective way. The High-Level Commission on Carbon Prices suggests that the carbon price should be in the range of USD 40 – 80 per tonne of CO_2e by 2020 and USD 50 – 100 by 2030 to hold global warming under 2°C relative to pre-industrial levels, provided complementary policies addressing other market failures are in place (High-Level Commission on Carbon Prices, 2017[48]). More recently, the International Monetary Fund (IMF) estimated that a carbon price of USD 75 per tonne of CO_2e by 2030 is needed to be compatible with the goals of the Paris Agreement (IMF, 2019[49]). Incorporating the external costs from air pollutants (e.g. SO_x, NO_x, PM, O_3 emissions) would further increase these figures. For example, Israel's Ministry of Environmental Protection calculates the electricity-related external costs of SO_x and NO_x emissions at NIS 46,260 and 26,791 (USD 12,588 and 7,290) per tonne, respectively (Ministry of Environmental Protection, 2019[50]). Pricing fugitive emissions from gas extraction provides strong incentives for gas operators to reduce emission leaks in the gas supply chain. Fugitive emissions from gas extraction are priced, among others, in the Californian emissions trading scheme based on the global warming potential (ICAP, 2018[51]).

Only 1% of Israel's *electricity-related* carbon emissions are priced above EUR 5, one of the lowest shares across OECD countries (Figure 2.2).[10] Israel uses excise taxes on coal at NIS 46.09 per ton and on natural gas at NIS 17.36 per ton, translating into implicit carbon rates of EUR 4.54 and EUR 1.91 per ton CO_2 respectively (OECD, 2019[52]). Recent developments suggest that the gap between the effective carbon rates of Israel and other OECD countries is widening (OECD, 2018[53]). For example, due to the rise of the permit price in the European Union emissions trading scheme increased from EUR 5 in 2017 to EUR 25 in 2019. Natural gas received public support of approximately NIS 500 million, equivalent to 0.04% of GDP in 2017 (OECD, 2018[53]). The major part of this producer support reflects a long-term gas agreement at guaranteed prices between the IEC and the investor consortium of the Tamar gas field (OECD, 2018[53]).

Introducing a carbon tax or gradually raising excise taxes on natural gas and coal would improve the incentives of independent power producers (IPPs) to invest in renewables. Cost-reflective prices for natural gas would increase the cost of the government to procure investments in new gas capacity. This, in turn, would decrease the relative costs of renewables vis-à-vis gas power plants, enhancing the competitiveness of renewables. In addition, higher taxes on natural gas would preserve the tax base since electricity generation is increasingly shifting towards gas with the announced coal phase out.

Figure 2.2. Share of electricity-related CO_2 emissions priced above EUR 5 in 2015

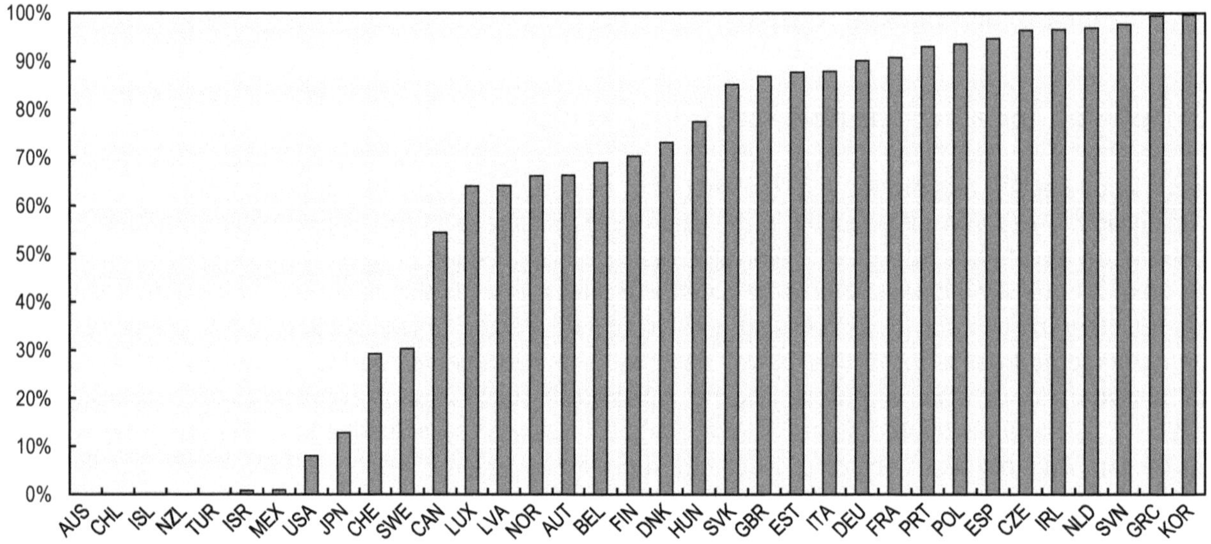

Note: Includes emissions from biomass firing. 99% of Israel's electricity-related CO_2 emissions are priced below EUR 5.
Source: Authors, based on (OECD, 2018[54]).

StatLink https://doi.org/10.1787/888934156067

Retail electricity prices would likely need to increase to reflect rising carbon costs of the IEC and IPPs. Electricity retail prices need to reflect the full cost of electricity, including the social cost of generation and the electricity system costs (storage, transmission and distribution network) (IEA, 2016[55]). Higher retail prices encourage private investments in energy efficient equipment, including air conditioners, refrigerators and electric heat pumps (Section 2.3.5). Higher prices also improve the payback time for investments in energy efficient buildings to reduce the heating and cooling needs in the first place (Chapter 3) while ensuring sufficient investments in distribution and transmission networks by the IEC. Finally, cost-reflective prices also provide more incentives to drive private investments into distributed solar PV (Section 2.3.3).

Residential electricity prices in Israel, administratively set by the Electricity Authority, have slightly increased from 0.462 NIS/kWh in 2015 to 0.472 NIS/kWh in 2018. They are, however, still below the levels of 2006 in real terms (0.502 NIS/kWh) (Electricity Authority, 2018[9]). Israel has one of the lowest residential retail rates among OECD countries, 40% lower than the EU average (EcoTraders, 2019[2]). Despite the low price levels, electricity price hikes can create affordability problems for low-income households. At current prices, the poorest 10% of the income distribution spend already 9% of the available income on electricity, gas and fuels compared to 3.4% for the 5th decile (EcoTraders, 2019[2]). Increasing electricity prices can also challenge the competitiveness of firms in the industry sector. However, complementary policies can alleviate some of the negative impacts for households and firms and can avoid carbon leakage.[11]

Addressing the problem of residential electricity affordability and energy poverty in general requires a two-step approach, identifying vulnerable population groups in the first step and using targeted policy support for these groups in a second. The low-income high-cost share (LIHCS) indicator is suitable for identifying vulnerable household groups and is used in a number of countries, including the UK (BEIS, 2019[56]). Countries are using different thresholds for the definition of low-income and high-cost share, depending on the country-specific circumstances, but commonly applied thresholds include an expenditure share of energy of more than 10% while being below the relative poverty line (i.e. 60% of median income) after expenditure on energy (Flues and van Dender, 2017[57]). LIHCS is one of the most selective indicator on affordability risks as it combines two criteria, identifying households in the low-income group that spend a high share of their income on energy products. However, LIHCS' data requirements are relatively high, preventing the calculation of this indicator for Israel with publicly available data.

In a second step, targeted support, including targeted deployment of distributed solar PV, targeted income transfers or dedicated programmes to enhance energy efficiency (Section 2.3.5) help reduce energy poverty. Deploying distributed solar PV on social housing units or in disadvantaged communities reduces the energy bill of low-income households while spurring renewable expansion. For example, California provides upfront financial incentives of USD 3,000 per kW for the installation of rooftop solar PV under the Disadvantaged Communities Single-family Solar Homes programme (CPUC, 2019[58]). Eligible customers must live in a disadvantaged community[12] and must be below a certain income threshold. Targeted transfers help low-income households to cope with energy poverty without distorting the price incentives for saving energy (as would be the case for preferential electricity tariffs). For example, in 2016 France switched from social energy tariffs to providing energy cheques to help households pay their energy bills (OECD, 2016[59]). Depending on the households' income and the characteristics of the dwelling, eligible households receive a cheque of up to EUR 277 per year (EUR 150 on average) to pay utility bills, in 90% of the cases electricity bills. In 2019, 5.8 million households were eligible for this programme (Ministry for the Ecological and Inclusive Transition, 2019[60]).

Addressing the burden of higher electricity prices for electricity-intensive industries also entails a two-step approach to reduce negative impacts on competitiveness and avoid carbon leakage. Up to today, the economics literature has not found negative effects of carbon prices on industrial firms' competitiveness, measured by revenue, jobs, profits or net imports (Ellis, Nachtigall and Venmans, 2019[61]). Yet, this finding is in part due to low carbon price levels levied on industrial installations either because of tax exemptions or allocation of free allowances. Rapidly rising electricity prices as a result of cost-pass through of carbon costs can have negative short-term adjustment effects, notably for electricity-intensive firms. These firms may receive support depending on their electricity and trade intensity. Support could be either in form of direct transfers or targeted support for energy efficiency improvements, allowing these firms to better cope with higher electricity prices while enhancing their competitiveness in the future.

Revenues from carbon pricing can be used for targeted support, alleviating the regressive distributional effects of carbon pricing while strengthening citizen support (Marten and van Dender, 2019[62]). Research in European economies suggests that it may be sufficient to use one third of the revenues from higher energy taxation for transfers to low-income households to improve energy affordability of these households (Flues and van Dender, 2017[57]). Using carbon tax revenues to improve environmental outcomes and reduce poverty also strengthens citizens' support (Kallbekken and Aasen, 2010[63]; Baranzini and Carattini, 2017[64]; Kallbekken, Kroll and Cherry, 2011[65]).

2.3.2. Accelerate utility-scale solar PV deployment and removing barriers

Utility-scale solar PV is already cheaper than natural gas, but long-term support remains important to reduce financing costs. Providing revenue certainty for private investors reduces risks of solar PV projects and helps channel private capital into renewables. Competitive auctions are more cost-effective than administratively set Feed-In-Tariffs (FIT) (IEA, 2018[66]). In 2017, the Electricity Authority switched its major support scheme from FiTs to competitive tenders (Gallo and Porath, 2017[31]). The Electricity Authority held the first solar PV auction in 2017, tendering a total capacity of 234 MW from 12 selected project developers at a price of NIS 199/MWh (USD 55/MWh) (IEA, 2019[67]).

Support mechanisms can be designed to account for various well-being dimensions, including jobs and the development of local industrial clusters. For example, South Africa's Renewable Energy Independent Power Procurement Program (REIPPP) assigned 70% of the auction score on the bid price whereas the remaining 30% are allocated based on socio-economic dimensions including job creation, black ownership and enterprise development (Ettmayr and Lloyd, 2017[68]). Between 2011 and 2015, the REIPPP is estimated to have created more than 100.000 direct full-time jobs (Eberhard and Naude, 2017[69]). As another example, the Contract for Differences programme in the UK requires projects larger than 300MW to submit a 'supply chain plan' (Fitch-Roy and Woodman, 2016[70]). This is to encourage the effective development of renewable energy supply chains, notably to enhance competition, support the development of local industrial clusters and to promote innovation and skills, all of which trigger further cost decreases in the long-term (BEIS, 2018[71]).

Remuneration of renewable projects must strike a balance between channelling private investments into sustainable infrastructure and risk-taking of private actors. As technologies become more mature and the share of renewables increases, support schemes need to be adjusted to hand over more risk to private actors. Notably, this includes increasingly exposing renewables to market risk in form of wholesale market remuneration to incentivise system-friendly behaviour, i.e. providing electricity at hours of the day when it is most beneficial for the power system. This requires a wholesale market that Israel does not yet have (Section 2.3.4).

Until recently, infrastructure development has not yet fully taken into account the potential for renewable generation away from the consumption centres, likely leading to bottlenecks in the transmission grid (Gallo and Porath, 2017[31]). Most of the available land is located far away from the main consumption centres, notably in the Negev desert. In 2018, the Ministry of Energy and the Electricity Authority approved a five year development plan that includes significant investment in the transmission grid and will expand the transmission network from 5.587 km in 2018 to 6.389 km in 2022 (Electricity Authority, 2018[9]). Investments in 2018 were NIS 0.9 billion, almost double the amount of the average in the last 10 years (Electricity Authority, 2018[9]). Tenders for transmission capacity have been found to be cost-effective for realising transmission projects (IEA, 2016[55]). Integrated long-term planning, including mapping of the geographical distribution of renewable energy resources and establishing project pipelines of bankable PV projects, improves the co-ordination between land-use planning and deployment of utility-scale solar PV while reducing the investment risk of project developers (OECD, 2015[72]). Long-term scenarios help evaluate the investment needs in network infrastructure. For example, ENTSO-E, the European transmission network operator, explores a range of long-term scenarios until 2050 (ENTSO-E and ENTSO-G, 2018[73]) and provides open access to all relevant electricity data through its Transparency Platform (Hirth, Mühlenpfordt and Bulkeley, 2018[74]).

Removing administrative barriers for project developers of solar PV (e.g. the lack of land allocation procedure, delays in obtaining installation permits) can also substantially lower the costs. One-stop shops, i.e. offices in charge of issuing all necessary permits, are effective in streamlining permit and licensing procedures (OECD, 2017[34]). Completing general environmental impact assessments before the competitive tender reduces the uncertainty of project developers, leaving only the project-specific risk related to environmental impact assessment to the bidder (OECD, 2017[34]). Israel has tendered pre-approved sites for solar PV deployment (Ministry of Environmental Protection, 2015[75]). Legal time limits for permit approval speeds up construction (Koźluk, 2014[76]) and helps address conflict of interest between project developers and the IEC that is responsible for issuing the installation permits. In addition, legal time limits for connecting generators to the distribution and transmission network would further strengthen the position of IPPs.

Market concentration of state-owned enterprises has been found to discourage investment in renewables (Prag, Röttgers and Scherrer, 2018[77]). The state-owned IEC is the dominant generator of electricity, accounting for 79% of installed capacity and 69% of generation in 2018 (Electricity Authority, 2018[9]). The major electricity sector reform, enacted in 2018, foresees to reduce IEC's share on installed capacity to 45% by 2025 through privatisation, requiring the IEC to sell half of its gas-fired power stations, equivalent to 4,500 MW (EcoTraders, 2019[2]). At the same time, the reform prevents the IEC from investing in new capacity further adding to a more competitive electricity sector. The electricity sector reform also transfers the operation of the electricity system from the IEC to an independent, but state-owned body (EcoTraders, 2019[2]). The system operator is responsible, among others, for the dispatch of power stations as well as long-term planning and forecasts of electricity demand. It will be important for the system manager to be fully independent of the incumbent to prevent discrimination against market entrants (Fuentes, 2009[78]).

2.3.3. Supporting distributed energy resources

Distributed generation, notably distributed solar PV, plays an increasingly important role in Israel's electricity system, overcoming bottlenecks in the transmission lines and preventing costly expansion of the transmission network. Investment costs of distributed solar PV has globally declined by 60-80% since 2010 and are expected to decline by a further 15-35% until 2024, making this technology cost-competitive in an increasing number of countries (IEA, 2019[32]). Even though the costs of utility-scale solar PV are between 10-50% lower than distributed solar PV, there is an economic argument for distributed generation due to its proximity to the consumption centres (IEA, 2019[32]). Generating electricity onsite or next to consumption centres reduces the investment need in transmission grid extension and distribution grid reinforcement with lower impacts on biodiversity and ecosystems.

In most countries, distributed solar PV's LCOE, ranging between USD 83 and USD 195/MWh, is well-below the variable part of the retail tariff, rendering distributed PV deployment profitable (IEA, 2019[32]). However, in Israel, the economic attractiveness of rooftop solar PV in the absence of policy support is not given under current electricity prices. The LCOE of rooftop solar in Israel, currently around USD 150/MWh (Ministry of Energy, 2019[7]), is higher than the electricity retail price at USD 120/MWh. A carbon price of USD 50/tCO_2 would equalise Israel's electricity retail price with the cost of rooftop solar PV, creating strong economic incentives for distributed PV deployment. This number is based on the assumption of full cost pass-through of carbon costs to electricity consumers, using Israel's carbon intensity of the electricity mix in 2018.

A carbon price of USD 50/tCO_2 would equalise Israel's electricity retail price with the cost of rooftop solar PV, creating strong economic incentives for distributed PV deployment.

Policy support would remain the key stimulant for distributed solar PV uptake even if retail prices fully reflected the social cost of electricity generation (IEA, 2019[32]). Israel uses a diverse set of policies to scale up distributed solar PV deployment. Israel's government increased investment incentives by granting small renewable energy installations exemptions from municipal tax, value-added tax, income tax, and betterment levies while streamlining the permit process. All of these measures have contributed to growth of distributed solar PV deployment (EcoTraders, 2019[2]). In addition, the Minister of Energy authorised a 1,600 MW framework for rooftop solar PV in 2018, valid for the next 3 years. The new framework stipulates competitive tenders for commercial rooftop solar, allowing the successful bidder to sell electricity at the winning bid to the grid under a long-term power purchase agreement. In addition, Israel switched from its net-metering scheme to administratively set FiTs for residential solar PV (IEA PVPS, 2018[79]). Households can apply for a 25-year FiT of 0.48 NIS (0.137 USD)/kWh while lower rates apply for larger project sizes (0.45 ILS or 0.129 USD/kWh for projects between 15kW and 100kW) (IEA PVPS, 2018[79]).[13] Too high levels of FiTs risk overcompensating generators, increasing the cost burden of the IEC as electricity buyer.

Real-time self-consumption models provide better incentives than time-invariant FiTs (IEA, 2019[32]). In real-time self-consumption models, the excess electricity generation is sold to the grid at the current electricity market price, in some cases adjusted by some other factors reflecting the benefits of self-consumption. Self-consumption can lead to a reduction of grid costs as grid reinforcement and extension can be deferred, notably when distributed solar PV can lower peak power loads (IEA, 2019[32]). Selling electricity at real-time prices (or at time-varying prices that reflect system value) provides incentives to maximise the market value of electricity generation, e.g. by investing in distributed storage (Section 2.3.4). Real-time self-consumption models already dominate in the commercial PV segment and are employed in the residential PV segment by an increasing number of countries, including Denmark, Germany and Australia (IEA, 2019[32]).

An increasing share of self-consumption, however, can raise concerns on the cost recovery of distribution network costs, requiring adjustment of the retail tariff (IEA, 2019[32]). In Israel, as in most countries, grid costs are recovered from the variable part of the electricity price (EcoTraders, 2019[2]). Lower grid consumption of PV-owners has two implications: First, it challenges the financial viability of the IEC because the (fixed) network costs need to be allocated over a lower number of kWh consumed. Second, ensuring cost recovery may force the Electricity Authority to approve higher tariffs, which poses questions on the fairness of allocating costs between PV-owners and non-owners. PV-owners are still using grid services when consumption exceeds generation, but do not pay the fair share when grid costs are entirely recovered from the variable part of the retail tariff (IEA, 2019[32]). As the share of distributed generation and self-consumption increases, grid costs might be increasingly recovered through the fixed part of a two-part tariff to mitigate this problem (IEA, 2016[55]). However, increasing the fixed part of the electricity tariff would be regressive and would imply that the share of the tariffs' variable part decreases. This reduces the economic incentives for energy efficiency and deploying distributed PV for self-consumption. The Electricity Authority, thus, needs to strike a balance between the two opposing effects as well as between the different stakeholders, including the IEC, IPPs, PV-owners and non-owners (IEA, 2019[32]).

The Israeli government can leverage the dynamics of sub-national governments, including cities and municipalities. Many cities have ambitious (100%) RE targets in the power sector (REN21, 2019[80]). In Israel, the southern city of Eilat aims to be energy independent by 2023 (Haaretz, 2018[81]). Sub-national governments can successfully activate the civil society, strengthening support for more rapid deployment of distributed solar PV or enact special regulations tailored to the preferences of citizens. For example, California and the German city Tübingen require rooftop solar deployment on new buildings. Mandatory deployment of rooftop solar, on a national or sub-national level, would increase deployment in Israel substantially as 1.5 mill houses are yet to be built until 2040 (Chapter 3). In fact, developers of new buildings need to choose whether they want to install solar water heaters or solar PV on their roofs. Currently, the Ministry of Energy is conducting a cost-benefit analysis of mandatory rooftop solar for new buildings (Ministry of Energy, 2019[7]). In addition, new PV technologies (e.g. building-integrated solar PV) would change building design even more drastically by replacing traditional building materials through PV materials.

2.3.4. *Increasing the flexibility of the power system to integrate VREs*

Integrating VREs into the grid by providing flexibility to ensure that supply meets demand at every hour of the day is not yet critical, but will become increasingly important as renewable penetration grows. In 2018, Israel's share of VREs in the electricity generation mix was 3%, putting Israel in the first or second category of the IEA's six phase framework, which categorises countries according to their flexibility needs (IEA, 2016[55]). In these stages, the penetration of VREs has no immediate impact on power system operations, requiring, if at all, only minor operational changes. However, some policy action needs to take place to address specific challenges (Table 2.2). It is important to keep in mind that the share of VREs on total electricity generation reflects the national average; some regions may already have higher shares, and thus facing different challenges.

Table 2.2. Policy action for system integration of VREs in early stages

Possible challenge	Actions
Can the grid accommodate VRE at the identified site?	Solve local grid issues and/or introduce flexibility provisions into the interconnection agreement
Is the grid connection code appropriate?	Develop or upgrade codes with stakeholders
Is VRE reflected in system operations?	Ensure transparency and controllability of power plants Install VRE forecast system
Is VRE being deployed in a system-friendly way?	Manage VRE deployment locations

Source: (IEA, 2019[32]).

With higher penetration of solar PV in the generation mix, flexibility needs are increasing (IEA, 2019[27]). High penetration of solar PV substantially challenges the functioning of the electricity system, leading to the so-called Duck Curve, which is exemplified on the net load of California (Figure 2.3). This curve shows the (expected) net load, i.e. total electricity demand minus the generation of VREs, on January 11 for the years 2012 to 2020, identifying four different ramp periods:

- 4am – 8am (duck's tail): people get up and start their daily routine, need for conventional power
- 8am – 4pm (duck's belly): the sun starts shining, solar power replaces conventional power
- 4pm – 7pm (duck's neck): sun sets, solar generation ends, people come home and start their evening routine, need for steep ramp up
- 7pm – 4am (duck's other parts): no sun, demand is approaching night level

Figure 2.3. Duck Curve and ramping requirements

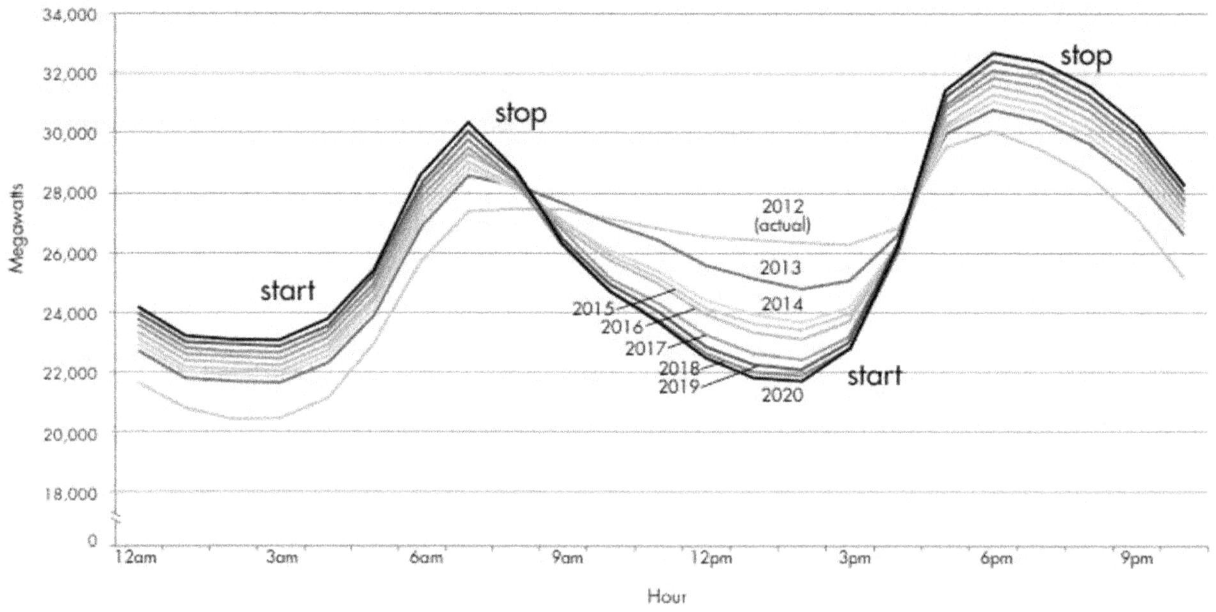

Note: Net load throughout the day on January 11 between 2012 and 2020. 'Stop' and 'start' refer to dispatchable power plants.
Source: (CAISO, 2016[82]).

There are three major challenges associated with the duck curve. First, the duck's belly entails a risk of over-generation where solar PV supply exceeds total demand, potentially necessitating curtailment of renewable electricity. Second, the steep ramp starting at 4pm where conventional power plants need to be brought online rapidly to avoid load curtailment and ensure grid reliability. Third, the demand peak around 7pm currently still needs to be satisfied with conventional power plants (after the sun has set).

A set of strategies and technologies can tackle the various challenges of the duck curve and provide power system flexibility, including storage (e.g. pumped hydro and battery), demand response (DR), and flexible power plants (IEA, 2019[83]). The Ministry of Energy set a quota of 800 MW to procure pumped storage, out of which 640 MW are expected to be built in the coming years (EcoTraders, 2019[2]). Battery storage is expected to be the fastest growing source of global flexibility provision over the next 20 years (IEA, 2019[27]). Batteries can be installed almost everywhere while the modularity allows for scaling according to the flexibility needs. The costs of battery storage declined by 45% between 2012 and 2018 and this trend is expected to continue, making them increasingly competitive with other sources of flexibility (IEA, 2019[27]). Energy arbitrage - buying electricity when solar PV is abundant and prices are low and selling electricity at peak prices - would reduce procurement costs and increase the market value of solar PV, but this requires the existence of an electricity market (see below).

Battery storage coupled with solar PV can also reduce the investments in peaking plants based on natural gas. For example, the Florida Power and Light Energy Storage Centre comprises a 409 MW battery that will be fed by electricity from utility-scale solar PV during the day and will deliver electricity during the evening peak demand. After coming online in 2021, the battery is expected is expected to replace two natural gas power plants. Besides the savings in investments costs associated with the replacement of the two natural gas peaking plants, the battery is also expected to save USD 100 million to customers in fuel costs and 1 million ton CO_2 emissions (IRENA, 2020[84]).

Demand response (DR) has huge potential for low-cost flexibility provision (IEA, 2019[27]). DR can reduce the peak load (duck's neck), typically by around 15%, by shifting load away from the peak towards hours of higher solar penetration (IEA, 2016[55]). Moreover, DR can also avoid curtailment of solar PV generation (filling the belly of the duck), reduce the steepness of the evening ramp and reduce carbon emissions by shifting load from relatively carbon-intense peak hours of the day to hours with high renewable shares (IEA, 2019[27]). The industry sector currently has the biggest potential to provide DR (IEA, 2016[55]). However, also electric appliances in the residential sector, including air conditioners, refrigerators and heat pumps, can shift their load through hours of the day without compromising the quality of their energy services. For these appliances, it is important to improve demand-response readiness, e.g. by introducing labels to inform customers about the capability of the appliances to be controllable by third parties, for example as done in Australia (IEA, 2018[85]). Korea's energy labelling even requires air conditioners to be controllable in order to receive the highest energy rating (IEA, 2018[85]).

With higher penetration of electric vehicles (EVs), demand response becomes almost inevitable, as most consumers are expected to charge their EVs at home after returning from work (IEA, 2018[86]). This would further elevate the peak load, increasing the ramping requirements (transition between duck's belly and duck's neck) and putting considerable strain on the distribution network (IEA, 2019[27]). However, EVs can be also a source for providing (distributed) low-cost flexibility through vehicle to grid technologies, allowing EVs to be charged and discharged at times when it is most beneficial for the power system (IEA, 2019[27]). Currently, vehicle to grid is discussed in California to make the power system more resilient to outages (WRI, 2019[87]).

Tapping the potential of DR, EVs and storage requires having the right incentives and infrastructure in place. Time-of use prices provide important financial incentives for consumers to shift their load towards hours where electricity supply is abundant. In Israel, time-of-use rates are mandatory for large electricity consumers, but not yet for residential consumers (EcoTraders, 2019[2]). Residential time-of use prices were piloted some years ago on a voluntary basis, but the pilots have been stopped (EcoTraders, 2019[2]). Based on a case study on dynamic pricing in Chicago, participating households saved 1-2% of the electricity cost on average and reduced electricity-related GHG emissions by 4% (Allcott, 2011[88]). However, these numbers from early case studies are expected to increase as new information and communication technologies, including smart meters and smart appliances, become available, reducing the transaction costs for electricity consumers and strengthening the effectiveness of dynamic pricing (IEA, 2017[89]). Demand response aggregators, i.e. third-party entities, managing multiple residential loads, could further enhance DR uptake while offering well-paid IT jobs. Creating adequate electricity markets and ensuring market access for a broad range of actors, including aggregators, facilitates the effectiveness of DR. At the same time, cybersecurity risks and other consumer concerns need to be addressed adequately (IEA, 2019[27]).

Electricity generators, including solar PV, can also provide flexibility if the right incentives are in place. Remuneration of solar electricity can increasingly incorporate market exposure, shifting the support mechanism towards feed-in premiums (FiPs) instead of having a fixed FiT with the IEC as guaranteed buyer (IEA, 2019[83]). Fixed FiPs, as in Denmark, are paid on top of the electricity wholesale price, providing incentives for system-friendly behaviour, but also exposes project developers to the highest market risks (Diacore, 2014[90]). Alternatively, sliding FiPs, as those used in Germany and the Netherlands, guarantee a fixed remuneration,[14] but let project developers benefit from electricity prices above the pre-determined remuneration. This incentivises system-friendly behaviour, e.g. by investing in on-site storage or adjusting the orientation of solar panels (Diacore, 2014[90]). Both FiPs and sliding FiPs, however, require a well-functioning electricity wholesale market.

In the absence of an electricity market, the auctioneer can announce, as in Mexico, a set of hourly adjustment factors that reflect the perceived and expected system value of the power system (IRENA, 2019[91]). In addition to a fixed remuneration determined by the auction bid, project developers receive the adjustment, providing incentives to align the generation profile with (expected) system needs while shielding developers from revenue risks. Determining the administratively set hourly adjustment factors is, however, complicated and requires vast amount of information on the generation costs of generators, which can be easier revealed through a market mechanism.

Electricity markets are key enabler for power system flexibility and support efficient co-ordination of a wide range of actors. Despite Israel's major electricity sector reform from 2018, the electricity sector is expected to continue to operate under central planning and not as an electricity market at least in the short and medium term (EcoTraders, 2019[2]). Efficient co-ordination of multiple actors will become even more important as the number and diversity of market participants, including distributed generation and providers of demand response, aggregators and storage is expected to increase. A market aligns the incentives of renewable energy producers with those of the power system and enables business models to provide flexibility, including storage and demand response (IEA, 2016[55]). Other electricity market elements, including scarcity pricing, ancillary service markets and capacity mechanisms, further enhance investments in flexibility (IEA, 2019[27]). Electricity markets also provide incentives for efficient short-term operation as well as investment decisions, potentially leading to lower system costs and lower electricity prices. Temporally and spatially differentiated market prices reflect grid constraints and further enhance operational efficiency while providing incentives to invest in new capacity at places where it is most needed (IEA, 2016[55]). For example, increasing the spatial resolution of the electricity market by switching from zonal to nodal pricing resulted in more efficient system operation of gas power plants of around 2.1% (and lower fuel consumption by 2.5%) in California (Wolak, 2011[92]) as well as lower prices for consumers of around 2% in Texas (Zarnikau, Woo and Baldick, 2014[93]).

Electricity markets are a key enabler for power system flexibility and support efficient co-ordination of a wide range of actors.

2.3.5. Energy efficiency and electrification of end-uses

Energy efficiency can cost-effectively reduce GHG emissions, deliver on a number of well-being goals, mitigate pressure on the power system and can ease the achievement of renewable energy and emission reduction targets, in particular by reducing investments in generating capacity. Yet, improving energy efficiency typically results in less than expected reductions in total electricity consumption and GHG emissions due to the rebound effect (Sorrell, Dimitropoulos and Sommerville, 2009[94]). For electricity, the rebound effect is estimated to be around 0.1, meaning that an initial 10kWh decrease of electricity consumption due to more efficient electric equipment would trigger a second-order increase of 1kWh due to consumer and market response, reducing the final saving to 9kWh (Gillingham, Rapson and Wagner, 2015[95]). The National Plan for Energy Efficiency-Electricity Consumption Reduction aims to reduce electricity consumption by 17% by 2030, relative to BAU consumption. The plan sets out key priorities for energy efficiency in the residential, commercial and industry sector and foresees most (47.2%) of the electricity reduction by 2020 to be achieved in the residential sector (Ministry of Energy, 2015[96]).

Electrification of end-uses (e.g. EVs in transport, heat pumps in buildings and electric motors in industry) is a key strategy to improve energy efficiency. For example, EVs are much more energy efficient than cars with internal combustion engines (IEA, 2018[86]). The Ministry of Energy is planning to ban the sales of new cars with internal combustion engines by 2030, which is expected to increase EV uptake (Chapter 4) and, thus, electricity consumption. Assuming the share of private electric vehicles, commercial vehicles and trucks to be 8%, 8% and 3% respectively by 2030 would increase electricity demand by 2.06TWh (EcoTraders, 2019[2]), equivalent to 2.6% of the targeted total electricity consumption in 2030. Higher EV shares would lead to higher electricity consumption. Yet, EVs can also be a major (low-cost) source of flexibility, improving the integration of renewables and the efficiency of the power system (Section 2.3.4). Mapping different EV pathways and electrification pathways is crucial to inform future power infrastructure needs (e.g. generation assets and networks) and to support long-term planning. Increasing electrification will also require distribution network upgrades. If upgrades are carried out, the network capacity may be expanded substantially as the cost of upgrading is relatively insensitive to the size of the capacity increase (Imperial College London and Vivid Economics, 2019[97]).

Israel uses a broad set of measures to improve energy efficiency. Many energy efficiency measures are related to the design and the insulation of buildings, which determine cooling and heating requirements of residential buildings, accounting for more than 50% in residential electricity consumption (BDO, 2017[98]). Chapter 3 will discuss these measures in detail. In addition, Israel also uses minimum energy performance standards (MEPS) for key equipment (see below), regulations on industry and large energy consumers that require periodical energy surveys and equipment efficiency tests, budgets and requirements for energy efficiency in the government sector as well as grants and loans (EcoTraders, 2019[2]). Israel has resumed the National Support Mechanism for Energy Efficiency and Emission Reduction with a renewed budget of NIS 300 million and will allocate NIS 500 million in loan guarantees over a ten-year period to leverage investment in the fields of energy efficiency. The government is currently discussing more stringent minimum performance standards for electric appliances as well as a set of market-based policy instruments, including a purchase mechanism for non-consumed megawatt and an energy efficiency certificates trade system (obligation) (EcoTraders, 2019[2]).

MEPS for key equipment and appliances, including air conditioners and refrigerators, are most effective for the diffusion of more energy efficient equipment (IEA, 2018[85]). Israel applies MEPS for a broad range of electric equipment, reducing electricity consumption and in turn saving money for private households and industry. MEPS can be complemented by labelling, which is a low-cost option to provide information and improve decisions of electricity customers (IEA, 2018[85]). Residential consumer savings on energy bills through MEPS and labels can be as high as EUR 490 a year on average as estimated for the European Union's updated Ecodesign MEPS (European Parliament, 2019[99]).

Market-based instruments (MBi), such as energy efficiency obligations and auctions, offer efficiency gains more cost-effectively as they leave the decision on how to save energy to market actors, discovering the most cost-effective way to achieve a given target (OECD and IEA, 2017[100]). Obligations would require the utility to deliver a pre-specified amount of energy savings whereas auctions seek market actors to bid for energy savings. Several approaches for calculating the savings exist, but most existing MBi programs are using deemed savings, i.e. estimates based on previous efficiency measures using the same technology. MBi have proven to stimulate private investment (with a leverage factor up to 3), reduce electricity consumption cost-effectively, deter investments in generation capacity and avoid investment in network upgrades (as in New York) (OECD and IEA, 2017[100]).

The IEC as the monopolistic retailer and owner of the distribution and transmission network could leverage on these network savings, further improving cost-effectiveness and easing short-term congestion problems. Raising funds from an energy company rather than from the government budget is likely to deliver more stable outcomes due to the annual budget reviews in the political process (OECD and IEA, 2017[100]). In addition, the IEC as a state-owned enterprise may benefit from preferential financing conditions due to better credit ratings, allowing for further cost-reductions (Prag, Röttgers and Scherrer, 2018[77]). For example, the IEC could use on-bill financing, financing upfront energy efficiency improvements and allowing repayment to be made as part of the monthly electricity bill. The IEC could also co-finance the installation of modern and smart air conditioners in private dwellings and reserve the right to remotely control the equipment under pre-specified conditions to shift load. In addition to conserving energy, this can reduce peak demand and can further defer grid reinforcement. It would also create new business opportunities for the IEC, likely easing the transition towards a low-carbon electricity sector for its employees. The IEC may also go one step further and provide energy services through long-term agreements with customers that stipulate the delivery of a specific energy service (e.g. lighting or cooling) instead of delivering just electricity. Energy service companies, such as Proven Lightning in the UK, are currently focussing predominantly on commercial clients as the residential sector is too heterogeneous (IEA, 2018[85]).

Some energy efficiency programmes are specifically targeted to low-income or fuel-poor households. The UK ECO Scheme restricts the energy efficiency obligation entirely to households subject to fuel poverty (OECD and IEA, 2017[100]). The Brazilian obligation scheme has required utilities to allocate at least 60%

of the investment to low-income communities or households since 2010. Most of the measures consisted in fully funded provision of energy efficient lightbulbs and refrigerators, reducing the electricity bill of low-income households (OECD and IEA, 2017[100]). Bulk procurement of equipment and appliances in competitive tenders as done under the Indian 'Unnat Jyoti by Affordable LEDs for All' (UJALA) programme can further reduce the costs. Combined with a public awareness campaign, India procured LEDs in large quantities and passed the reduced rates on to the customers. The scheme is responsible for annual energy savings of around 100 TWh and 790 Mt CO_2 emissions while avoiding 20.000 MW of generation capacity (EESL, 2019[101]). India is currently exploring bulk procurement for highly energy efficient air conditioners.

Non-targeted energy efficiency investments can also be beneficial for low-income households even if they are not directly enrolled. This is because the social returns of energy efficiency improvements in terms of reduced system costs, including avoided distribution and transmission grid upgrades and avoided environmental costs, are returned to all customers, including low-income households, and can be larger than the direct costs associated with the investment (OECD and IEA, 2017[100]). Based on a study in Vermont, the social benefits of energy saving (USD 147/MWh) clearly outweighed the costs incurred by the obligation (USD 39/MWh) (OECD and IEA, 2017[100]). Part of the benefits (USD 47/MWh) was passed on to all participants, outweighing the initial increase in the electricity price, including for low-income households. Of course, this effect varies across programmes and crucially depends on whether and how the social benefits are returned to customers.

References

Allcott, H. (2011), "Rethinking real-time electricity pricing", *Resource and Energy Economics*, Vol. 33/4, pp. 820-842, http://dx.doi.org/10.1016/J.RESENEECO.2011.06.003. [88]

Baranzini, A. and S. Carattini (2017), "Effectiveness, earmarking and labeling: testing the acceptability of carbon taxes with survey data", *Environmental Economics and Policy Studies*, Vol. 19/1, pp. 197-227, https://doi.org/10.1007/s10018-016-0144-7. [64]

BDO (2017), *Israel Natural Gas Demand Forecast 2017-2040*, https://www.delek-group.com/wp-content/uploads/2017/09/BDO-Gas-Market-Forecast-2-07-2017-for-Delek-Group-with-final-letter-1.pdf (accessed on 15 November 2019). [98]

BEIS (2019), *Annual Fuel Poverty Statistics in England*, Department for Business, Energy and Industrial Strategy, https://www.gov.uk/government/publications/fuel-poverty-statistics-methodology-handbook (accessed on 15 November 2019). [56]

BEIS (2018), *Supply Chain Plan Guidance*, Department for Business, Energy & Industrial Strategy, http://www.nationalarchives.gov.uk/doc/open-government-licence/ (accessed on 16 December 2019). [71]

CAISO (2016), *What the duck curve tells us about managing a green grid*, http://www.caiso.com (accessed on 16 December 2019). [82]

CPUC (2019), *Solar in Disadvantaged Communities*, https://www.cpuc.ca.gov/SolarInDACs/ (accessed on 16 December 2019). [58]

Dechezleprêtre, A., N. Rivers and B. Stadler (2019), "The economic cost of air pollution: Evidence from Europe", *OECD Economics Department Working Papers*, No. 1584, OECD Publishing, Paris, https://dx.doi.org/10.1787/56119490-en. [17]

Diacore (2014), *Best practice design features for RES-E support schemes and best practice methodologies to determine remuneration levels.* [90]

Eastmed (2017), *Eastmed Policy Brief*, http://eastmedproject.eu/files/IO6-1stpolicybrief.pdf (accessed on 16 December 2019). [33]

Eberhard, A. and R. Naude (2017), *THE SOUTH AFRICAN RENEWABLE ENERGY IPP PROCUREMENT PROGRAMME: Review, Lessons Learned & Proposals to Reduce Transaction Costs*, https://www.gsb.uct.ac.za/files/EberhardNaude_REIPPPPReview_2017_1_1.pdf (accessed on 12 February 2019). [69]

EcoTraders (2019), *The Electricity Sector: Main policies, barriers and opportunities.* [2]

EESL (2019), *About UJALA*, https://eeslindia.org/content/raj/eesl/en/Programmes/UJALA/About-UJALA.html (accessed on 20 June 2019). [101]

Electricity Authority (2018), *Market Report for 2018*, https://pua.gov.il/English/Pages/default.aspx. [9]

Ellis, J., D. Nachtigall and F. Venmans (2019), "Carbon pricing and competitiveness: Are they at odds?", *OECD Environment Working Papers*, No. 152, OECD Publishing, Paris, https://dx.doi.org/10.1787/f79a75ab-en. [61]

ENTSO-E and ENTSO-G (2018), *TYNDP 2018: Scenario Report*, https://ec.eur (accessed on 9 December 2019). [73]

Ettmayr, C. and H. Lloyd (2017), "Local content requirements and the impact on the South African renewable energy sector", *South African Journal of Economic and Management Sciences*, Vol. 20/1, pp. 1-11, http://dx.doi.org/10.4102/sajems. [68]

European Parliament (2019), *Ecodesign directive: From energy efficiency to recycling | News | European Parliament*, http://www.europarl.europa.eu/news/en/headlines/society/20180522STO04021/ecodesign-directive-from-energy-efficiency-to-recycling (accessed on 20 June 2019). [99]

Fantidis, J. et al. (2012), "Financial Analysis of Solar Water Heating Systems during the Depression: Case Study of Greece", *Engineering Economics*, Vol. 23/1, http://dx.doi.org/10.5755/j01.ee.23.1.1222. [42]

Fischhendler, I., D. Nathan and D. Boymel (2015), "Marketing Renewable Energy through Geopolitics: Solar Farms in Israel", *Global Environmental Politics*, Vol. 15/2, pp. 98-120, http://dx.doi.org/10.1162/glep_a_00300. [45]

Fitch-Roy, O. and B. Woodman (2016), *Auctions for Renewable Energy Support in the United Kingdom: Instruments and lessons learnt*, http://dx.doi.org/10.13140/RG.2.1.4462.1686. [70]

Flues, F. and K. van Dender (2017), "The impact of energy taxes on the affordability of domestic energy", *OECD Taxation Working Papers*, No. 30, OECD Publishing, Paris, https://dx.doi.org/10.1787/08705547-en. [57]

Fuentes, A. (2009), "Reforms to Open Sheltered Sectors to Competition in Switzerland", *OECD Economics Department Working Papers*, No. 667, OECD Publishing, Paris, https://dx.doi.org/10.1787/226785745104. [78]

Gallo, L. and Y. Porath (2017), *The Development of the Electricity Market in Israel: Toward a Sustainable Electricity Market*, Bank of Israel Research Department. [31]

Gillingham, K., D. Rapson and G. Wagner (2015), "The Rebound Effect and Energy Efficiency Policy", *Review of Environmental Economics and Policy*, Vol. 10/1, pp. 68-88, http://dx.doi.org/10.1093/reep/rev017. [95]

Haaretz (2018), *Israeli cities take the lead in recycling and renewable energy*, https://www.haaretz.com/israel-news/israeli-cities-take-the-lead-in-recycling-and-renewable-energy-1.5867242 (accessed on 16 December 2019). [81]

High-Level Commission on Carbon Prices (2017), *Report of the High-Level Commission on Carbon Prices*, World Bank, Washington, DC, http://www.carbonpricingleadership.org. (accessed on 3 August 2018). [48]

Hirth, L., J. Mühlenpfordt and M. Bulkeley (2018), "The ENTSO-E Transparency Platform – A review of Europe's most ambitious electricity data platform", *Applied Energy*, Vol. 225, pp. 1054-1067, http://dx.doi.org/10.1016/j.apenergy.2018.04.048. [74]

ICAP (2018), *Emissions Trading Worldwide: Status Report 2018*, https://icapcarbonaction.com/en/?option=com_attach&task=download&id=547 (accessed on 1 June 2018). [51]

IEA (2019), *Electricity Information 2019*, OECD Publishing, Paris, https://dx.doi.org/10.1787/e0ebb7e9-en. [44]

IEA (2019), *Israel solar PV auction*, https://www.iea.org/policies/6385-israel-solar-pv-auction?country=Israel&qs=Israel&sector=Electricity (accessed on 16 December 2019). [67]

IEA (2019), *Renewables 2019: Analysis and forecasts to 2024*, International Energy Agency, Paris, https://dx.doi.org/10.1787/b3911209-en. [32]

IEA (2019), *Status of Power System Transformation 2019: Power system flexibility*, OECD Publishing, Paris, https://dx.doi.org/10.1787/7c49400a-en. [83]

IEA (2019), *The Future of Hydrogen: Seizing today's opportunities*, OECD, Paris Cedex 16, https://dx.doi.org/10.1787/1e0514c4-en. [28]

IEA (2019), *World Energy Outlook 2019*, OECD Publishing, Paris, https://dx.doi.org/10.1787/caf32f3b-en. [27]

IEA (2018), "Emissions per kWh of electricity and heat output (Edition 2018)", *IEA CO2 Emissions from Fuel Combustion Statistics* (database), https://dx.doi.org/10.1787/5f382d97-en (accessed on 4 March 2020). [3]

IEA (2018), *Energy Efficiency 2018: Analysis and outlooks to 2040*, International Energy Agency, Paris, https://dx.doi.org/10.1787/9789264024304-en. [85]

IEA (2018), *Global EV Outlook 2018: Towards cross-modal electrification*, International Energy Agency, Paris, https://dx.doi.org/10.1787/9789264302365-en. [86]

IEA (2018), *Renewables 2018: Analysis and Forecasts to 2023*, International Energy Agency, Paris, https://dx.doi.org/10.1787/re_mar-2018-en. [66]

IEA (2018), *World Energy Outlook 2018*, International Energy Agency, Paris, https://dx.doi.org/10.1787/weo-2018-en. [10]

IEA (2017), *Digitalization & Energy*, International Energy Agency, Paris, https://dx.doi.org/10.1787/9789264286276-en. [89]

IEA (2016), *Re-powering Markets: Market design and regulation during the transition to low-carbon power systems*, Electricity Market Series, International Energy Agency, Paris, https://dx.doi.org/10.1787/9789264209596-en. [55]

IEA (2016), *World Energy Outlook 2016*, International Energy Agency, Paris, https://dx.doi.org/10.1787/weo-2016-en. [6]

IEA and CEEW (2019), *Women working in the rooftop solar sector*, IEA, Paris, http://www.iea.org/publications/reports/womeninindiasrooftopsolarsector/. [39]

IEA PVPS (2018), *Annual Report 2018*, International Energy Agency, Paris. [79]

IMF (2019), *Fiscal Monitor: How to Mitigate Climate Change*, International Monetary Fund, Washington. [49]

Imperial College London and Vivid Economics (2019), *Accelerated Electrification and the GB Electricity System*. [97]

IPCC (2014), “Energy Systems”, in *Climate Change 2014: Mitigation of Climate Change. Contribution of Working Group III to the Fifth Assessment Report of the Intergovernmental Panel on Climate Change*, Cambridge University Press, Cambridge, https://www.ipcc.ch/pdf/assessment-report/ar5/wg3/ipcc_wg3_ar5_chapter7.pdf. [4]

IPCC (2014), “Energy Systems”, in *Climate Change 2014: Mitigation of Climate Change. Contribution of Working Group III to the Fifth Assessment Report of the Intergovernmental Panel on Climate Change*, Cambridge University Press, Cambridge, https://www.ipcc.ch/pdf/assessment-report/ar5/wg3/ipcc_wg3_ar5_chapter7.pdf. [29]

IRENA (2020), *Electricity Storage Valuation Framework*, International Renewable Energy Agency, Abu Dhabi. [84]

IRENA (2019), *Renewable energy auctions: Status and trends beyond price*, International Renewable Energy Agency, Abu Dhabi. [91]

IRENA (2018), *Renewable Energy and Jobs: Annual Review 2018*, http://irena.org/-/media/Files/IRENA/Agency/Publication/2018/May/IRENA_RE_Jobs_Annual_Review_2018.pdf (accessed on 14 June 2018). [37]

Kallbekken, S. and M. Aasen (2010), “The demand for earmarking: Results from a focus group study”, *Ecological Economics*, Vol. 69/11, pp. 2183-2190, https://doi.org/10.1016/j.ecolecon.2010.06.003. [63]

Kallbekken, S., S. Kroll and T. Cherry (2011), “Do you not like Pigou, or do you not understand him? Tax aversion and revenue recycling in the lab”, *Elsevier Journal of Environmental Economics and Management*, Vol. 62/1, pp. 53-64, https://doi.org/10.1016/j.jeem.2010.10.006. [65]

Koźluk, T. (2014), "The Indicators of the Economic Burdens of Environmental Policy Design: Results from the OECD Questionnaire", *OECD Economics Department Working Papers*, No. 1178, OECD Publishing, Paris, https://dx.doi.org/10.1787/5jxrjnbnbm8v-en. [76]

Lavy, V., A. Ebenstein and S. Roth (2014), *The Impact of Short Term Exposure to Ambient Air Pollution on Cognitive Performance and Human Capital Formation*, National Bureau of Economic Research, Cambridge, MA, http://dx.doi.org/10.3386/w20648. [16]

Ludin, N. et al. (2018), "Prospects of life cycle assessment of renewable energy from solar photovoltaic technologies: A review", *Renewable and Sustainable Energy Reviews*, Vol. 96, pp. 11-28, http://dx.doi.org/10.1016/j.rser.2018.07.048. [102]

Marten, M. and K. van Dender (2019), "The use of revenues from carbon pricing", *OECD Taxation Working Papers*, No. 43, OECD Publishing, Paris, https://dx.doi.org/10.1787/3cb265e4-en. [62]

Ministry for the Ecological and Inclusive Transition (2019), *Chèque Energie*, https://chequeenergie.gouv.fr/beneficiaire/eligibilite (accessed on 16 December 2019). [60]

Ministry of Energy (2019), *Written Information from Israel's Ministry of Energy*. [7]

Ministry of Energy (2018), *Historical Signing: Israel joins the PPCA, a Global Agreement to Reduce the Use of Coal; Declares the Cessation of Coal Use by 2030*, https://www.gov.il/en/departments/news/ppca (accessed on 15 November 2019). [18]

Ministry of Energy (2017), *Israel's income from royalties from natural resources is expected to be multiplied by four by 2020*, https://www.gov.il/en/departments/news/royalties_from_natural_resources (accessed on 15 November 2019). [19]

Ministry of Energy (2015), *National Energy Efficiency Plan*. [96]

Ministry of Environmental Protection (2019), *Natural Gas Production in Israel: Leviathan*, http://www.sviva.gov.il/English/env_topics/climatechange/fossil_fuels/Pages/Natural-Gas-Production-in-Israel.aspx (accessed on 15 November 2019). [30]

Ministry of Environmental Protection (2019), *The external cost of air pollution*, http://www.sviva.gov.il/subjectsenv/svivaair/documents/airexternalcost/airexternalcoast-2019.docx. [50]

Ministry of Environmental Protection (2019), *איכות האוויר במפרץ חיפה*. [14]

Ministry of Environmental Protection (2018), *A Comparative Study of the Carbon Capture Alternatives in the Production of Natural Gas-based Transportation Fuels*, http://www.sviva.gov.il/infoservices/reservoirinfo/doclib4/r0401-r0500/r0459.pdf (accessed on 15 November 2019). [26]

Ministry of Environmental Protection (2018), *Israel's Third National Communication on Climate Change*. [12]

Ministry of Environmental Protection (2015), *Israel's first biennial update report*. [75]

Ministry of Finance (2019), *Energy Stocks in the Government Pension Fund Global*. [23]

Ministry of Finance (2014), *Guidelines for observation and exclusion from the Government Pension Fund Global.* [22]

Ministry of Health (2017), *Environmental Health in Israel | 2017*, http://www.ehf.org.il/en (accessed on 4 November 2019). [15]

Ministry of National Infrastructures (2010), *POLICY ON THE INTEGRATION OF RENEWABLE ENERGY SOURCES INTO THE ISRAELI ELECTRICITY SECTOR*, http://archive.energy.gov.il/English/PublicationsLibraryE/REPolicy.pdf (accessed on 15 November 2019). [41]

Norges Bank (2019), *Norway's Government Pension Fund Global*, https://www.nbim.no/ (accessed on 16 December 2019). [21]

OECD (2019), *Accelerating Climate Action: Refocusing Policies through a Well-being Lens*, OECD Publishing, Paris, https://dx.doi.org/10.1787/2f4c8c9a-en. [8]

OECD (2019), "Air and climate: Air and greenhouse gas emissions by industry - OECD Estimates", *OECD Environment Statistics* (database), https://dx.doi.org/10.1787/68a25273-en (accessed on 15 November 2019). [1]

OECD (2019), "Labour Force Statistics: Employment by activities and status", *OECD Employment and Labour Market Statistics* (database), https://dx.doi.org/10.1787/data-00289-en (accessed on 15 November 2019). [35]

OECD (2019), *Revenue Statistics 2019*, OECD Publishing, Paris, https://dx.doi.org/10.1787/0bbc27da-en. [105]

OECD (2019), *Taxing Energy Use 2019: Using Taxes for Climate Action*, OECD Publishing, Paris, https://dx.doi.org/10.1787/058ca239-en. [52]

OECD (2018), "Air and climate: Air emissions by source (Edition 2018)", *OECD Environment Statistics* (database), https://dx.doi.org/10.1787/33987876-en (accessed on 15 November 2019). [13]

OECD (2018), *Effective Carbon Rates 2018: Pricing Carbon Emissions Through Taxes and Emissions Trading*, OECD Publishing, Paris, https://dx.doi.org/10.1787/9789264305304-en. [54]

OECD (2018), *Human Acceleration of the Nitrogen Cycle: Managing Risks and Uncertainty*, OECD Publishing, Paris, https://dx.doi.org/10.1787/9789264307438-en. [5]

OECD (2018), *OECD Companion to the Inventory of Support Measures for Fossil Fuels 2018*, OECD Publishing, Paris, https://dx.doi.org/10.1787/9789264286061-en. [53]

OECD (2018), *OECD Economic Surveys: Israel 2018*, OECD Publishing, Paris, https://dx.doi.org/10.1787/eco_surveys-isr-2018-en. [20]

OECD (2017), *Investing in Climate, Investing in Growth*, OECD Publishing, Paris, https://dx.doi.org/10.1787/9789264273528-en. [34]

OECD (2017), "The environmental case for natural gas", in *World Energy Outlook 2017*, OECD Publishing, Paris, https://dx.doi.org/10.1787/weo-2017-12-en. [24]

OECD (2016), *OECD Environmental Performance Reviews: France 2016*, OECD Environmental Performance Reviews, OECD Publishing, Paris, https://dx.doi.org/10.1787/9789264252714-en. [59]

OECD (2015), *Policy Guidance for Investment in Clean Energy Infrastructure: Expanding Access to Clean Energy for Green Growth and Development*, OECD Publishing, Paris, https://dx.doi.org/10.1787/9789264212664-en. [72]

OECD (2012), *Linking Renewable Energy to Rural Development*, OECD Green Growth Studies, OECD Publishing, Paris, https://dx.doi.org/10.1787/9789264180444-en. [36]

OECD and IEA (2017), *Market-based Instruments for Energy Efficiency*. [100]

Potter, J. et al. (2012), "Clean-Tech Clustering as an Engine for Local Development: The Negev Region, Israel", *OECD Local Economic and Employment Development (LEED) Working Papers*, No. 2012/11, OECD Publishing, Paris, https://dx.doi.org/10.1787/5k98p4wm6kmv-en. [38]

Prag, A., D. Röttgers and I. Scherrer (2018), "State-Owned Enterprises and the Low-Carbon Transition", *OECD Environment Working Papers*, No. 129, OECD Publishing, Paris, https://dx.doi.org/10.1787/06ff826b-en. [77]

Quarton, C. and S. Samsatli (2018), "Power-to-gas for injection into the gas grid: What can we learn from real-life projects, economic assessments and systems modelling?", *Renewable and Sustainable Energy Reviews*, Vol. 98, pp. 302-316, http://dx.doi.org/10.1016/j.rser.2018.09.007. [104]

REN21 (2019), *Renewables in Cities Global Status Report*, Renewable Energy Policy Network for the 21st Century, Paris. [80]

RFF (2019), *PG&E Power Outages Reduce Just a Portion of Wildfire Risk*, https://www.rff.org/news/press-releases/new-blog-post-pge-power-outages-reduce-just-portion-wildfire-risk/ (accessed on 15 November 2019). [43]

Schiebahn, S. et al. (2015), "Power to gas: Technological overview, systems analysis and economic assessment for a case study in Germany", *International Journal of Hydrogen Energy*, Vol. 40/12, pp. 4285-4294, http://dx.doi.org/10.1016/j.ijhydene.2015.01.123. [103]

Shindell, D. et al. (2012), "Simultaneously Mitigating Near-Term Climate Change and Improving Human Health and Food Security", *Science*, Vol. 335/6065, pp. 183-189, http://dx.doi.org/10.1126/science.1210026. [25]

Solomon, A., D. Bogdanov and C. Breyer (2018), "Solar driven net zero emission electricity supply with negligible carbon cost: Israel as a case study for Sun Belt countries", *Energy*, Vol. 155, pp. 87-104, http://dx.doi.org/10.1016/j.energy.2018.05.014. [40]

Sorrell, S., J. Dimitropoulos and M. Sommerville (2009), "Empirical estimates of the direct rebound effect: A review", *Energy Policy*, Vol. 37/4, pp. 1356-1371, http://dx.doi.org/10.1016/j.enpol.2008.11.026. [94]

Spencer, R. et al. (2018), "Floating Photovoltaic Systems: Assessing the Technical Potential of Photovoltaic Systems on Man-Made Water Bodies in the Continental United States", *Environmental Science & Technology*, Vol. 53/3, pp. 1680-1689, http://dx.doi.org/10.1021/acs.est.8b04735. [47]

Taboada, M. et al. (2017), "Solar water heating system and photovoltaic floating cover to reduce evaporation: Experimental results and modeling", *Renewable Energy*, Vol. 105, pp. 601-615, http://dx.doi.org/10.1016/j.renene.2016.12.094. [46]

Vardimon, R. (2011), "Assessment of the potential for distributed photovoltaic electricity production in Israel", *Renewable Energy*, Vol. 36/2, pp. 591-594, http://dx.doi.org/10.1016/j.renene.2010.07.030. [11]

Wolak, F. (2011), "Measuring the benefits of greater spatial granularity in short-term pricing in wholesale electricity markets", *American Economic Review*, Vol. 101/3, pp. 247-252. [92]

WRI (2019), *How California Can Use Electric Vehicles to Keep the Lights On*, https://www.wri.org/blog/2019/11/how-california-can-use-electric-vehicles-keep-lights?utm_campaign=wridigest&utm_source=wridigest-2019-11-12&utm_medium=email&utm_content=readmore (accessed on 16 December 2019). [87]

Zarnikau, J., C. Woo and R. Baldick (2014), "Did the introduction of a nodal market structure impact wholesale electricity prices in the Texas (ERCOT) market?", *Journal of Regulatory Economics*, Vol. 45/2, pp. 194-208. [93]

Notes

[1] Note that electricity-related GHG emissions spiked in 2012 at 48.9 Mt CO2e due to the anomalous disruption of the gas supply and the following higher generation through coal plants. Hence, the year 2012 does not represent an appropriate reference year to indicate emission trends.

[2] The 2019 budget of Israel sees government expenses of NIS 480 bill.

[3] This figure is based on the 2018 carbon intensity of natural gas (393g/kWh, (Electricity Authority, 2018[9])) and assumes electricity consumption growth to continue at a rate of 2.1% until 2050. Electricity-related CO_2 emissions in 2018 were 37.8 Mt CO_2 (EcoTraders, 2019[2]).

[4] Lifecycle emissions from solar PV originate predominantly from the construction phase and range from 18 to 180gCO_2e/kWh with a median of 50gCO_2e/kWh (IPCC, 2014[4]). More recent studies suggest that this range has narrowed to 6 to 87gCO2e/kWh (Ludin et al., 2018[102]).

[5] A hydrogen blend of 5% in the gas mix is currently the maximum threshold in some countries, including Germany (Schiebahn et al., 2015[103]). However, most technological studies suggest that this share could be increased to 15 – 20% (Quarton and Samsatli, 2018[104]). Beyond these shares, hydrogen would need to be transmitted through a dedicated network.

[6] Note that these figures refer to the period before the COVID-19 crisis.

[7] The unemployment and poverty rates in the Negev is higher than in the rest of Israel (Potter et al., 2012[38]). Levels of education are lower and the economic structure weaker, with manufacturing and agriculture accounting for 22% of total employment (Potter et al., 2012[38]). While the Negev has a diversity of skills in the labour force, albeit with a relatively low share of high-skilled labour suitable for renewable energy, there is a need for training to accommodate for growth in solar PV deployment (Potter et al., 2012[38]).

[8] Annual required capacity addition post 2020 is based on expected renewable capacity of 3,800 MW in 2020. Expected capacity addition in 2020 is 1,367 MW (Electricity Authority, 2018[9]).

[9] However, this number rather represents a lower bound as technological improvements in the panel efficiency are not taken into account and the available rooftop area was estimated conservatively and has since increased.

[10] Note that this figure applies to the electricity sector only. This figure may contradict the fact that the share of Israel's environmentally related tax revenues on total tax revenue or GDP are one of the highest across OECD countries (OECD, 2019[105]). However, the high share for Israel is primarily driven by the high tax rates and revenues in the transport sector (Section 4.3).

[11] See the upcoming second part of the OECD report "Accelerating Climate Action: Refocusing Policies through a Well-being lens" for further discussion.

[12] California defines disadvantaged communities as communities that are disproportionately burdened by and vulnerable to multiple sources of pollution (CPUC, 2019[58]).

[13] Distributed solar PV for self-consumption outside the framework can sell the excess generation at NIS 0.16 (USD 0.045) kWh to the grid.

[14] Typically, the premium is defined as difference between the winning bid and a reference electricity price, in most cases defined as the average electricity market value of solar plants in a given period.

3 Policies for a sustainable residential sector

This chapter discusses how to accelerate climate mitigation in the residential sector whilst delivering broader well-being goals, such as affordable housing. Building 1.5 million new homes by 2040 under the Strategic Housing Programme may resolve the shortage of affordable housing, but runs the risk of drastically increasing emissions across the lifecycle of a building and indirect emissions (e.g., transport). The first section sets out a number of policies and recommendations to decarbonise dwellings, such as green and circular public procurement, and financing mechanisms for retrofits of the existing building stock. The following section presents recommendations for decarbonising beyond the dwelling to foster smart urban planning especially given the projected population growth in Israel and increasing heat island effects due to climate change; in addition to ways to relieve the financial burden placed on municipalities, for example, via greater decentralisation and the creation of Metropolitan authorities.

In Brief

Key findings and recommendations for Israel's residential sector

Residential emissions plateaued over the last decade, but could dramatically increase due to planned housing developments in the next two decades. 1.5 million dwellings will be constructed by 2040, increasing the housing supply by 60% relative to 2011 (EcoTraders, 2019[1]). If poorly and hastily constructed, these new dwellings could lock-in emission-intensive infrastructure until mid-century; putting pressure on other sectors (e.g. energy) to help reach the Paris Agreement targets.

At the dwelling-level, generating demand for sustainable dwellings whilst upgrading the existing supply of housing will be key.

- By using green and circular public procurement for the 1.5 million homes under the Strategic Housing Programme, the government can generate demand for sustainable house and establish a sustainable construction sector. Analyses show that this does not need to cost more meaning it could be feasible.
- To improve the existing supply of housing, establishing emissions limit values for existing and new dwellings is one tool to lower emissions.
- High upfront costs and long payback periods can make retrofits unattractive to property owners. Innovative financial instruments could catalyse retrofits, e.g. soft loans. Providing information on green leases to property owners and tenants could be another means of fostering retrofits.

Beyond the dwelling, steer smart growth both in existing urban cores and in peripheral areas.

- Minimum density regulations, urban infill and brownfield redevelopments with the use of land value capture mechanisms, land assembly mechanisms, and split-rate property taxation, can contribute to making cities more compact and sustainable.
- Promoting the uptake of eco-neighbourhoods, by directing adequate funds (both from the national government and municipalities) and linking them to compliance with more ambitious standards will be important.
- Planning and anticipating the inevitable growth that will occur in less – or non- urbanized zones will be paramount for ensuring urban areas expand in a sustainable way. This entails putting in place policies that guide developments along existing or future transport lines, e.g. planning for sufficiently spaced arterial grids, incorporating transport considerations into development standards.
- Providing an adequate level of infrastructure and services, such as green space, water and waste management systems, and connections to accessible and frequent transport, will ensure the liveability of dense and compact urban areas. Israel can put in place standards that can ensure the provision of this infrastructure (e.g. using green space factors or transport accessibility indicators).
- Simplifying and enhancing existing affordable housing assistance schemes is key to align the climate and equity agendas. Ways forward include widening the beneficiaries, determining assistance by need (i.e. backed by affordability analysis) whilst increasing rental supply through the removal of existing barriers (e.g. discouraging vacant homes by better enforcing the taxation on empty homes).

Decrease financial burden of municipalities and attract innovative sources of finance.

- Overcoming the budgetary constraints of Israeli municipalities calls for greater devolution of power, funding and responsibilities to local governments. Building on good practice across the OECD, Israel can embark in a decentralisation process, providing greater autonomy and capacity to municipalities while ensuring coherence in planning and investment. The creation of metropolitan bodies could, for instance, be part of new institutional framework.
- In addition to gaining financial capacity through a decentralisation process, Israeli municipalities could look at innovative ways to promote cooperation of a range of public and private actors, (e.g. inter-ministerial pool funding or Business Improvement Districts).

3.1. Introduction

Israel faces two seemingly competing challenges in the residential sector, on the one hand, is a dire need for affordable housing, and on the other, is the necessity to decarbonise the sector. The housing shortage came to a head in the summer of 2011, when millions protested rising rents and lack of housing throughout the country.[1] A decade later, the problem persists today.[2] Rents have risen nearly 60% since 2010, a drastic increase for the 33.5% of Israelis who rent. In response, the Israeli government is building as many dwellings as quickly and cheaply as possible, but without adequate regulation of key sustainability determinants (EcoTraders, 2019[1]).

Pursuing only one of these priorities in policymaking could undermine the attainment of the other. Building dwellings as rapidly and inexpensively as possible, without due consideration of their sustainability, will increase GHG emissions (OECD, 2019[2]). Emissions will accumulate from carbon-intensive materials (e.g., cement, steel), energy use during the building's occupation and its eventual demolition (WorldGBC, 2019[3]). Likewise, optimising policies for decarbonisation, for example, the creation of eco-districts, without taking into account the adverse impacts for affordability due to increases in value of land and property, could price out low-income families, further entrenching social inequalities and aggravating the problem of unaffordable housing (OECD, 2019[2]).

Policymaking in the residential sector should create affordable low-carbon housing that is also safe, comfortable, and equitable. Failure to do so could lead to irrevocable trade-offs (OECD, 2019[2]), locking in emission-intensive infrastructure for decades to come (see the discussion in Chapter 1). A well-being approach helps policymakers assess trade-offs and synergies between affordability and sustainability, or other priorities, signalling where complementary policies are needed (OECD, 2019[2]). Well-crafted policy packages can accelerate climate action in the residential sector by helping garner widespread political and social support.

A well-being approach to policymaking in the residential sector starts by recognising the spatial dimensions of housing – at the dwelling, neighbourhood and city-level (OECD, 2019[2]). Affordable housing is more than providing a shelter, but is contingent on whether there is nearby access to opportunities and services. If housing is location inefficient – without such access - then transport costs may render it unaffordable. Worse for mitigation, inaccessible housing further entrenches life around private vehicles, thereby raising emissions. Moreover, constructing dense housing developments in neighbourhoods without enough green infrastructure can exacerbate urban heat islands increasing energy demand from dwellings to use for cooling, especially during hot days, thereby increasing emissions. Because choices made at one level impact mitigation and well-being at other spatial scales, it is crucial to analyse polices at the neighbourhood and city-level in addition to the dwelling (OECD, 2019[2]; OECD, 2018[4]). Ignoring these spatial implications could lead to a self-reinforcing dynamic that creates unaffordable (for a large portion of the population) and carbon-intensive dwellings, neighbourhoods and cities. Conversely, climate policies that take a comprehensive vision can contribute to building resilient cities; helping them cope and adapt to acute shocks (e.g., natural disasters, pandemic) and chronic stresses (e.g., rising temperatures, affordability of housing) (100 Resilient Cities, 2020[5]).

The next section provides an overview of the situation in Israel, exploring the causes behind the housing shortage and the sources of emissions coming from residential dwellings. The following section evaluates policy and financial instruments that can help reduce emissions at the dwelling-level. The subsequent section discusses policies that go beyond the dwelling-level to tackle emissions by developing dense cities with mixed land-uses and integrated infrastructure –transport, waste, water and energy – to foster well-being.

3.2. State of play: Housing shortage and emissions from residential dwellings

3.2.1. What led to the housing shortage?

Private landownership in urban centres, skewed budgetary incentives at the local level, and long approval times for building permits – averaging 12 years in 2011 – catalysed the housing crisis (OECD, 2017[6]; EcoTraders, 2019[1]). Municipalities rely on property taxes for revenue - the *arnona* system. These are taxes on the *use* of a property, rather than its value. These taxes are far higher for commercial and industrial properties than for residential ones, since the national government heavily regulates the latter (OECD, 2017[6]). This incentivises local governments to build industrial and commercial properties, in order to reap greater revenues. As of 2019, Israel has yet to change this, even though correcting municipal incentives for residential property development would make the supply of housing more responsive to demand in a lasting manner (IMF, 2017[7]).

Israel's response to the housing crisis has been to implement two overarching programmes shortly after the protests in 2011 to increase the supply of housing – the *Strategic Housing Programme* and the *Urban Renewal Programme.* Neither of the two programmes developed is statutory. The Strategic Housing Programme aims to build approximately 60,000 dwellings per year, to reach an additional 1.5 million homes by 2040, which is a 60% increase in the existing housing supply from the 2,308,000 dwellings in 2013. The National Economic Council set this overarching target, along with an in-depth analysis of the potential for adding dwellings in each district (EcoTraders, 2019[1]).[3] The Strategic Programme places public calls to tender dwellings, yet for the most part, omits criteria on the type of buildings (number of floors, number of rooms in a dwelling) along with any sustainability criteria (EcoTraders, 2019[1]). Specificities of the dwelling remain in the purview of local authorities. The key exception is the Planning and Building law (Amendment 101), which requires plans that add more than 100 housing units, or plans with a density of 7 units per acre, to have at least 20% of units be 80m^2 or less (Israel Planning Administration, 2020[8]). In the absence of any sustainability criteria, these tenders could drastically increase emissions across the buildings' lifecycle (EcoTraders, 2019[1]), discussed in detail below. The Urban Renewal Programme is a densification strategy to: (1) renovate existing buildings by adding floors on top of the existing structure; and (2) to demolish especially old buildings to build new ones with additional units. Uptake of this is very low, since all of the building's tenants and property owners must agree to participate (EcoTraders, 2019[1]). The government offers loans for retrofits but these are primarily for commercial and industrial buildings. Alternative schemes will be necessary to catalyse retrofits in the existing residential dwellings.

The government also began subsidising housing purchases. Since the housing shortage is leading to mounting prices for would-be homeowners. The price-to-income ratio captures the price of housing relative to annual income, and this is far higher in Israel than for other countries such as the USA, Canada, and Singapore (OECD, 2018[9]). In the US and Canada, the price-to-income ratio is typically around three, while in Singapore it is around five (OECD, 2018[9]). In Israel, it is around eight. In response, the Israeli government launched the *"occupant price (mechir lamishtaken)" programme,* in parallel to the two programmes above, which sells new housing at a fixed, reduced price, and raffles off the right to purchase the apartments to those without any rights to a home; instead of basing purely on need. The raffle includes married couples, individuals above 35 (those who are bachelors, divorced or widowers), single parents, divorced (without a child) and below 35, handicapped individuals (above 21), and individuals from 26 to 35 (if extra housing units available) (Israel Planning Administration, 2020[8]). There is the option for local authorities to prioritise individuals who live in the local authority for at least 25 to 35 % of available units (EcoTraders, 2019[1]). However, the *Times of Israel* claims that, "The plan has backfired, failing to deliver on promises of rapid construction and skewing in favour of the more affluent social echelons, who are the only ones who can afford to enrol in lotteries for the more expensive apartments offered in central Israel," in September 2019.[4]

Finally, the government also reformed the building permit process. More specifically, it decentralised the process for building permits, so that it only takes approximately five years under Master Plan 1, instead of a decade or longer (OECD, 2017[6]).

3.2.2. Emissions from energy use are stable, but it is difficult to estimate embodied carbon in residential dwellings

The picture of emissions from residential dwellings in Israel is largely incomplete. Emissions accrue throughout a building's lifecycle from the (1) pre-use phase, (2) the operational phase (i.e., when people are living in the building), and (3) the end-of-life phase (WorldGBC, 2019[3]). Israel only tracks emissions from energy use during the operational phase, which gives a skewed picture of the sector's contribution to climate change.

- Emissions from the **pre-use phase** of a building include emissions from the extraction and manufacturing of raw materials into primary materials (e.g., cement, steel, aluminium, and glass), the transportation of materials to the construction site, and the emissions from the construction of the building (WorldGBC, 2019[3]).
- During the **operational phase,** emissions come from energy use (e.g., electricity, heating, cooling) and from the repair and refurbishment of the dwellings (WorldGBC, 2019[3]).
- **End of life** emissions occur at the end of a building's useful life from its demolition and disposal (Abd Rashid and Yusoff, 2015[10]; WorldGBC, 2019[3]).

"Embodied carbon" is the catchall term for all of the emissions from the pre-use, operational, and end-use phase, *excluding emissions from energy use in the operational phase*. Embodied carbon can account for 10 to 20% of a building's lifecycle emissions, whilst the rest accrue from energy use (WorldGBC, 2019[3]). Given that the building stock in Israel will rise rapidly under the Strategic Housing Programme and the Urban Renewal Programme, embodied carbon will rise with it. Overlooking this could grossly underestimate emissions; since steel and cement are energy-intensive industries, whose high temperature processes have yet to be decarbonised with commercially viable technology (OECD, 2019[2]). Therefore, better data is needed to grasp the contribution of the sector to Israel's heavy industry emissions and the rest of embodied carbon. To transition to a low-carbon economy, *Israel will need to reduce embodied carbon and emissions from energy-use, aiming to minimise embodied carbon throughout the lifecycle of the building, which will require better data.*

It is possible to calculate expected emissions from energy use from residential dwellings, separately from commercial and industrial buildings. The Ministry of Environmental Protection combines all buildings' emissions in its *Assessment of GHG Reduction Potential and Recommended National Targets for Israel* (Ministry of Environmental Protection, Eco Traders Ltd. and Ricardo Energy and Environment, 2015[11]). In Brief sets out the assumptions used by that report to understand exactly the emissions that could come from the energy use from residential buildings. Figure 3.1 plots these emissions over time under a BAU scenario; there are two projections to represent emissions from the minimum and maximum number of dwellings that the government expects to build in a given year. Emissions from residential dwellings would *cumulatively* increase by **278.9** to **281.58 ktCO_2e under BAU from 2005 to 2030**. Said differently, by 2030, emissions from residential dwellings would equal 0.88 to 0.90 tCO_2e per capita.[1] Israel's 2030 NDC target is 7.7tCO_2 per capita, which means that emissions from energy use in residential dwellings per capita would account for 11 to 12 % of the 2030 target. Continuing in a BAU trajectory for residential dwellings would place a greater burden on other sectors to meet NDC targets, given the projections below and that embodied carbon is excluded.

Box 3.1. Projecting GHG emissions from energy use in the residential sector

The Business-As-Usual (BAU) scenario projects a 1.1% reduction in the energy intensity per dwelling annually until 2030, and specifies an indicative range of the expected increase in residential dwellings. The BAU scenario also assumes 40,000 to 50,000 new dwellings annually until 2020 and 50,000 to 65,000 new dwellings annually until 2035 (Ministry of Environmental Protection, Eco Traders Ltd. and Ricardo Energy and Environment, 2015[11]).The Ministry of Environmental Protection then forecasted future values of the emissions intensity of energy based on historic values from 2000 to 2011 (2012 and 2013 omitted by Israel as outliers). With this information, it is feasible to estimate total emissions from energy use from residential dwellings.

Source: (Ministry of Environmental Protection, Eco Traders Ltd. and Ricardo Energy and Environment, 2015[11])

Figure 3.1. Projected BAU GHG emissions MtCO_2e from the use phase of residential dwellings

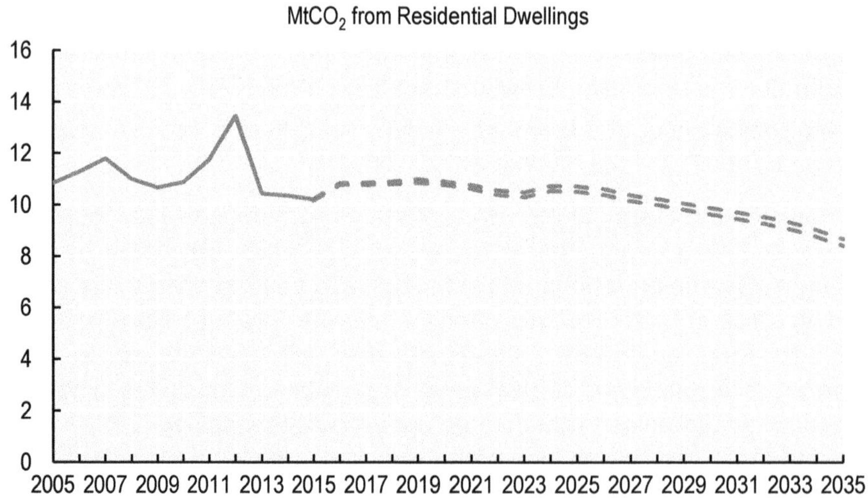

Note: Solid line represents observed values and the dotted line projected. Two projections result from the range of dwellings that could be built each year.
Source: Based on the assumptions in (Ministry of Environmental Protection, Eco Traders Ltd. and Ricardo Energy and Environment, 2015[11]).

StatLink https://doi.org/10.1787/888934156086

3.2.3. Location matters: the residential sector can lead to rising emissions in transport

Whether the location of a dwelling is accessible to services and opportunities nearby – e.g. school, work, shopping – directly links to emissions from transport (discussed in detail in Chapter 4). Developing housing in neighbourhoods with access to services and opportunities - whether by public transport, walking, or cycling – avoids private vehicle use (OECD, 2019[2]). In contrast, developing housing without access to such opportunities and services - by means of public transport, cycling, or walking - means households will need to rely on cars, thereby increasing emissions from private vehicle use (OECD, 2019[2]). The greater proportion of location inefficient housing in cities, the higher annual household emissions from car use, as shown in the US in Figure 3.2.

Figure 3.2. Percent of location efficient neighbourhoods and annual household emissions

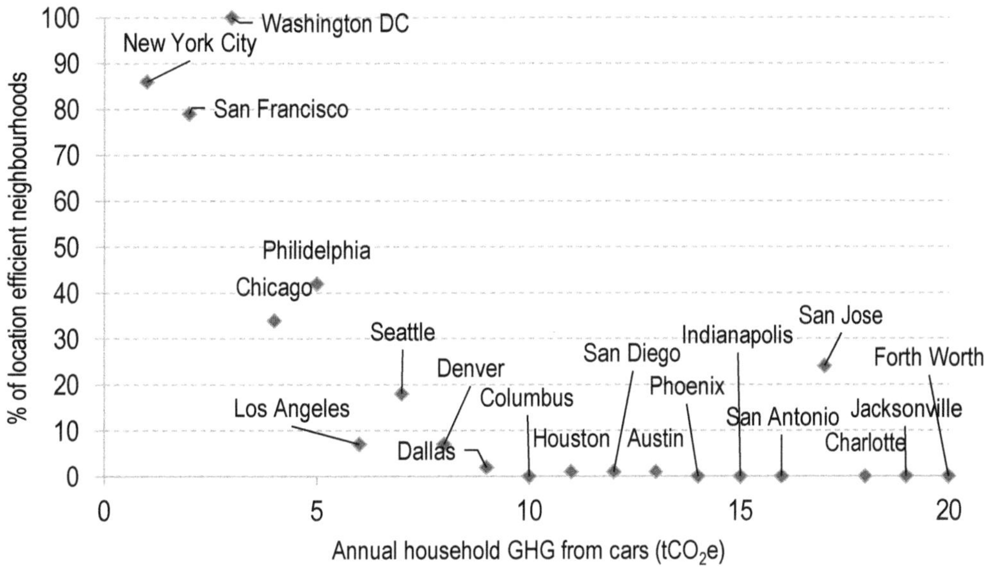

Source: (Center for Neighborhood Technology, 2019[12]).

StatLink https://doi.org/10.1787/888934156105

3.3. Tackling emissions at the dwelling-level: Deep retrofits and sustainable new builds

This section poses two relevant questions for Israeli policymakers to consider when creating policies to decarbonise dwellings. Even though, these questions appear sequentially, in reality, policymakers will need to think about these in parallel.

- *What policy packages are needed to decarbonise residential dwellings across the lifecycle of a building?* This subsection shows that building green does not necessarily cost more for developers and overviews a set of supply-side and demand-side instruments to catalyse sustainable buildings.
- *Who should pay for retrofits of exiting dwellings?* This subsection estimates the total financing needed to retrofit existing dwellings, along with possible financial instruments to catalyse this.

Answering these questions will be necessary to ensure that the decisions made in the near-term align with the LT-LEDS low-carbon transition.

3.3.1. What policy packages are needed to decarbonise residential dwellings across the lifecycle of a building?

A suite of policy instruments tackle emissions at different points of a building's lifecycle. The far left column of Table 3.1 lists the instrument, the rest of columns are labelled by phase and whether the dwelling is existing or new. If the box is coloured, then this means that the instrument could reduce emissions in this phase. Each of the instruments listed in Table 3.1 is explained below in the subsections on demand-side and supply-side policy instruments.

Table 3.1. Instruments for reducing emissions from residential buildings

		Existing residential dwellings		New residential dwellings		
	Emissions →	Operational phase	Post-use phase	Pre-use phase	Operational phase	Post-use phase
Supply-side policy instruments	Existing Green Building Standards in Israel	■		■	■	
	Emission limits on dwellings	■			■	
	Carbon pricing on emissions from production	■		■	■	
	Waste directives, circular economy principles		■	■		■
Demand-side policy instruments	Green and Circular Public Procurement			■	■	■
	Green Mortgages				■	

Supply side policy instruments for existing and new dwellings – standards, emission limits, and carbon pricing

Israel could require existing and new dwellings to comply with the currently voluntary Green Building standards as recommended by the Ministry of Environmental Protection (2015[11]) and the World Green Building Council (2013[13]). So far, the uptake of these standards is relatively low and rarely applied to the new buildings under the Strategic Housing Program (EcoTraders, 2019[1]). Israel's main green building standard - *SI 5281: Sustainable Building* – already sets criteria for energy, land, water, waste, environmental management, transportation, materials, innovation and well-being (e.g., health). Moreover, experts revise this every two years to ensure criteria stays up-to-date and aligns with the Leadership in Energy and Environmental Design (LEED) from the United States. The Department of Energy in the United States reviewed 22 LEED-certified buildings and found CO_2 emissions were 34 percent lower and used 25 percent less energy. The buildings also presented 11 percent less water consumption, and diverted more than 80 million tons of waste from landfills.[5] Two other noteworthy standards in Israel are *SI 5282: Energy Rating of Buildings* and *SI 1045: Thermal Insulation of Buildings*. The former defines specific criteria for a building's energy consumption including energy-use in the construction phase, while the latter ensures comfortable temperatures in a dwelling while minimising energy consumption for heating and cooling. The advantage of using these is that there is already a procedure in place to review these standards along with technical guidance in Israel, so it is a low hanging fruit.

Better new buildings in line with Green Building standards or alternative designs (e.g., passive house design, for example, using the natural environment for heating and cooling) could drastically lower the emissions in Israel. For example, Pearlmutter, Freidin and Huberman (2007[14]) calculated the lifecycle emissions of different materials for a hypothetical house in the Negev Desert in Israel[6] and found that switching building materials significantly lowers demand for energy in the pre-use and operational phases. Replacing clinker (the most emission intensive portion of cement) with fly ash leads to 75% fewer emissions than the traditional Portland concrete – in other words, reducing emissions in the pre-use phase. Moreover, Fly Ash Blocks with or without double insulation – the more sustainable one - also reduces energy demand of a hypothetical building over time compared to the traditional Hollow Concrete Blocks – the solid line – even though, both have the same structural performance in Figure 3.3.

Figure 3.3. Energy demand over time for hypothetical dwelling in Negev Desert

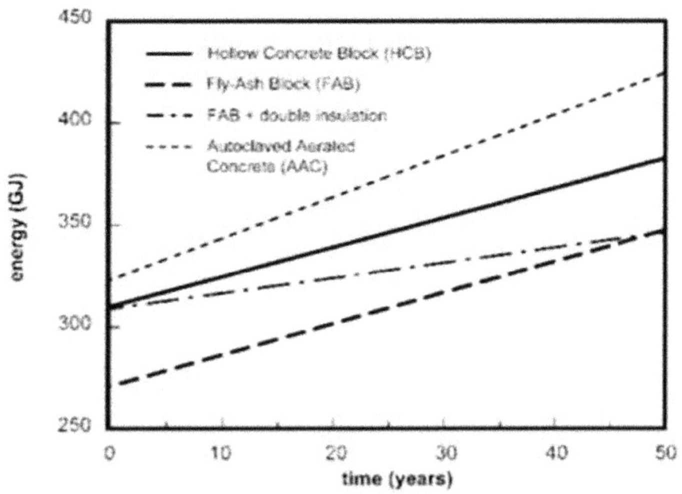

Figure 7 Cumulative life cycle energy consumption for the case study house as built (with conventional concrete block) and in hypothetical scenarios with alternative fly-ash block (with insulation as originally designed, and of double thickness). Also compared is an option with the original wall section modified by replacing the concrete block with a lightweight aerated autoclave concrete (AAC) block

Source: (Pearlmutter, Freidin and Huberman, 2007[14]).

A major barrier to adopting these designs and materials is that the costs for green buildings are often overestimated. A meta-review by the World Green Building Council (2013[13]) shows that building green – technically, meaning compliant with the LEED standards mentioned above – does not necessarily need to cost more, particularly when cost strategies, programme management and environmental strategies are integrated into the development process right from the start. While there can be additional costs associated with building green as compared to a conventional building, the cost premium is typically not as high as is perceived by developers. Moreover, studies around the world show green buildings – LEED certified – more easily attract tenants and command higher rents and sale prices (WorldGBC, 2013[13]). In the World Green Building Council's meta-review of the academic literature, the actual cost premiums for green buildings falls within the 0% - 12.5% range (WorldGBC, 2013[13]). The World Green Building Council states Standard 5281 in Israel – Sustainable Building standard - only increases costs by about 3% (WorldGBC, 2013[13]).

The World Green Building Council states Standard 5281 in Israel – Sustainable Building standard - only increases costs by about 3%.

That said, the World Green Building Council points out that a major obstacle globally is that many industry professionals operate under the general assumption that building green increases design and construction cost by approximately 10-20% (with estimates as high as 29%) compared to the cost of conventional code compliant buildings (WorldGBC, 2013[13]). Therefore, increasing awareness amongst professionals should be a top priority. *Educating stakeholders across the supply chain will be essential in the next five years to increase the uptake of these standards.*

A complementary action could be to set emission limits for dwellings to catalyse retrofits as well as sustainable new dwellings – these emission limits typically apply to energy use in the operational phase. For example, UK building regulations now target CO_2 emissions directly; by setting a Target carbon dioxide Emission Rate (TER), which is an emissions cap of kg CO_2 per year per square meter by building type (e.g., dwelling, commercial), size and shape.[7] The TER of the building is then used to calculate a Dwelling Emissions Rate (DER) or the Building Emissions Rate (BER) for commercial or industrial properties, again expressed as kg CO_2 per m^2 per year. Before construction, any new building must undergo a design stage assessment by Building Control Body setting out the expected TER and DER/BER. Within five days of completion, the Building Control Body conducts an "as-built" assessment to verify standards stay within the allotted cap. A similar regulation exists in New York City under the Climate Mobilization Act, which sets emission caps on buildings – residential and commercial/industrial - of more than 25,000 ft^2, by requiring them to reduce emissions by 40% below 2005 by 2030.[8] Failure to submit an annual report to the City Council leads to 0.50 USD per square foot per month until a report is filed. If the building emissions per square foot are higher than allowed, there is a penalty of 268 USD per square foot. Accompanying these emissions limit is NYC's retrofit accelerator programme that provides free assistance to property owners on how to reduce emissions – e.g., insulation of walls and roof, better lightbulbs, and so on. The advantage of setting an emissions limit or cap is it enables each homeowner to determine how to best achieve emissions reductions; in contrast, to the Green Building codes above. A similar standard in Israel – 40 % reduction below 2005 levels by 2030 – would save between 3.13 and 3.38 $MtCO_2e$ from residential dwellings. In other words, with these savings, total emissions would be 6.5$MtCO_2e$ in 2030 compared to the 9.63 to 9.88 $MtCO_2e$ under BAU.

An emissions limit on residential dwellings in Israel – 40 % reduction below 2005 levels by 2030 - would save 3.13 to 3.38 $MtCO_2e$ compared to BAU.

Carbon pricing will also indirectly reduce emissions from residential dwellings. Only 1% of Israel's electricity-related carbon emissions are priced above EUR 5, one of the lowest shares across OECD countries (as discussed in Chapter 2). The bulk of households meet their energy needs with electricity, the price of which is kept artificially low. Putting a carbon price will likely require the Electricity Authority to approve higher (residential) electricity tariffs, improving incentives for more energy efficiency and resulting in less energy during the operational phase of a dwelling (OECD, 2019[2]), which is discussed in detail in the Chapter 2. Likewise, increasing the carbon price on energy would reduce industrial emissions from heavy industry – e.g., steel, cement, and aluminium – during the manufacturing of primary materials (Dechezleprêtre, Nachtigall and Venmans, 2018[15]), thereby reducing the embodied carbon in residential buildings.

Creating demand for sustainable homes – whether retrofitted or new builds

The other side of the coin is to catalyse sustainable houses by creating demand either via (1) green and circular public procurement, (2) green mortgages (also known as energy efficient mortgages), and (3) variable property taxes – i.e., adjusting property taxes based on the property's sustainability.

The Israeli government is already releasing calls for tenders to build housing, which only specify the number of dwellings but not the quality. *A low hanging fruit for Israel is to engage in circular and green public procurement, which will bring wider well-being benefits, while reducing emissions.* Israel can use its purchasing power to choose dwellings – and construction practices – that decrease emissions, and could even extend this to circular economy criteria to decreases waste across the lifecycle of the building and increase recycled materials to the greatest extent possible (European Commission, 2017[16]). Moreover, green and circular public procurement can be a major driver for innovation, providing industry with real incentives for developing greener practices and offers (Baron, 2016[17]; IISD and i2-4c, 2017[18]). This is especially true in Israel since 1.5 million homes are planned under the Strategic Housing Programme.

The Netherlands is a best practice example of green and circular public procurement. The government uses the MEAT procedure (Most Economically Advantageous Tender), which awards the tender to the bidder with the "lowest" price. It wavers from traditional tender calls, since bidders monetise two sustainability criteria, (1) CO_2e emissions and (2) overall environmental impact, using a standardised methodology (OECD/The World Bank/UN Environment, 2018[19]). This amount – money saved from less CO_2e and greater environment sustainability – is then subtracted from the bidders' offer; thereby, reducing the bidders' overall price.[9] The greater level of ambition, the greater value, and lower bid. *In the next five years, Israel could also establish criteria for monetising these gains, so that Israel awards bidders with greater sustainability.*

These practices help avoid emissions. For example, closed loop town hall construction in the Netherlands – leased a building for twenty years – that was designed for disassembly, meaning it can be easily taken apart (Kaiser, 2016[20]). This practice helps to recycle these materials at the end of a building's life, and reduce emissions from the post-use phase of a building during demolition. In addition, Humboldt University in Berlin used recycled aggregates in construction, that saved 880m^2 of virgin gravel (i.e., saved raw materials), which reduced emissions by 7% (European Commission, 2017[16]). An example of green public procurement in a climate similar to Israel's is the Navarra Social Housing[10] project in Spain, which reduces emissions from the use-phase of the dwelling. It is building 524 social flats for rent in line with the 'passive house' sustainable construction standard between 2018 and 2021. These flats will achieve the highest levels of energy efficiency, with savings of up to 90% and nearly zero consumption. The units are for young and elderly people on low incomes, families with limited means and people in critical need of accommodation. In addition, the construction work will create 298 jobs until 2021.

Green mortgages is yet another tool that Israel can consider using. Better borrowing rates on mortgages if purchasing more energy efficient homes. Thirty-seven major European banks launched a new energy efficiency mortgage pilot scheme;[11] about a third of the European banking sector's assets are in mortgages (WorldGBC and European Commission, 2018[21]). Investments in building performance improvements can help to free-up disposable income for borrowers through lower utility bills and can enhance property value (WorldGBC and European Commission, 2018[21]). As a result, they can reduce credit risk, so they are a win-win for lenders, investors, consumers and climate. Mortgage lenders are uniquely positioned to intervene at critical moments in a property's lifecycle to support improvement of its quality and energy performance (i.e. when it is built, bought or refinanced). The energy and environmental performance of buildings is not often accounted for in credit risk assessments conducted for mortgages (WorldGBC and European Commission, 2018[21]). *Mortgage loans account for 47 % of bank loans in Israel in 2018* (S&P Global Rating, 2019[22])*; green mortgages could be a major opportunity for Israel in the next five years.*

A related idea is variable tax rates for property based on energy performance. Local authorities use best available data to establish a baseline level of energy efficiency. Properties above a given amount receive a discount on their tax bill, while those below the baseline would have a percentage added. Such a scheme could be constructed to be revenue neutral, with the potential for local authorities to revise the baseline overtime. A number of councils in the UK have put this into practice. Typically, it is a two-phase process: (1) all households have energy performance assessment, and (2) local authorities adopt the relevant thresholds (UK GBC, 2013[23]). In theory, it can also be one-sided where only the reduction is provided instead of a penalty. However, this is no longer revenue neutral, and could be difficult for local authorities who already have constrained budgets. While this does nothing to mitigate the high upfront costs, this could increase the rates of return if the reduction in property taxes were high enough. Of course, then local budgets would need to be supplemented via different means.

3.3.2. Who should pay financing deep retrofits of exiting dwellings?

The starting point when tackling emissions from existing dwellings is whether to retrofit or demolish; methodologies to do this are explored in greater detail in Box 3.1. If retrofitting is the best option, high upfront costs and long payback periods can make retrofits unattractive for homeowners. The rest of this section estimates the financing needs for retrofits and reviews financial instruments to catalyse retrofits.

What are the financing needs for retrofits in Israel?

In the 2015 *Assessment of Greenhouse Gas Emission Reduction Potential* report, Israel identified abatement measures for existing residential dwellings, all of which were extracted from the Green Building standards mentioned above (Ministry of Environmental Protection, Eco Traders Ltd. and Ricardo Energy and Environment, 2015[11]). Some of these pertain to the building envelope – e.g., improving wall and roof insulation, reflective coatings on windows; while others pertain to the inside of the dwelling – e.g., energy efficient appliances. Table 3.2 lists each abatement measure, along with experts' estimations of the technology's present penetration in the existing stock, its potential uptake, and costs. The last column is the emissions reduction potential of each retrofit.

Table 3.2. How to retrofit existing dwellings

Abatement measures	Current technology	How many dwellings currently use which technology?	How many more dwellings could uptake the new technology?	Costs per dwelling (NIS)	Emissions reduction potential
Install air source heat pumps	Electric resistance heaters	20%	80% of electric resistance heaters could be replaced	6000	Air source heat pumps have COP 3.5, electric resistance of 1, and diesel 0.65
	Diesel	7.6%	50% of diesel heaters could be replaced		
Improve energy efficiency of appliances	EE Refrigerators	Close to 0%	90%	4510	BAU is 290 kWh, abatement technology 135 kWh.
	EE Dryers	Close to 0%	90%	1845	BAU is 350lWh and abatement technology is 300.
	EE Dishwashers	Close to 0%	90%	3034	BAU is 529kWh and abatement technology is 441.
Reduce heat losses and gains through insulation of wall and roof	Updated to the Green Building Standard	93.5%	2%	10,000-40,000	Insulation reduces energy consumption for HVAC by 20% in existing buildings.
Reduce heat losses through window glazing	Updated to the Green Building Standard	Close to 0%	2%	5,000 – 20,000	Insulation reduces energy consumption for HVAC by 4% in existing buildings.
Improve efficiency of air conditioners	Updated to the Green Building Standard	84% of dwellings have AC units	90%	750	COP 3.8
Install ground source heat pumps	Updated to the Green Building Standard	Close to 0%	2%	8800	Can be 30-70% less energy for heating, 20-50% in cooling
Solar shading of windows	Reflective coatings	Close to 0%	10%	1800	6% reduction HVAC energy consumption
	Brises soleil	Close to 0%	5%	4800	6% reduction HVAC energy consumption
Install solar heaters with closed water cycle	Updated to the Green Building Standard	86%	90%	300	15% reduction in energy consumption

Note: COP stands for Coefficient of Performance. The COP of air source heat pump is the ratio heating and cooling output for the energy that is input. A COP greater than one means that heat pump is performing very efficiency. HVAC is an acronym for heating, ventilating and air conditioning.

Source: (Ministry of Environmental Protection, Eco Traders Ltd. and Ricardo Energy and Environment, 2015[11]).

It is possible to calculate a rough estimate of the total financing needed to retrofit existing dwellings as of 2015 – with the existing building stock of 2,386,000 apartments. We already know the total number of dwellings in 2015; therefore, it is possible to estimate how many dwellings presently use which technologies, what the potential uptake of the technology could be, and a price range from Table 3.2. Using this information, the *total* financing needed – to implement the abatement measures in Table 3.2 with estimated uptake potential - is roughly 5.5 to 7.55 billion NIS to completely retrofit; roughly **1.4** to **1.9%** of **GDP in 2019**. The cost of a complete retrofit for a single dwelling would be approximately **39,000** to **85,000 NIS**. Not every dwelling will need each abatement measure; however, this provides an indicative range of what the upper echelon of a complete retrofit could be (if all the abatement measures in Table 3.2 were implemented).

The total financing needed to retrofit existing residential dwellings is approximately 1.4 to 1.9% of annual GDP (5.5 to 7.5 billion NIS).

Box 3.2. Should existing dwellings be demolished or retrofitted?

This question is presented as a dichotomy, but in actuality, practitioners will likely use both approaches to existing building stock, depending on the characteristics of the building. Demolishing and rebuilding will undoubtedly increase emissions from demolition in the post-use phase and in the pre-use phase – e.g., from demolition, material production, and construction (WorldGBC, 2019[3]). Nevertheless, it can be an attractive option for certain buildings since it can drastically reduce emissions from the operational phase of a building via energy efficiency improvements. Retrofitting existing buildings could still be preferable to rebuild depending on the building's age and characteristics (WorldGBC, 2019[3]). For example, weighing the benefits and costs of retrofits vs. rebuilds by building type in Toronto (Canada), led to the conclusion that basement plus air leakage sealing retrofit is preferable for a 1930s house, basement retrofit for the 1960s house, and no retrofitting for 1980s house (WorldGBC, 2019[3]).

Urban planners, architects, policymakers, typically, do this by using models to compare buildings' energy and environmental performance (e.g., GHGs, water usage, waste), along with costs (capital expenditures, operational expenditures, capital appraisal for the future), over the existing and new building's lifetime from construction to demolition (UCL Urban Lab and Engineers Exchange, 2014[24]). Nevertheless, these calculations require assumptions – e.g., the lifetime of buildings, the emissions intensity of energy, even the costs of carbon. Assumptions can be faulty, for example, predicted and actual performance of buildings often differs (referred to as "performance gaps") (UCL Urban Lab and Engineers Exchange, 2014[24]). This picture is even more complex when assigning value to non-monetary costs and benefits – e.g., quality of life, health, and so on. These models often exclude peoples' behavioural biases, for example, increases in consumption after an energy efficiency project (the rebound effect). University of College London's Urban Lab conducted an analysis of different methodologies to evaluate whether to demolish or retrofit – Demolish or Refurbishment for Social Housing: A review of the evidence – which can serve as a guide for Israel (UCL Urban Lab and Engineers Exchange, 2014[24]). Given that, the Urban Renewal Programme incorporates an option for demolition enriching the capacity of local stakeholders to properly evaluate the risks and benefits will be pivotal in the forthcoming years.

The first obstacle to deep retrofits is high upfront costs for households**.** To place these upfront costs in perspective for homeowners (66.5% of Israelis own their home), Figure 3.4 shows these costs in terms of households' monthly disposable income (net of mortgage payments and transportation costs). For any household in the bottom three deciles of the income distribution, it is equivalent to more than a year's disposable income.

High upfront costs are not insurmountable but the payback periods on investment for many of these retrofits are very long, making them unappealing for property owners. Friedman, Becker and Erell (2014[25]) estimate the rates of return on two retrofits to building envelopes for different building types and climatic conditions – (1) roof insulation and (2) insulating the walls. Given current electricity prices and building construction costs, insulating the roof could be a cost-effective strategy but the payback period is 15-30 years in Israel, making it unattractive to most homeowners. Insulating the external walls of a typical apartment results in electricity savings comparable to only one third of the retrofit cost in some cases, and is thus not economically viable.

Figure 3.4. Upfront capital costs of complete retrofits in terms of monthly household disposable income of property owners in Israel (by income decile)

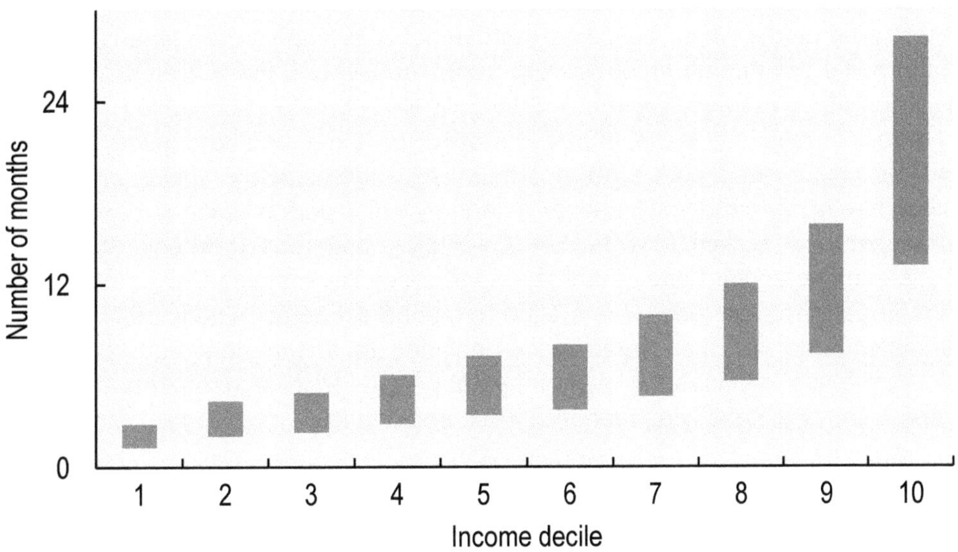

Note: Disposal income is what is left over after mortgage and transport payments.

StatLink https://doi.org/10.1787/888934156124

Table 3.3 estimates the payback periods for insulating the external walls for two types of dwellings – 2-family detached house and apartment building - in the four climate zones of Israel, where payback periods fall anywhere between 12 to 70 years. The table shows the result for the *'private'* individual (i.e. disregarding the value of the external benefits to society from the resulting reduction in electricity demand), and the *'total'* benefit to society (which is the sum of the private and external benefits[12]). A point for future work by Israel is to extend this analysis to estimate payback periods for complete retrofits, as specified under the Green Building Standards.

Table 3.3. Payback time in years on wall and roof insulation in Israel's four climate zones

	Tel Aviv		Beer Sheva		Jerusalem		Eilat	
	Private	Total	Private	Total	Private	Total	Private	Total
2-family Detached house	68	37	41	28	32	22	24	18
Apartment building	29	21	23	17	20	15	16	12

Note: In the apartment building, the effect of roof insulation was only reflected in the energy budget of the upper floor.
Source: (Friedman, Becker and Erell, 2014[25]).

One reason for these very long payback periods is because the residential price of electricity is so low – only 0.135 EUR per kWh on average while the average price in Europe is 0.2 EUR per kWh (see Chapter 2). Presumably, if the price of electricity were increased, e.g., to better reflect the social cost of electricity generation via a carbon price, then the payback periods would be shorter. Electricity bills could also increase because of greater use of air conditioning, as temperatures start to increases in Israel with climate change, thereby reducing the payback period.

On top of the long payback periods and high upfront costs, there is even less incentive to retrofit if property owners let out the dwelling. Property owners typically pay for retrofits, but the renters will be the ones who stand to benefit from lower electricity bills, better temperatures, and so on creating split incentives. One way to resolve this is via green leases. Essentially, this involves including provisions in a lease to enable building owners to pass on the costs of building improvements to tenants if the tenants benefit from energy savings. Singapore is a frontrunner in introducing green leases, and the Building Construction Authority even provides a toolkit for property owners and tenants to co-create such leases.[13] This toolkit defines three types of greens leases: soft lease, mutual-performance lease, and hard lease. A soft lease is when the tenant and the landowner create a Memorandum of Understanding where each party commits to improving environmental performance, identifies criteria by which performance is measured, and opens an opportunity for property owners and tenants to mutually share their respective environmental performance – i.e., the actions that the landlord and tenant take to improve the sustainability of the dwelling. One step further – a mutual performance lease –sets a performance schedule, where both parties aim to meet targets. Other safeguards will likely need to be included to ensure that both parties share truthful information. A "hard lease" includes the environmental performance requirements as part of the normal lease framework, along with identifying responsibilities and financial obligations.

Green leases could cause affordability challenges for some renters if location is ignored; this could also overestimate GHG reductions. About 33.5% of Israelis rent their homes. Figure 3.5, shows that in 2016, *only households in the top three income deciles had access to affordable housing.* In other words, only those households spent less than 30% of monthly income on rent (blue bars and blue line in Figure 3.5) (Central Bureau of Statistics, 2019[26]).[14] These estimates overlook, however, a key cost for households, which is transport. As stated above, if housing is in inaccessible neighbourhoods, then transport costs will rise for renters. Including public transport and private vehicle costs into these calculations, then *households in the top four deciles had affordable housing and transport in 2016* (Central Bureau of Statistics, 2019[26]). In other words, only these households spent less than 45% of their monthly income in these two items, which is the threshold used by the Housing Transport and Affordability Index (red bars and red line in Figure 3.5) (Center for Neighborhood Technology, 2019[12]). Monthly housing and transport costs actually exceeded the monthly income of the lowest income decile in 2016 (these households likely rely on rental assistance or public housing). *Therefore, any set up for green leases will need to make sure that transport costs are not underestimated when analysing renters' payment.* In addition, as highlighted above Figure 3.2, location-efficient neighbourhoods are associated with lower car use and emissions. Thus, *promoting green leases schemes in areas that are location efficient or are being upgraded to be so, will ensure wider mitigation benefits.*

Figure 3.5. Rent and transport is only affordable for the top four income deciles in 2016

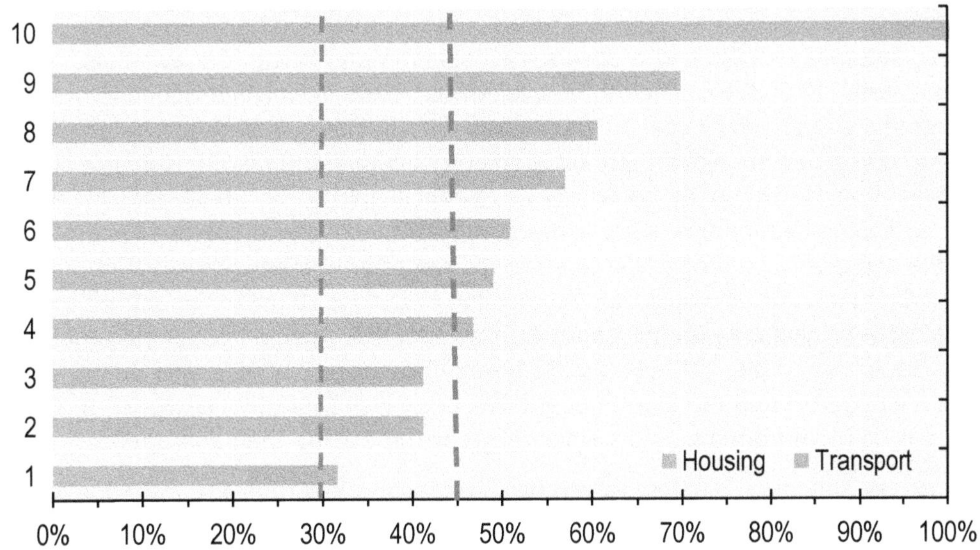

Note: Blue bars represent % of monthly income spent on housing costs - includes monthly rent, utilities, plus dwelling and household maintenance per income decile divided by the net income per household in 2016. The blue line is 30%, which is the rule of thumb for how much of a household's monthly income should go to rent. Red bars represent percent of monthly income on transport. Transport includes public transportation and private vehicle expenditure. The rule of thumb for housing and transport affordability is 45%.
Source: Authors' calculations using Israeli Census Data from 2016.

StatLink https://doi.org/10.1787/888934156143

Further linking the affordable and sustainable housing agendas through retrofits

As seen above, rental and transport costs remain unaffordable for many Israelis, with access to assistance limited. Herein lies an opportunity for Israel to be innovative and surmount the twin challenges of housing affordability whilst catalysing retrofits. Local governments around the world are crafting innovative solutions to catalyse retrofits; while creating affordable housing. For example, in Rhode Island (USA), House of Hope, a non-profit community-based agency, will pay for retrofits of buildings, e.g., roof replacement or insulation of walls, if the property owner agrees to provide affordable housing units at a rate (equal to that of rental assistance) for a certain period of time.[15] Other municipalities in Northeast United States use retrofitting programmes that are part of historical preservation schemes as means to provide affordable housing. Preserving historic properties can revitalise neighbourhoods, enriching the community by creating jobs and even stimulating the local economy (Housing Works RI, 2013[27]). Several states offer a tax credit for up to 25% of the cost for retrofitting historic properties in Rhode Island, Connecticut and in Massachusetts. Such a credit could be increased – or only accessible – if the preservation project includes affordable housing (Housing Works RI, 2013[27]). Certain affordable housing agencies have already adopted this strategy, even though, it is not formalised in the policy. For example, House of Hope in Rhode Island (which faces similar land scarcity issues to Israel) retrofitted an existing historical property, Fair House, where all units are allocated to affordable housing, and managed to recoup 125,000 USD of their investment via the tax credit for rehabilitating historic properties.[16]

Other opportunities to incentivise property owners to retrofit existing dwellings

Even with green leases, financing instruments will likely be needed to catalyse and incentivise property owners to retrofit. Three such financing instruments are described in detail below: utility on-bill financing, cash-back schemes, and soft loans. The analysis includes an assessment of their feasibility in Israel along with other well-being implications. The findings are summarised in Table 3.4.

Utility on-bill financing, also known as Energy Performance Contracting, is when a utility, such as Israel Electric Company, finances retrofits and recovers the costs through billing. For example, in Nova Scotia, over the past four years, 13,000 households have taken out loans from Nova Scotia Power as part of its Heat Pump programme and paid back on their utility bill (Ministry of Energy Mines and Resources (Canada), 2016[28]). Even though, Nova Scotia is a different climate, the funding scheme should still work in Israel. The Israel Electric Company could offer to finance any of the abatement measures listed in Table 3.2 – e.g., air source heat pumps, solar heaters with a closed water cycle, even improving insulation. The onus is on the occupant of a property – whether the renter or homeowner - to take out the loan from the Israel Electric Company, which could help resolve the challenge of the initial upfront cost for retrofits. Nevertheless, utility on-bill finance may still be unaffordable for low-income households such as happened in the UK Green Deal. In principle, if a household's energy bills were £1,000 a year when applying for the loan, the reduced energy bill and the loan should have been less than this, however, many low-income users ended up paying more from the outset since they consumed less than average.

Similar to utility on-bill financing, local improvement charges work so that the municipality finances the retrofits and the property owner repays the municipality for the loan through their property tax bill. For example, nearly 400 households installed solar hot water systems using a loan from the city of Halifax, in its Solar City programme (Ministry of Energy Mines and Resources (Canada), 2016[28]). Given the tight constraints on local budgets in Israel already, covering these expenses could be challenging. One of the key sources of revenue for local budgets in Israel is property taxes (as mentioned above). The federal government, however, sets a mandatory range for residential property taxes, which could serve as an obstacle if these improvements push property taxes outside of this predefined band. In addition, such a mechanism may be impossible for households living in the lower deciles of the population (see Figure 3.5).

Another option is to cooperate with third-party investors to provide soft loans for retrofits, which is very different from green mortgages (that offer lower interest rates for more energy efficient homes). The basic principle of soft loans is to enable homeowners to borrow money for retrofits at lower interest rates than standard market conditions. Other amenities that render such loans attractive are longer maturity (enables homeowners to adjust monthly payments according to their financial resources), longer grace periods, and lower administrative as well as insurance costs. Many of these loans enable even low-income households, who would generally be denied loans, the same opportunities as more affluent households by reducing the risk of default on the mortgage (European Commission, 2014[29]). The nature of the relationship between the bank, homeowner, and local government can vary.

- The first setup is traditional, the city or municipality identifies partner banks to provide the soft loans; the banks check the homeowners creditworthiness, manage the loan (reducing the administrative costs for the locality), but ultimately, *the banks decide who can take out a loan*, potentially excluding low-income households. This setup is already used in Germany. For example, "Kreditanstalt für Wiederaufbau" (KfW) is state-owned bank, that offers subsidised loans for entire retrofits (up to 75,000 EUR) at interest rates as low as 1% (European Commission, 2014[29]). Scheme started in 2001, now; 2.1 million housing units received finance. The evaluation of KfW programmes for the funding years 2005 to 2009 have shown very positive results, in terms of not only investment, energy savings, CO_2 reduction and employment, but also a positive net impact on public budgets (UK GBC, 2013[23]). The refinancing rates of KfW are low due to the good credit rating of Germany; Israel's credit rating is not as high, meaning that rates would likely be higher than 1%, or Israel could use public budgets to keep rates low.
- The second setup is when partner banks provide the loans, for example, as used in the Brussels Capital Region (European Commission, 2014[29]), but *any homeowner can take out a loan* even those with very low income and people with no access to commercial loans are eligible. Brussels

Green Loan, a zero to low-interest loan, which helps homeowners to pre-finance energy renovation work.[17] Homeowners have a choice between a short-term consumer loan with an interest rate of 0% or 1%, which they have to reimburse in up to 10 years. In this setup, the Brussels Capital Region takes on the risk of payment defaults. This loan is offered by Crédal, a financial cooperative that aims to promote a fairer and more supportive society.

- A third option is for the locality to disburse soft loans as found in Riga and Delft (Infinite Solutions, 2017[30]). This already exists in some cities in Israel. Tel-Aviv tenants who are interested in renovation can get an attractive loan from the Tel-Aviv Municipality's economic company to do it with provisions in place for tenants that cannot afford to repay the loan.

Cash-back schemes are popular tools since they drive action, but these come with major challenges such as the significant cost for government and questionable efficacy. Therefore, these instruments may not be the best use of limited resources. Because of high costs, such schemes tend to be a time-limited. For example, the UK's boiler scrappage scheme; offered vouchers of 400 GBP to encourage the installation of energy efficient boilers; matched by installers – for 800 GBP discount. Take-up of the scheme was quite significant, of the 125,000 vouchers given out, 95% were cashed in (UK GBC, 2013[23]). Cash-back schemes, however, often incentivise single retrofit measures, which can be less efficient in terms of costs and energy, when compared to a harmonised deep retrofit package (Streicher et al., 2020[31]). Deep retrofit package examine a dwelling as a single, integrated system rather than as a collection of standalone systems. With respect to costs, single retrofit measures can lock-in technologies, increasing costs of retrofits in the future as seen in United States and Germany (Streicher et al., 2020[31]). With respect to energy, neglecting to look at the system as whole means that potential synergies may be overlooked. For example, "improving the building envelope, providing solar heat gain control, and improving lighting systems could substantially reduce a building's heating and cooling energy demand. This would in turn reduce the required size of duct systems, air-handling units, boilers, and chiller," (Alexander Zhivov et al., 2017[32]).

Table 3.4. Summary table of financing options for deep retrofits

Instrument	Who loans?	Who repays?	Well-being implications	Feasibility in Israel
Utility on-bill financing	Utility company	Resident of property via utility bills	Affordability for low income residents due to increased utility bills	
Local improvement charges	Municipality	Property owner via property taxes	Affordability for low-income property owners due to higher property taxes	Constrained budgets of municipalities in Israel; split incentives between property owners and tenants since the property owner pays, but the tenant benefits from less utility bills
Soft loans	Bank (identified by the municipalities); typically offering loans at very low interest rates	Property owners	Excludes low-income households (e.g., elderly, the young)	
	Banks	Municipalities subsidise interest rates, guarantee fund, and pay the banks' operating costs. Property owners pay the loan		Split incentives problem remains, and overcoming the constraints on local budgets
	Locality	Property owners		Split incentives problem remains, and overcoming the constraints on local budgets

3.4. Beyond the dwelling: Compact development with integrated infrastructure and green space considerations

So far, Israel's response to the housing shortage is leading to greater sprawl, low-density development and poorly integrated infrastructure across municipalities/cities; all of which generates growing emissions (OECD, 2017[6]). The Israeli Ministry of Planning Administration revised its guidelines to permit construction in the periphery of cities in response to the housing crisis - re-appropriating considerable land reserves. In addition to rezoning agricultural land,[18] leading to a gradual degradation of the land around cities. Moreover, there is a mismatch between the location of these newly built dwellings and where Israelis wants to live (OECD, 2017[6]; EcoTraders, 2019[1]). New housing is being developed on state-owned land in rural areas, while the majority Israelis prefer to be in urban centres, where the land is under private ownership (OECD, 2017[6]).

A two-way strategy to accommodate future growth in a sustainable way will be needed (see Section 3.4.1). On the one hand, revising minimum density requirements (presently ongoing in Israel) in addition to incentivizing land infill and redevelopment in urban cores[19] can help create compact cities that not only help to attain mitigation objectives but also advance wider well-being by providing better connectivity to goods, services, job and leisure opportunities. However, given the expected future growth in cities, all of these strategies will need to be accompanied by sound actions to plan for some peripheral development, so that this is also consistent with the objective of building compact cities. Moreover, increasing densification brings the need for services and infrastructure to support it, and green space to curb heat island effects. Heat islands can inadvertently increase emissions because of rising energy needs for cooling on hot days. Ideally, housing developments would not only be integrated with green infrastructure, but also with sustainable mobility, embedded energy, water and waste infrastructure; i.e. it would be planned as eco-districts.

One catalyst of urban sprawl is strained local finances, which will be discussed in Section 3.4.2. Israel would benefit from enhancing local financial and technical capacities. Besides decentralising the budget and increasing the local tax base, the frameworks for a number of financial instruments could also be developed to widen local financial capacity. Among these are development charges, land value capture mechanisms, pool funding, and business improvement districts (all of which are explained in Section 3.4.2).

3.4.1. Managing growth to develop compact and sustainable cities

The population in Israel's urban areas is expected to grow exponentially in the coming decades. Under these conditions, both curbing urban sprawl and accommodating inevitable growth will be paramount to creating sustainable cities. A wide range of cities in OECD countries physically contain growth through urban containment boundaries, such as green belts or urban growth boundaries, but this may not be the optimal response in Israel. Angel et al (2010[33]) shows that strictly limiting growth by setting containment policies can be counter-productive, especially in fast-growing urban areas. Greenbelts can cause leapfrogging, i.e. developments "jumping" the belt and can also increase housing and land prices, as in Korea and the UK (OECD, 2015[34]). Pressing demand for housing or ineffective policies inside city cores, such as slow permitting processes or stringent regulations can further exacerbate this challenge. Therefore, a two-way strategy to accommodate future growth in a sustainable way should be adopted. In the next sections, we will, first, present policies that foster compactness and allow to sustainably absorb growth inside urban areas, and then strategies to smartly guide additional growth in the periphery. It is important to signal that even when not using explicit green belts, protecting and restoring green areas and ecosystem services should be part of strategic planning for urban core redevelopment as well as development of any peripheral areas.

Renewing and densifying urban cores

It is paramount that existing urban cores in Israel develop in a pattern that is compact and sustainable. This requires development to be dense with mixed land-uses, both of which are important enablers to create proximity and facilitate sustainable mobility, which ultimately allow enabling access to services and opportunities (see Box 3.2) (OECD, 2012[35]). However, compact cities can generate trade-offs with respect to the affordability of housing, as well as heat island effects. In addition, increased densities in cities should be supported by an adequate level of infrastructure, such as water and waste management as well as public services.

Box 3.3. The role of urban form on cities' GHG emissions

Urban form is an important determinant of GHG emissions from cities. Several empirical piece of work have found that the urban form and related characteristics such as density, land-use diversity, destination accessibility, and distance to transit also influence mode choice, trip frequency, trip distance and then vehicle kilometres and GHG emissions (Lee and Lee, 2014[36]). Urban form can be characterized through three dimensions: (i) population density and its geographical distribution; (ii) centrality i.e. which measures the concentration of an urban area population near the central location, as opposed to being located at urban fringes; and (iii) polycentricity i.e. the extent to which services and functions of urban centres (economic, commercial, recreational) are distributed between the main business centres and subcentres (Lee and Lee, 2014[36]). These dimensions shape urban areas either in a sprawled or compact way. The OECD defines urban sprawl as an urban development pattern characterised by low population density that can be manifested in multiple ways: (i) low population density; (ii) high average population density but unequally distributed, leading to zones with extremely low density levels; (iii) fragmented, discontinued and decentralized developments (OECD, 2018[4]). Compact cities are characterized by density and proximity in terms of development patterns, strong urban linkages to public transport systems, and accessibility to services and jobs (OECD, 2012[35]). In addition to these density-related features, diversity of land-uses is also an important feature of compact and smart cities.

Density and mixed-land uses are an enabler of proximity as well as of an integrated and viable mobility system, both of which enhance accessibility - defined as the ability to reach destinations using a given transport mode (ITF, 2019[37]) - and ultimately foster compactness. Based on this definition, Figure 3.6 outlines a framework which illustrates the interlinkages between (i) density and mixed land-uses, (ii) proximity and well-functioning urban mobility systems, (iii) accessibility and (iv) compactness and overall sustainability (which includes climate change mitigation objectives). The dynamics created by these different elements allows in particular to reduce GHG emissions, since it allows people and goods to move in an optimal manner and privileging more sustainable transport modes, which are under these circumstances more competitive for reaching destinations than private cars. As such, population living in compact and transit-oriented cities tend to drive less that those living in sprawling ones.

Figure 3.6. Framework for compact and sustainable cities

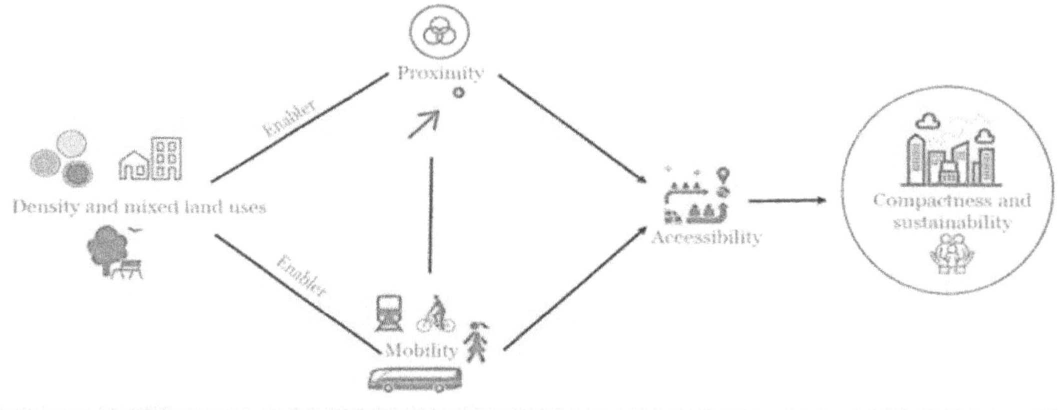

Note: Proximity is measured by the number of opportunities within a certain distance (ITF, 2019[37]); The quality of mobility by the ratio of absolute accessibility to proximity; accessibility by the easiness to reach destination within a number of minutes.

The rest of this subsection will outline policies that foster compactness and allow for absorbing urban growth as much as possible, while maintaining affordability and ensuring the provision of green space and adequate level of infrastructure to keep pace with densification.

Relaxing stringent density regulations

Maximum density restrictions are common in urban areas inside OECD countries - e.g., building height restrictions or limits on building floor-to-area ratios - but these often stymie densification. Israel already uses minimum density requirements, which are presently undergoing revision to be increased. Zoning with minimum densities in cities helps to cluster services and opportunities for residents, as well as to generate economic gains over time within the designated area (OECD, 2017[38]). In particular for public transport, minimum density standards help advance the development of functional and economically successful transit-oriented districts by creating a sufficient population of residents in proximity to transit stops (OECD/ITF, 2017[39]). Minimum densities catalyse transit investments and expand opportunities for accessible housing developments, both of which reduce emissions. The average density in Israeli cities is far lower than other European cities, which makes it challenging to have integrated infrastructure with transport. Tel Aviv has a density of 8,565 people per square kilometre and Jerusalem, 7,186 people per square kilometre. In comparison, the density of Paris is nearly triple the average of that in Jerusalem and Tel Aviv, while that of Barcelona is four times higher.[20] The Israeli government is raising the permissible density, for example, as part of the Urban Renewal Programme, which targets old neighbourhoods constructed before the 1950s, and allow the demolition of old neighbourhoods to reconstruct at much higher densities (OECD, 2017[38]). If the densities in cities remain too low, and public transport and facilities for active modes are not significantly enhanced, residents will continue to rely on car ownership, and anyone without a car will have difficulty accessing facilities and services. *Fostering density, mix land-uses and proximity will be as important as improving public transport and facilities for active transport for reducing emissions form Israel's urban areas.*

Fostering sustainable urban infill by incentivising land development and promoting urban regeneration that revitalizes neighbourhoods

An obstacle to higher densities in cities in Israel is private landownership, since these owners can hold on to their land to speculate for higher prices (OECD, 2017[38]); therefore, policies incentivizing land development, such as land assembly or targeted fiscal tools will be needed in the next five years. Assembling land means combining private smaller parcels of privately owned land. The key feature of land assembly is that it changes land ownership to enable property development and infrastructure provision (OECD, 2018[4]), by ensuring that holding onto land is less attractive than selling. Arch (2014[40]) argues that the key to solving this hold out problem in Israel is for the municipalities to develop a clear plan outlining what they project to do with the land[21]. Announcing these plans publicly means private owners can capture the value increase of the land when selling, so that holding on to their plot of undeveloped land will be far less desirable. In parallel though, municipalities will need to start taxing the owners on the new monetary value of the property (Arch, 2014[40]). In the case of Tel Aviv, increasing the value of a parcel of land to allow for six stories from an undeveloped plot would raise taxes six fold (Arch, 2014[40]). The potential changes in tax rates can also open an opportunity for mechanisms such as Tax Increment Finance (TIF), which is a tool that anticipates future tax revenues increases and raises capital for investments occurring in the present. TIF is, for instance, used in London to fund transport infrastructure such as the Northern Line underground extension (ITF/OECD, 2017[41]).

The increase in land value can be an important element to incentivise private owners to sell rather than keep hold of undeveloped land. Land assembly (and other land-value capture mechanisms) can also be strategically used by the government or local municipalities in Israel to capture a portion of the land value increase, which can then be channelled towards well-being objectives. The logic being that infrastructure developed by the government to support redevelopment is paid for using public funds; therefore, a portion of the increase in land value should also be invested to advance general well-being.

One good practice example is the Metrovivienda programme in Bogota, which aimed at providing affordable housing to low-income populations, especially those living in informal settlements (OECD, 2014[42]). In the first phase of the programme, the government used a land-banking mechanism and acquired privately-owned land, by negotiating with landowners in areas that were to be served by the future Bus Rapid Transit (BRT), the Transmilenio (Cullen-Cheung, 2003[43]). It then sold the land to private developers for the construction of affordable housing near the BRT stations (Cullen-Cheung, 2003[43]). In the second phase, after having faced a certain number of challenges, Metrovivienda associated with landowners instead of buying parcels directly (Gilbert, 2009[44]). Through this association, the government serviced the land by developing infrastructure, schools and parks, and provided landowners the difference between the final sales price and the cost of servicing the area (Gilbert, 2009[44]). Landowners received compensation in nature, i.e. serviced land (Gilbert, 2009[44]).

Overall, through this land value capture programme, the city managed to provide needed infrastructure and relocate low-income households, that used to live in informal and illegal settlements in the periphery, into liveable and transit-friendly neighbourhoods well connected to the rest of the city (OECD, 2014[42]), contributing thereby to GHG emissions reduction from transport. Overall, Metrovivienda improved populations' livelihoods, thanks to enhanced accessibility to opportunities and decreased transport expenditures, while fostering transit-oriented development. Developing and communicating long-term plans in the short-term will be an important basis for implementing successful land assembly programmes. In addition, exploring the potential of using different land-value capture mechanisms and developing comprehensive standards will be key to unlocking the potential for redevelopment projects to meet multiple well-being goals (including climate).

Urban infill can also incentivize land development, especially of privately-owned parcels in city cores in Israel. A national tax on vacant land used to be applied but was rescinded in 2000 (OECD, 2017[38]). The Knesset[22] found it questionable, and it was perceived as generally unfair for landowners who were unable to develop their land (e.g. lack of permitting procedures, or when situated near sensitive areas such as archaeological or industrial sites) but were still charged a tax (Haarets, 2012[45]). The cancellation of this tax, however, allows private landowners to speculate and keep their land undeveloped. An alternative policy tool that for Israel is split-rate property tax, which sets a higher rate on the value of land, and a lower rate on the value of a dwelling and its improvements (OECD, 2018[4]). Applying a higher rate on land discourages undeveloped land, prevents land speculation, thereby curbing urban expansion outside the city (OECD, 2018[4]), in addition, to incentivising developers and owners to build higher buildings or to upgrade their properties.

However, implementing such split-rate property taxes can be challenging. First, one difficulty lies in the fact that it can be administratively complex to assess the value of land and to separate it from the value of the dwelling built on it (OECD, 2018[4]). In addition, their implementation can raise political economy issues, as developments that have a high land-to-improvement ratio, i.e. the ratio of the land value to its improvements, such as car dealerships and other land-intensive uses, tend to face higher levels of taxation with a split-rate tax (Cohen and Coughlin, 2005[46]). In contrast, developments with low land-to-improvement ratio such as high-rise residential buildings tend to be advantaged (Cohen and Coughlin, 2005[46]). Despite these challenges and the low level of awareness and application so far - mostly concentrated in the United States (OECD, 2018[4]) - their potential for incentivizing densification are strong, especially when applied to the residential sector.

Regenerating cities' urban cores in Israel, especially in old ones, will be paramount in reaching desirable levels of density and compactness. The Ministry of Construction and Housing already includes an Urban Renewal Government Authority (Israel Planning Administration, 2020[8]). Their activities could include the redevelopment of brownfields, which can bring significant benefits to communities and cities by increasing housing supply. Putting in place planning tools that identify and promote the redevelopment of brownfields will be central to reinforce regeneration strategies. The Israeli Planning Administration (IPA) already promotes leading projects and guidelines.

An example of a policy tool that the IPA or Israel's cities could put in place is the Opportunity Area Planning Framework (OAPF) in London. The OAPF aims at transforming and regenerating "opportunity areas", which are identified brownfield land in town centres that have "significant capacity to accommodate new housing, commercial and other development linked to existing or potential improvements to public transport accessibility," (Greater London Authority, 2019[47]). The OAPF document sets guidance for both developers and local communities on the way planning decisions and developments should resolve a wide range of issues such as density optimization, infrastructure provision, accessibility enhancement, and overall design (Designing Buildings, 2016[48]). Opportunity Areas can accommodate around 2,500 homes and 5,000 jobs or a combination of the two, and can support additional infrastructure (Greater London Authority, 2019[47]). Feasibility for implementing the OAPF is made possible thanks to the strong role the London Mayor has in encouraging and incentivizing their development through support and leadership, by providing in-house expertise or partnering with boroughs in steering groups (Greater London Authority, 2019[47]).

Another good practice example is the Stockholm Royal Seaport project, which is a formerly contaminated brownfield, transformed into a vibrant and energy-efficient district offering a variety of mixed-uses and integrated infrastructure (ECODISTRICTS, 2013[49]). The aim of the Royal Seaport project was to address both projected population growth and climate change. While Stockholm is planning to become fossil-fuel free by 2040 (City of Stockholm, 2016[50]), the Royal Seaport has set a more ambitious target to become fossil-free by 2030 (ECODISTRICTS, 2013[49]). The City Council invested more than 150 million USD to decontaminate the land, and sold the land, at a price higher than the invested funds, to private developers who should meet requirements in line with the city's sustainability targets, building and planning requirements (ECODISTRICTS, 2013[49]). While affordability remains an important issue due to the high land prices, the Royal Seaport has gained worldwide recognition for being an example of urban design that contributes to both GHG emissions reductions and overall wellbeing.

Along the same lines, fostering the development of eco-districts (also called eco-neighbourhoods or sustainable neighbourhoods) that embed integrated planning systems for buildings, transport, and supporting infrastructure such as energy (in particular through the deployment of renewable energy), waste and water (Fraker, 2013[51]) is an opportunity to redevelop brownfields and decarbonize existing neighbourhoods, and also to promote them in new areas. The eco-district concept is gaining momentum in Israel, even though their nature varies. The Northwest District in Tel Aviv envisions a transformation into a neighbourhood that will produce its own renewable energy, mainly from solar sources (City of Tel Aviv-Yafo, 2017[52]). The Municipality of Tel Aviv, with the support of the Environmental Protection Authority, the Education Administration and Community Administration, strongly promotes the upgrading of neighbourhoods into sustainable ones, through its "From an existing Neighbourhood to a Sustainable Neighbourhood" Programme (Tel Aviv-Yafo Municipality Environment and Sustainability Authority, 2018[53]). This initiative is based on the One Planet Living model, which is a worldwide programme promoting sustainable modes of living, the protection of natural areas and renewable energy generation (Tel Aviv-Yafo Municipality Environment and Sustainability Authority, 2018[53]). To date, there are seven neighbourhoods, such as Bizaron and Yad Eliyazu committed to the Sustainable Neighbourhood programme[23] (Tel Aviv-Yafo Municipality Environment and Sustainability Authority, 2018[53]), financed from the municipality's own funds[24], and the aim is to progressively extend it to all neighbourhoods across the city. Therefore, *in the next five years, Israel could upscale the transformation of neighbourhoods into eco-districts.*

The Israeli government could catalyse this by providing a centralised stream of funding as occurred in Malmo (in Sweden), a former industrial city turned into an eco-district. The city applied for funding from national and European sources to realise their vision. A total of SEK 250,000,000 (91,497,500 NIS) was awarded to the city for various projects – e.g., green infrastructure, construction of more energy efficient buildings, or information and knowledge dissemination (Fraker, 2013[51]). An European grant (included in the total) helped to finance the energy system in the Western Harbour, which allows the city, in cooperation with Skydraft, the utility company, to come up with a plan to locally produce electricity with wind, solar, and geothermal (European Commission and European Environment Agency, 2016[54]).

In other cities (with similar climates to Israel's), eco-neighbourhoods not only resulted in environmental benefits, but also helped residents save money, for example, Trinitat Nova, a neighbourhood in Barcelona (Spain). In the 1990s, the residents of Trinitat Nova agreed on a major regeneration project to transform their rundown neighbourhood into a sustainable, eco-neighbourhood place to live (Flurin, 2017[55]). Trinitat Nova was constructed in the 1950s for rural immigrants, without proper urban planning and poorly connected to the rest of the city (European Urban Knowledge Network, 2010[56]). It had around 3,200 dwellings built with poor quality and energy inefficient materials (European Urban Knowledge Network, 2010[56]). The upgrade of Trinitat Nova to an eco-neighbourhood cost approximately EUR 16.2 million, 50% funding from the municipality of Barcelona and the rest from the European Regional Development Fund (LPED, n.d.[57]). The regeneration of Trinitat Nova rebuilt dwellings in a sustainable way by integrating passive designs, thereby reducing energy demand (and related expenditures) from cooling during hot summers, and heating during winter. The project set out clear objectives in terms of energy efficiency: (i) reduction of energy demand, (ii) replacement of fossil-fuel energy with renewables when technically possible, and (iii) promotion of solar energy for hot water (Alternativas, 2004[58]). The neighbourhood added green infrastructure, and it is estimated that the vegetation of Trinitat Nova sequesters up to 150 tonnes of CO_2 annually (Alternativas, 2004[58]). All of which increases the life quality of residents, in addition to extending the public transport network to make the neighbourhood accessible.

Putting in place similar frameworks or programmes in Israel can allow it to transform rundown neighbourhoods into vibrant areas offering housing, economic and environmental opportunities, while enhancing inhabitants' well-being.

Removing existing barriers that hamper the provision of affordable housing

In addition to relaxing density restrictions and urban infill, removing structural barriers that dampen the provision of affordable housing in Israel will be key for inclusive urban areas. The availability of public housing is rather limited as noted by Israel Planning Administration (2020[8]); available housing is intended for population in financial (lowest social-economic status) or functional disadvantages (i.e., disabled persons), who do not own a home, lack housing and meet housing criteria. One important barrier for low-income population, according to OECD (2011[59]), is the complex point system that rewards access to public housing, where households need to score at least 1400 points to be eligible. For example, a couple married for five years (receives 450 points) with three children (500 points) will pass the points test for public housing if they have at least five brothers and sisters (600 points), but not if they have four or less siblings (400 points) (OECD, 2011[59]). The reason used to justify this is that children of large families are likely to receive less support than children from small families (OECD, 2011[59]). The eligibility system should be simpler; according to recommendations from the 2011 and 2018 OECD Economic Surveys (OECD, 2011[59]), (OECD, 2018[60]), for instance by removing points for siblings, since this is an inaccurate measure of parental support.

However, purchasing a home is not always feasible nor a priority for certain segments of the population (e.g. young students), which makes the provision of rental a key area of policy intervention. Strengthening rental opportunities for low-income population across cities and enhancing existing targeted rental assistance will be an important area of action in the short term. Rental assistance from the Ministry of Construction and Housing is the most common form of support (accounting for approximately 36% of the ministry's budget in 2010); however, the system is complex with narrow eligibility (OECD, 2011[59]). Rental assistance is primarily targeted at new immigrants who, regardless of need, receive rental support for the first five years of settlement in Israel (OECD, 2011[59]).

The availability of Public Housing is also rather limited and is mainly reserved for population in financial (low income) or functional disadvantages (i.e. individuals with some kind of physical or mental limitation), who do not own a home and lack housing. The Ministry offers additional support for the wider population through: a)"Supervised" Long-Term rental apartments at market prices for up to five years (no eligibility criteria); and b) "Reduced" Long-Term rental apartments below market prices and according to the eligibility criteria set out by the "Buyer's Price" programme (Israel Planning Administration, 2020[8]). The latter is a programme that targets those without any rights to homes, namely married couples; individuals above 35 (bachelors, divorced or widowers); single parents, divorced (without a child) and below 35; handicapped individuals (above 21), and individuals from 26 to 35 (if extra housing units available) (Israel Planning Administration, 2020[8]). Putting in place a mean-tested uniform scheme that widened the range of beneficiaries across the society – e.g. by including students, young households – and based on affordability analysis would help making the policy more effective in terms of use of public funds.

In addition, the challenge of providing rental opportunities is exacerbated by the phenomenon of vacant homes i.e. that are empty most of the year - so called" ghost homes". Vacant apartments limit rental opportunities for low-income population and artificially increase housing prices, especially in big cities such as Jerusalem, Haifa, and Tel-Aviv which have the most important concentration of ghost homes (Haaretz, 2016[61]). In addition, land scarcity and high prices can discourage developers to build affordable housing in central areas. More people outside the city and living far from opportunities and services can lead to increased GHG emissions from transport and higher transport expenditures. Policies supporting rental and incentivizing developers to construct affordable housing in central areas will therefore be key.

In 2011, a national commission, the Trajtenberg Committee, was put in place in response to the housing crisis occurred during the same year, and one of its task was to examine the magnitude of the phenomenon of ghost homes. The Committee has found that more the 46,000 homes were empty (Haaretz, 2013[62]). As a response and in line with the Committee's recommendations, the Ministry of Interior has put in place in 2013, a strong policy to double-tax vacant homes, as a way to encourage homeowners to either sell or rent (Haaretz, 2013[62]). However, this law has proved to be ineffective, as only a very small number of homeowners[25] had been formally identified and received notifications that their tax would be doubled. Officials have not been able to identify the majority of ghost apartments, because the only tool at their disposal was water bills (Haaretz, 2016[61]). One solution proposed to the Knesset by a deputy was to give city officials access to electricity and gas bills to be able to find more empty homes (Haaretz, 2016[61]). However, using utility bills can be inefficient, as homeowners can set automated lighting or watering systems in order to avoid paying this tax (OECD, 2017[38]). Moreover, as of end of 2018, new estimations have been made by the Central Bureau of Statistics and the number of empty homes was thoroughly revised to more than 170,000 (Globes, 2019[63]). This has further emphasised the urgency of putting in place effective measures and strengthening the administrative capacity of municipalities for better implementing the double-tax policy. One option authorities in Israel should consider is to provide more budget transfer from national government to face this additional administrative burden at municipal level. Another option for tax authorities would be to use existing treaties with other countries that would allow to have access to more exploitable administrative information beyond utility bills - so the proof of non-residency can be established using rules that govern tax residency in Israel (OECD, 2019[64]) - such as the international framework as part of the OECD/The Global Forum on Transparency and Exchange of Information for Tax Purposes underlying a convention for automated tax information sharing (OECD, 2018[65]).

Inclusionary Zoning policy can also be a policy option to promote the provision of affordable housing inside urban cores, especially for rental. Inclusionary zoning encourages developers to include, for new developments, a proportion of affordable units for low income population, either for homeownership or for rent. In exchange, it allows for denser construction (see related discussions above on relaxing stringent density restrictions) or an accelerated permitting through a fast-track process that reduces the time and costs for new developments (New York University, 2008[66]). The incentives can also be tax abatements

(OECD, 2015[34]). The affordable units can be part of new developments in the same site, or be located elsewhere (off-site) (New York University, 2008[66]). As an alternative, developers can also pay in-lieu fees to local authorities, who can use them to build affordable housing (New York University, 2008[66]). However, mandatory affordable housing provision can cause developers to build in other localities where such regulations are not imposed, thereby causing urban sprawl. Alternatively, there are programmes that use a voluntary approach, i.e. requiring developers to build affordable units only if they choose to use the incentives (Lincoln Institute of Land Policy, 2015[67]). Inclusionary zoning that uses the permission to build with a higher density as an incentive should apply in areas where higher level of density or new constructions are desirable and feasible, with respect to the capacity of maintaining or upgrading existing infrastructure, and looking at other social considerations such as the potential added crime level (OECD, 2015[34]).

Guiding future development by planning for smart urban growth

As explained in the previous section, physically containing urban growth is not an effective climate mitigation strategy in Israel, as urban areas will need to expand to accommodate population growth. To illustrate, in 2004, despite pressures from environmental advocacy groups, a greenbelt in West Jerusalem was transformed into a neighbourhood, in order to face enormous demand for housing (Haaretz, 2004[68]). Therefore, anticipating future urban growth by putting in place timely planning strategies is key for cities in Israel to make sure that their urban footprint evolves within a sustainable pattern. Complementing density regulations and urban regeneration policies outlined in the section above with strategies that anticipate and allow for sustainable growth in peripheral and less urbanized areas will be paramount. This needs to be done while ensuring sound coordination across relevant sectors and actors through enhanced integrated planning (OECD, 2015[34]).

According to Angel (2008[69]), preparing for growth in less urbanized zones or peripheral areas entails establishing visionary planning through an arterial grid of roads, sufficiently spaced one from each other by 1 kilometre (OECD, 2015[34]). This spacing will allow to carry, in the future, public transport infrastructure, and will ensure that residents, will be less than a ten-minute walk from transport stations, which have both environmental and well-being benefits. Guiding future residential developments along large arterial grids would ensure that residential developments are sufficiently dense to sustain public transport, while contributing to lower GHG emission from transports due to transit-oriented developments. In addition, the roads should be sufficiently large (from 60 to 100 feet wide) so that they can include bus and bike lanes (Fuller, 2012[70]), i.e. so that a *complete street* approach can be adopted (see chapter on transport). In order to support the growth, cities will need to create green space, water and waste management (see next section), and telecommunication networks (Fuller, 2012[70]). This planning is particularly relevant in Israel, where most of peripheral land is publicly owned. The Israel Planning Administration already developed policies for densification along mass transportation lines in the Tel Aviv and Jerusalem metropolitan areas. Areas along these routes will reportedly be developed as dense and mixed-use areas (Israel Planning Administration, 2020[8]).

When planning for future growth, as already recognised in the cities of Tel Aviv and Jerusalem, setting zoning plans that require mixed land uses is pivotal in fostering climate-friendly developments. Mixing residential buildings with shops, services and jobs create vibrant communities and allow cross-fertilisation of ideas and cities' economic vitality. Curitiba, has put in place pioneering transit-oriented developments approach by setting zoning regulations that foster mixed-used, high-density, and vibrant communities along the main public transport corridors (ICLEI, 2016[71]). For example, the City's Zoning Plan requires that at least 50% of ground, first and second floors buildings near transport corridors be occupied by commercial services, shops and restaurants, creating thereby lively communities (ICLEI, 2016[71]). In addition, Curitiba put in place an inclusive zoning by designating Special Social Interest Housing Sectors for low-income population, and no-car zones dedicated to walking, contributing thereby to social inclusiveness and climate protection (ICLEI, 2016[71]).Following these principles will be especially important when developing any new peripheral developments to ensure they contribute rather than hinder climate and other well-being goals.

Furthermore, guiding future developments along existing or future transport infrastructure is an opportunity to promote integrated planning encompassing land use, housing, environment, and to align policy priorities around accessibility to jobs and opportunities, affordability of housing, sustainability and economic growth (OECD/ITF, 2018[72]). The development of long-term strategic planning tools is key to ensuring co-ordination between residential, transport and other key infrastructure as cities grow and evolve. In the UK, London shows a strong planning framework composed of three main pillars: the London Plan (the spatial development strategy), the Economic Development Strategy (EDS) and the Mayor's Transport Strategy (MTS). The three documents are developed with strong links between them (e.g. the MTS is based on emerging policies set out in the both the London Plan and the EDS, while the London Plan addresses planning policies and the way these can facilitate or hinder the transport's system capacity to cope with emerging trends) (OECD, 2016[73]).

Transport for London (the Metropolitan Transport Authority) has also put in place tools explicitly linking transport, housing and wider land use and thus supporting coordinated planning for new development. This is done using the Public Transport Accessibility Levels (PTAL) indicator and the Sustainable Residential Quality Matrix (see next subsection for further explanation) (OECD/ITF, 2018[72]). In France, the Île-de-France Mobilités (the MTA in charge of the Paris metropolitan region) develops the Plan de Développement Urbain Île-de-France (PDUIF), which is the Île-de-France's region mobility plan (OECD/ITF, 2018[72]), promoting a sustainable transport sector, and strongly linked to the Territorial Coherence Scheme, the SCoT, the region's strategic plan for urban planning, housing, and economic development (OECD/ITF, 2018[72]). Metropolitan level bodies (addressed further in Section 3.4.2 and Chapter 4 on transport) have proven successful in developing strategic planning capacity, which on the one hand builds on relevant knowledge of local issues but on the other is embedded in a wider vision that can better balance priorities and strategies across metropolitan areas.

At neighbourhood level, fostering the uptake of eco-districts, which present similar features in terms of integrated infrastructure planning (discussed in above section) can be a strategy for Israeli municipalities when expanding into non-urbanized or less urbanized areas.

Accompanying urban growth with the provision of infrastructure

With denser cities and neighbourhoods comes the need to provide adequate levels of infrastructure, such as public services for transport, water and waste management, educational and health facilities, and green space to avoid urban heat islands effects. In particular, after the government's decision to increase minimum density requirements, the provision of infrastructure became a hot topic in the public realm (Globes, 2019[74]). In order to avoid situations where infrastructure is lacking as cities densify, residents in a wide range of cities are advocated for "retrained construction", i.e. infrastructure before construction (Globes, 2019[74]). In some cities, mayors who focused on constructions rather that the provision of infrastructure was sanctioned during elections (Globes, 2019[74]).

Therefore, strengthening the existing rules for infrastructure provision when providing housing in Israel will be paramount for sustaining the exponential urban growth projected. The London City Hall put in place a policy for optimising housing potential, using a Sustainable Residential Quality (SRQ) density matrix that sets ranges of acceptable housing density, depending on the urban zone features (suburban, urban, or central) and accessibility to public transport through the Public Transport Accessibility Level (PTAL) developed by Transport for London (see Chapter 4 on transport) (Greater London Authority, 2019[75]). As such, the higher the PTAL is, the higher the residential density can be. The SRQ is also in line with the City's wider policy guidance that requires the adequate provision of social infrastructures such as health services, water facilities or green space (Greater London Authority, 2019[76]). Incorporating transport considerations into development standards is also a good way of aligning planning of transport and development and can be done by building in indices like the PTAL.

Land value capture mechanisms, such as betterment levies, can also be put in place to provide or maintain infrastructure as cities densify. Betterment levies are a tax paid by landowners or beneficiaries, and applied on land or properties that have seen an appreciation of their value thanks to public infrastructure investments (The World Bank, 2019[77]). The levy can be paid on a one-off or a recurrent basis, and aims at sharing the benefits of public investment to the overall community. A wide range of countries have implemented the betterment charges in various forms. For example, in Colombia, the levy is called Contribución de Valorización (CV) and is a main source of municipal revenue, which has been implemented since 1921 (Borrero Ochoa, 2011[78]). Local authorities in Israel already implement betterment levies (also called capital gain taxes) in order to fund public facilities (OECD, 2017[38]). As set by the Law in Israel, a levy of 50% on the value the property has gained is applied, if this betterment is a result of actions from local authorities (OECD, 2017[38]). However, as part of urban renewal programmes such as the NMP38[26], and public housing projects, a betterment levy exemption is applied, on a full or partial basis, in order to incentivize higher density (additional floors to a building) or demolish and rebuild (OECD, 2017[38]). While this is an interesting incentive for property owners and developers, such exemptions are a missed opportunity for municipalities to raise revenues that can serve to make further investments. Also, as already mentioned, government investment in infrastructure as part of urban renewal programmes comes from the public budget. Betterment levies allow to balance out the fact that owners in the area have a direct gain from it, recuperating a portion of the value created for the public budget. Israel could rescind this betterment levy exemption or adjust it, so that more funds can be collected.

In addition, putting in place policies that foster the creation and maintenance of green infrastructure[27] - e.g., trees, parks, and lawns – will be key in order to reduce urban heat island effects as urban areas densify. Green infrastructure lower temperatures in the surrounding microclimate, thereby reducing energy demand for cooling in surrounding buildings; less energy means less emissions. Cohen, Potchter and Matzarakis (2012[79]) show that dense canopy tree cover in an urban park in Tel Aviv reduced temperatures by up to 3.8°C in the summer. A 3.8°C decrease in the summer temperature is estimated to reduce energy consumption by 20% from air conditioning in Israel[28] in residential and commercial buildings (Herzog, Shalabna and Maor, 2017[80]). Reductions in energy consumption, by consequence, reduce emissions, given the dominance of natural gas in Israel's electricity (Chapter 2). In addition, one acre of new forest can sequester about 2.5 tons of carbon annually, not to mention that it improves of air quality, by filtering pollutants, thereby reducing respiratory illnesses and health expenditure. For example, in the District of Victoria, London estimated that 1,225 trees - covering 8.8% of surface area - remove 1.2 tonnes of pollutants (e.g. PM10, PM2.5, Ozone) annually, and saved GBP 85,149 in health related expenditures[29], and stored nearly 850 tonnes of CO_2, corresponding to a value of GBP 44,895[30] (Rogers, Jaluzot and Neilan, 2012[81]). In addition, it has been estimated that urban trees in Barcelona - for a population of more than 210,000 trees - could remove up to 305 tonnes of air pollutants in a year, providing a value to the society estimated at EUR 1.12 million annually (Chaparro and Terradas, 2009[82]).

The protection of natural assets and the integration of green space in urban settings is already part of the agenda for some cities in Israel, for example, Tel Aviv and Jerusalem. In 2016, Tel-Aviv, approved a master plan for the protection of natural sites; in addition to the TA/5000 Zoning Plan, which set rules on how the city will develop until 2025, in terms of building density, including residential, mixed-land use, public open space and wider environmental guidelines (Tel Aviv-Yafo Municipality Environment and Sustainability Authority, 2018[53]). Likewise, the municipality of Jerusalem developed a Master Plan based on sustainable urban development with a focus on preserving ecological assets, green open spaces and metropolitan parks. However, the initiatives and master plans set out in cities such as Jerusalem and Tel Aviv are insufficient, as their outlined recommendations are not compulsory.

Green Space Factor (GSF) is a regulation for developers that requires green infrastructure in new housing developments. A wide range of cities use this, including Berlin, Malmö, Seattle, Southampton, and North

West England[31] (Vartholomaios, 2013[83]). The Green Space Factor is an indicator that usually goes from 0 to 1, which is a weighted average of different green surface types (using different factors assigned) and the area of each of these green surfaces (Kruuse, 2011[84]). For example, the minimum legally binding GSF is set to 0.6 in Malmö and Berlin, whereas in Seattle, the GSF has differentiated values (e.g. for multi-family mid-rise and high-rise buildings a score of 0.5 is required; for multifamily low-rise buildings 0.6). Some cities, such as Malmö, complement it by a list of Green Points (from which developers have to choose a certain number) that display unquantifiable green space qualities, e.g. "all buildings have green roofs" (Kruuse, 2011[84]). Developing tools to show these broader well-being benefits could be useful to help municipalities garner support for green space factors (see Box 3.3).

Betterment levies (discussed above) can also be used to provide green infrastructure. In certain areas of London, Putney Commons and Wimbledon, parks are maintained thanks to a betterment levy paid by residents living in proximity, additionally to existing council tax (Drayson, 2014[85]). In addition, the mechanism has been applied in Melbourne, via the Melbourne Metropolitan Parks Charge, which is levied on a one-off basis, and calculated by the local council to capture the value some of the city's parks provide to residents and businesses (Trinomics and IUCN, 2019[86]). The charge is used to maintain and manage large urban parks, gardens and trails, thereby contributing to greening neighbourhoods and ensuring their liveability for current and future residents.

Box 3.4. Incorporating the value of green infrastructure into decision-making

Developing tools that allow local authorities or developers in Israel to showcase the environmental and socioeconomic benefits of green infrastructure can help attract more public or private funding by showing positive outcomes that can reduce payback period of projects, thereby making their business case more appealing; or reduce public health expenditures.

The green infrastructure valuation toolkit (GIVAT) is a tool developed by a consortium of organisations across the UK, with the support of the Department for Environment, Food and Rural Affairs (DEFRA). As a response to economic, social and environmental challenges faced by the UK, it aims at evaluating the economic value of green infrastructure (The Mersey Forest et al., 2018[87]). The GIVAT showcases the benefits of green infrastructure in economic terms and wider returns for the environment and communities. The benefits are estimated in terms of climate change (mitigation and adaptation), health, land and property values (The Mersey Forest et al., 2018[87]). The current used prototype include modules estimating climate mitigation and air quality benefits, and uses parameters such as energy consumption, domestic price of electricity, amount of green space (surface). It has been already used for assessing the benefits of green space in some cities across the UK (The Mersey Forest et al., 2018[87]).

Source: (The Mersey Forest et al., 2018[87]).

3.4.2. Decreasing the strain on municipalities budgets and developing local technical capacity

Constrained budgets and private land-ownership exacerbate urban sprawl and poorly integrated infrastructure

Constrained local budgets – along with lingering debt – restricts municipalities' ability to develop housing in the city centre. The largest proportion of municipalities' budgets comes from property taxes – typically, about 46% (S&P Global Rating, 2019[22]). The Arnona rates – taxes on the use of buildings - change between municipalities, but the national government restricts the upper bound of taxes on the use of residential properties, leading to a state where municipalities are chronically in debt. The absolute level of debt is fairly constant, but as a percentage of operating revenues, it is equal or less than 30% (S&P Global Rating, 2019[22]).

This precarious but perpetual condition means that municipalities often cannot afford the upfront costs of infrastructure to develop privately owned land (which is one of municipalities' responsibilities), and instead, opt to develop state-owned land in the periphery, for which it has support from the national government. This lead to low-density development and sprawl, thereby increasing GHG emissions (OECD, 2018[4]). For example, in Netanya, the municipality needs upfront financing to develop the infrastructure for private land, but lacks the financial capacity to do so (OECD, 2017[6]). In contrast, it is possible for municipalities to develop state-owned land in collaboration with the national government as part of large-scale residential projects where financing for infrastructure and public facilities is provided by the Israel Land Authority (OECD, 2017[6]). As part of these agreements, the state usually provides pre-funding and assistance in planning, while the municipality is in charge of construction and providing building permits in a timely manner. In Netanya, these incentives have resulted in an urban core rampant with undeveloped private land (OECD, 2017[6]).

Exploring decentralisation and building on good practice

At the moment, spending in Israel is highly centralised, and local tax revenues are very low (in comparison with other OECD countries) (OECD, 2019[88]); a configuration that has exacerbated among other problems the housing shortage, as described above. Empowering local governments – whether at the municipal, district or regional level – with greater autonomy may help Israel address these chronic budgetary constraints. Locally elected authorities are generally better positioned to understand local needs and to respond to local demands (OECD/ITF, 2018[72]). Decentralisation has occurred throughout OECD countries, bringing a reconfiguration of power and responsibilities between levels of government. This has led to a different role for national governments, one that is less prominent in directly delivering local services and infrastructure, but which instead (at least ideally) needs to ensure coordination and alignment of local decisions with national policy objectives, as well as ensuring balanced development across territories. The experience with decentralisation in other OECD countries shows an improvement in the quality and efficiency of public services as a result. Revenue decentralisation, in particular, is associated with smaller regional economic disparities (OECD, 2019[88]). The OECD (2019[88]) already created a handbook for policymakers on how to decentralise, crucial steps include, "(1) clarifying the responsibilities assigned to different levels of government, (2) ensuring that these responsibilities are sufficiently funded, (3) strengthen subnational fiscal autonomy to enhance accountability, (4) support subnational capacity building," amongst others.

Israel could also build on international experience if engaging in a decentralisation process by ensuring the new governance framework allows (and even requires) for the creation of metropolitan level bodies. This type of bodies can avoid a common downside of decentralisation, which is generating a high level of fragmentation in responsibilities, for instance those for transport or urban development, across an array of actors. These bodies can strike a good balance, by on the one hand, allowing local authorities to perform a relevant role in the decision-making process and, on the other, making it possible to guarantee coherence and cohesion across a territory-the metropolitan area or region- which in many cases is also composed of urban and rural territories (which also generates important challenges). The creation of these bodies is in particular important where cities have evolved into economic units that do not necessarily coincide with administrative boundaries (OECD/ITF, 2018[72]).

The creation of Metropolitan Transport Authorities has, for instance, proven successful in delivering important improvements in transport policy and its integration with housing and land-use. The following chapter offers guidance on how to establish Metropolitan Transport Authorities. Transport has indeed been a common responsibility assigned to these types of bodies. However, in several cases metropolitan bodies have also been assigned other responsibilities. Among these are environment and urban development, like in the case of the Àrea Metropolitana de Barcelona (AMB) in Spain (OECD/ITF, 2018[72]), or economic development, as in the case of the Metropole Region Rotterdam The Hague (MRDH) in the Netherlands (OECD, 2016[73]). In both these cases, these responsibilities are additional to transport responsibilities.

Leveraging innovative financial instruments to further expand local financial capacity

A number of financial instruments – in addition to decentralisation - can be used to finance eco-districts and or simply green infrastructure, for example, via development charges. This is a one-time compulsory levy paid by developers as a condition to receiving building permit (Merk et al., 2012[89]). It aims at financing infrastructure and services costs incurred by new developments. Such a levy is particularly relevant for residential developments in new neighbourhoods to finance public facilities such as green space, sidewalks, or even transport. Israel's central government allows municipalities to exert development charges, but not all localities apply or promote them in an optimal way, due to capacity and knowledge gaps, thereby causing difficulties in raising funds. One solution the government proposed was to enact a national law that would standardise the calculation of development charges in all localities, depending on local density and topography (OECD, 2017[38]). Development charges are implemented and systematically used in a wide range of OECD countries, such as in the UK, which has put in place the Community Infrastructure Levy (CIL), that allow local authorities to charge developers for new developments in their areas. The CIL is applicable to any new development that creates new dwellings or additional floor space of a minimum of 100 square meters to help fund local infrastructure that provide services to residents (UK Government, 2014[90]). In London, the Mayoral CIL (MCIL) was put in place in 2012 to help fund the Crossrail, the new high capacity rail that will cross London[32]. The MCIL charge rate is calculated depending on the distance from the Crossrail: the closer the development to the stations, the higher the charge is, thereby charging more the more developments will benefit from the project (OECD/ITF, 2018[72]). Israel could also consider such variables integrating the distance to major transport stations with frequent transport services into the charges' formula. S*tandardising development charges could be a priority for Israel in the next five years.*

Municipalities in Israel could also strengthen inter-ministerial co-operation to attract public funds through pool funding (Trinomics and IUCN, 2019[86]). For example, Israeli municipalities could collaborate with public health departments to create or preserve green spaces in a given area. Green infrastructure positively influences public health – e.g., decreasing pollution, improving quality of life - thereby decreasing health related expenditures. This additional health-related funding can then be used to protect or add green spaces. For example, the city of Liverpool (in the UK) uses public health budget to improve green spaces in deprived residential areas, through the Liverpool Primary Care trust, which funds the Natural Choice for Health and well-being programme (Drayson, 2014[85]). In total, 38 projects in poor neighbourhoods were granted between GBP 1,000 and GBP 38,000 (for a total of GBP 380,000 granted) to create green space across neighbourhoods. The programme substantially enhanced the residents living conditions, as they self-reported an increase of wellbeing by 18% (Drayson, 2014[85]).

Israeli municipalities can also harness the potential of local businesses to fund green and accessible neighbourhoods. Business Improvement Districts (BID) are public-private organisations based on an agreement between local government and businesses who accept to pay an additional levy to finance projects in the district - e.g. green spaces, pedestrian facilities, cycling paths, and so on. In San Francisco, the BID model extended to residential areas to create the "Green Business District" (GBD) in the Dogpatch and Potrero Hill neighbourhoods. Residents and businesses agreed (by vote) to pay an additional compulsory levy aiming at supporting the maintenance or improvement of green space in the residential neighbourhood, augmenting thereby the actions of the local authority. In order to be effective, BIDs (or GBDs) need to be composed by a critical number of businesses (and/or residents) that are willing to pay for similar services (Merk et al., 2012[89]). BID is a tool that can be used in Israel, especially in newly built neighbourhoods or regenerated urban areas that foster mixed land uses, local economic activity and high business concentration. Awareness raising toward environmental concerns and a clear demonstration of wider wellbeing benefits can help obtaining commitment from businesses and landowners.

Similar to the cash-back schemes at the dwelling level, Israel's municipalities can subsidise private landowners to create or maintain green space on their properties, by partly covering their cost, but subsidies and tax rebates are more feasible in municipalities that do not encounter budgetary constraints. In Rotterdam, Netherlands, in order to promote the installation of green roofs, the City provide a subsidy of EUR 30 per square meters for roofs of at least 10 square meters. In 2018, around 360,000 square meters had been installed across the city (City of Rotterdam, 2018[91]). In Hamburg, Germany, in order to reduce urban heat island effects and buildings energy demands, the Ministry for Environment and Energy, through its Green Roof Strategy[33], decided to support building owners by providing subsidies covering up to 60% of green roofs costs, The Strategy aims at planting a total of 100 hectares of urban green roofs in 10-year time (Climate ADAPT, 2016[92]).

Table 3.5. Summary financing instruments at the neighbourhood and city-level

Type of land	Instrument	Who bears the costs ?	Who repays ?	Wellbeing implications	Feasibility in Israel
Public	Pool funding from different ministries or departments in local governments	Relevant ministries	No repayment	Synergies Cross-sectoral benefits – Public health, mental wellbeing, physical health Less public health expenditures due to improved public health Climate change mitigation Trade-offs Other challenges in other sectors might be less prioritized	Availability of funds in targeted ministries Clear quantification of benefits across sectors Monitoring tools that guide funding decisions Awareness raising
Public	Development charges	Developers	NA	Synergies More public funds available Enhanced public health Climate change mitigation Trade-offs Can be perceived as an imposed tax by developers	Regulatory changes Carefully designed in order to avoid "double" similar taxation
Public or private	Betterment levies	Landowners	NA	Synergies More public funds available Wealth sharing Benefits returned to society Trade-offs Some population might be unable to afford the levy	Accurate calculation tools and resources Targeted treatment for people who cannot pay for the levy
Private	Split-rate property tax	Landowners, property owners	NA	Synergies More public funds available Incentivize land development Increase density and curb urban sprawl Trade-offs Some population might be unable to afford the tax Administrative costs to isolate the value of land from the value of the dwelling	Accurate tools and resources to calculate the tax Targeted treatment for people who cannot pay for the tax
Public or private	Business Improvement Districts	Private sector: businesses or residents	No repay	Synergies The municipality "delegates" some responsibility, relaxing thereby budget constraints The wider community will benefit from the green infrastructure Trade-offs Small business or poor households might not be able to afford the additional tax	"Law of large numbers" Level of awareness and concern toward environmental issues
Private	Subsidies and tax rebates	Municipalities	NA	Synergies Can promote investments Wider benefits for the community (e.g. cooling and filtering of ambient air nearby) Trade-offs The price of subsidized solutions can be hold at a price artificially high Additional administrative costs	Availability of funds Transparency and verification with regard to solutions chosen by the beneficiary

References

100 Resilient Cities (2020), *Urban Resilience - 100 Resilient Cities*, http://www.100resilientcities.org/resources/ (accessed on 19 May 2020). [5]

Abd Rashid, A. and S. Yusoff (2015), *A review of life cycle assessment method for building industry*, Elsevier Ltd, http://dx.doi.org/10.1016/j.rser.2015.01.043. [10]

Alexander Zhivov, A. et al. (2017), *Deep Energy Retrofit-A Guide for Decision Makers*. [32]

Alternativas, G. (2004), *Ecobarrio de Trinitat Nova PROPUESTAS DE SOSTENIBILIDAD URBANA*. [58]

Angel, S. (2008), "An arterial grid of dirt roads", *Cities*, Vol. 25/3, pp. 146-162, http://dx.doi.org/10.1016/J.CITIES.2008.03.005. [69]

Angel, S. et al. (2010), *Atlas of Urban Expansion*, https://www.lincolninst.edu/research-data/data/atlas-urban-expansion (accessed on 4 March 2020). [33]

Arch, A. (2014), "Sustainable Urban Renewal: The Tel Aviv Dilemma", *Sustainability*, Vol. 6/5, pp. 2527-2537, http://dx.doi.org/10.3390/su6052527. [40]

Baron, R. (2016), "The Role of Public Procurement in Low-carbon Innovation", *33rd Round Table on Sustainable Development*, OECD, Paris, https://www.oecd.org/sd-roundtable/papersandpublications/The%20Role%20of%20Public%20Procurement%20in%20Low-carbon%20Innovation.pdf. [17]

Borrero Ochoa, O. (2011), "Betterment Levy in Colombia", Lincoln Institute of Land Policy, https://www.lincolninst.edu/publications/articles/betterment-levy-colombia (accessed on 5 August 2019). [78]

Center for Neighborhood Technology (2019), *Housing and Transport Affordability Index*, https://htaindex.cnt.org/ (accessed on 17 December 2019). [12]

Central Bureau of Statistics (2019), *2016 Household Census Data*, The State of Israel, https://old.cbs.gov.il/reader/cw_usr_view_Folder?ID=141. [26]

Chaparro, L. and J. Terradas (2009), *Ecological Services of Urban Forest in Barcelona*, https://www.itreetools.org/documents/302/Barcelona%20Ecosystem%20Analysis.pdf (accessed on 11 May 2020). [82]

City of Rotterdam (2018), *Rotterdam.nl | Green roofs*, https://www.rotterdam.nl/wonen-leven/groene-daken/ (accessed on 13 November 2019). [91]

City of Stockholm (2016), "Strategy for a fossil-fuel free Stockholm by 2040", https://international.stockholm.se/globalassets/rapporter/strategy-for-a-fossil-fuel-free-stockholm-by-2040.pdf (accessed on 18 May 2020). [50]

City of Tel Aviv-Yafo (2017), "The strategic Plan for Tel Aviv-Yafo", https://www.tel-aviv.gov.il/Residents/Development/DocLib1/City%20Vision%202017.pdf (accessed on 18 May 2020). [52]

Climate ADAPT (2016), *Four pillars to Hamburg's Green Roof Strategy: financial incentive, dialogue, regulation and science — Climate-ADAPT*, https://climate-adapt.eea.europa.eu/metadata/case-studies/four-pillars-to-hamburg2019s-green-roof-strategy-financial-incentive-dialogue-regulation-and-science (accessed on 13 November 2019). [92]

Cohen, J. and C. Coughlin (2005), *An Introduction to Two-Rate Taxation of Land and Buildings*, https://files.stlouisfed.org/files/htdocs/publications/review/05/05/CohenCoughlin.pdf (accessed on 16 July 2019). [46]

Cohen, P., O. Potchter and A. Matzarakis (2012), "Daily and seasonal climatic conditions of green urban open spaces in the Mediterranean climate and their impact on human comfort", *Building and Environment*, http://dx.doi.org/10.1016/j.buildenv.2011.11.020. [79]

Cullen-Cheung, J. (2003), *MetroVivienda: New Urban Renewal in Bogotá*, http://www.bogotalab.com/articles/metrovivienda.htm (accessed on 12 March 2020). [43]

Dechezleprêtre, A., D. Nachtigall and F. Venmans (2018), "THE JOINT IMPACT OF THE EUROPEAN UNION EMISSIONS TRADING SYSTEM ON CARBON EMISSIONS AND ECONOMIC PERFORMANCE", No. ENV/EPOC/WPIEEP(2017)7/REV1 3, OECD, https://one.oecd.org/document/ENV/EPOC/WPIEEP(2017)7/REV1/en/pdf (accessed on 21 August 2018). [15]

Designing Buildings (2016), *Opportunity Area Planning Framework (OAPF)*, https://www.designingbuildings.co.uk/wiki/Opportunity_Area_Planning_Framework_(OAPF) (accessed on 9 March 2020). [48]

Drayson, K. (2014), "Policies to improve the UK's urban green spaces", https://policyexchange.org.uk/wp-content/uploads/2016/09/green-society.pdf (accessed on 13 November 2019). [85]

ECODISTRICTS (2013), *Stockholm Royal Seaport - NEIGHBORHOOD CASE STUDY*, http://miljobarometern. (accessed on 8 March 2019). [49]

EcoTraders (2019), *Buildings and Urban Planning – the main policies, barriers and opportunities*, EcoTraders Energy and Environment. [1]

European Commission (2017), *PUBLIC PROCUREMENT FOR A CIRCULAR ECONOMY G o o d p r act i ce an d g u i d an c e*, European Commission, Brussels, https://ec.europa.eu/environment/gpp/pdf/CP_European_Commission_Brochure_webversion_small.pdf. [16]

European Commission (2014), *Technical Guidance: Financing the energy renovation of buildings*, European Commission, https://ec.europa.eu/energy/sites/ener/files/documents/2014_guidance_energy_renovation_buildings.pdf. [29]

European Commission and European Environment Agency (2016), *Optimization of the mix of private and public funding to realise climate adaptation measures in Malmö (2016)*, https://climate-adapt.eea.europa.eu/metadata/case-studies/optimization-of-the-mix-of-private-and-public-funding-to-realise-climate-adaptation-measures-in-malmo (accessed on 2 March 2020). [54]

European Urban Knowledge Network (2010), *Urban Regeneration in Trinitat Nova - Barcelona, ES*, https://www.eukn.eu/news/detail/urban-regeneration-in-trinitat-nova-barcelona-es-1/ (accessed on 15 November 2019). [56]

Flurin, C. (2017), "Eco-districts: Development and Evaluation. A European Case Study", *Procedia Environmental Sciences*, Vol. 37, pp. 34-45, http://dx.doi.org/10.1016/j.proenv.2017.03.012. [55]

Fraker, H. (2013), *The hidden potential of sustainable neighborhoods : lessons from low-carbon communities.* [51]

Friedman, C., N. Becker and E. Erell (2014), "Energy retrofit of residential building envelopes in Israel: A cost-benefit analysis", *Energy*, Vol. 77, pp. 183-193, http://dx.doi.org/10.1016/j.energy.2014.06.019. [25]

Fuller, B. (2012), *The Genius of Dirt Roads: Why the growing cities of the developing world need New York–style street grids*, City Journal, https://www.city-journal.org/html/genius-dirt-roads-13519.html (accessed on 12 March 2020). [70]

Gilbert, A. (2009), "The rise (and fall?) of a state land bank", *Habitat International*, Vol. 33/4, pp. 425-435, http://dx.doi.org/10.1016/J.HABITATINT.2009.01.003. [44]

Globes (2019), *Israeli gov't plans more densely populated cities*, https://en.globes.co.il/en/article-israeli-govt-plans-more-densely-populated-cities-1001289270 (accessed on 13 March 2020). [74]

Globes (2019), *Number of empty homes in Israel up 24% since 2012*, https://en.globes.co.il/en/article-number-of-empty-homes-in-israel-up-24-1001302710 (accessed on 9 March 2020). [63]

Greater London Authority (2019), *Policy 2.13 Opportunity Areas and Intensification Areas | London City Hall*, https://www.london.gov.uk/what-we-do/planning/london-plan/current-london-plan/london-plan-chapter-two-londons-places/policy-0 (accessed on 4 June 2019). [47]

Greater London Authority (2019), *Policy 3.16 Protection and enhancement of social infrastructure | London City Hall*, https://www.london.gov.uk/what-we-do/planning/london-plan/current-london-plan/london-plan-chapter-3/policy-316-protection-and (accessed on 4 June 2019). [76]

Greater London Authority (2019), *Policy 3.4 Optimising housing potential | London City Hall*, https://www.london.gov.uk/what-we-do/planning/london-plan/current-london-plan/london-plan-chapter-3/policy-34-optimising (accessed on 4 June 2019). [75]

Haarets (2012), *Israel's housing minister considering new tax on vacant land*, https://www.haaretz.com/housing-minister-proposes-taxing-vacant-land-1.5287161 (accessed on 10 March 2020). [45]

Haaretz (2016), *Plan to double tax on Israel's 'ghost homes' falls flat*, https://www.haaretz.com/israel-news/business/.premium-plan-to-double-tax-on-israel-s-ghost-homes-falls-flat-1.5462215 (accessed on 6 March 2020). [61]

Haaretz (2013), *Interior minister approves doubling property taxes on vacant Israeli apartments*, https://www.haaretz.com/israel-news/business/.premium-israel-doubling-tax-on-vacant-homes-1.5243415 (accessed on 6 March 2020). [62]

Haaretz (2004), *From a greenbelt to a neighborhood*, https://www.haaretz.com/1.4831198 (accessed on 24 February 2020). [68]

Herzog, C., N. Shalabna and G. Maor (2017), "Israel Natural Gas Demand Forecast 2017-2040", https://www.delek-group.com/wp-content/uploads/2017/09/BDO-Gas-Market-Forecast-2-07-2017-for-Delek-Group-with-final-letter-1.pdf (accessed on 16 December 2019). [80]

Housing Works RI (2013), *Historic Preservation and Affordable Housing A smart investment for Rhode Island's economy*, Housing Works RI, https://www.housingworksri.org/Portals/0/Uploads/Documents/HWRI-HRTCIssueBrief-FINAL.pdf (accessed on 2 March 2020). [27]

ICLEI (2016), "Curitiba, Brazil - A model for Transit Orient Development", https://www.thegpsc.org/sites/gpsc/files/iclei_cs_190_curitiba_urban-leds_0.pdf (accessed on 20 January 2020). [71]

IISD and i2-4c (2017), *Low-carbon innovation for sustainable infrastructure: The role of public procurement*, International Institute for Sustainable Development, https://www.iisd.org/project/public-procurement-and-innovation-low-carbon-infrastructure. [18]

IMF (2017), *Israel: Housing's Too Tight to Mention*, https://www.imf.org/en/News/Articles/2017/04/19/na042517-israel-housings-too-tight-to-mention (accessed on 16 December 2019). [7]

Infinite Solutions (2017), *Financing the energy renovation of residential buildings through soft loans and third-party investment schemes*, Infinite Solutions, https://energy-cities.eu/wp-content/uploads/2019/01/PUBLI_infinite_solutions_guidebook_softloans_2017_en.pdf. [30]

Israel Planning Administration (2020), *Affordable Housing*, Israeli Planning Administration. [8]

ITF (2019), "Benchmarking Accessibility in Cities Measuring the Impact of Proximity and Transport Performance", http://www.itf-oecd.org. [37]

ITF/OECD (2017), *Income Inequality, Social Inclusion and Mobility*, https://www.itf-oecd.org/sites/default/files/docs/income-inequality-social-inclusion-mobility.pdf (accessed on 2 October 2018). [41]

Kaiser, B. (2016), "Circular economy: Getting the circulation going", *Nature*, Vol. 531/7595, pp. 443-446, http://dx.doi.org/10.1038/531443a. [20]

Kruuse, A. (2011), *The green space factor and the green points system*, http://www.grabs-eu.org (accessed on 25 March 2019). [84]

Lee, S. and B. Lee (2014), "The influence of urban form on GHG emissions in the U.S. household sector", *Energy Policy*, Vol. 68, pp. 534-549, http://dx.doi.org/10.1016/j.enpol.2014.01.024. [36]

Lincoln Institute of Land Policy (2015), *Inclusionary Housing Creating and Maintaining Equitable Communities*, http://www.lincolninst.edu (accessed on 17 July 2019). [67]

LPED (n.d.), *Ecobarrio Trinitat Nova*, http://mc3.lped.fr/Ecobarrio-Trinitat-Nova?lang=en&thematique=160 (accessed on 15 November 2019). [57]

Merk, O. et al. (2012), "Financing Green Urban Infrastructure", *OECD Publishing*, http://www.oecd.org/cfe/regional-policy/WP_Financing_Green_Urban_Infrastructure.pdf (accessed on 13 November 2019). [89]

Ministry of Energy Mines and Resources (Canada) (2016), *Financing Energy Efficiency Retrofits in the Built Environment*, Canadian Government, Winnipeg, https://www.nrcan.gc.ca/sites/www.nrcan.gc.ca/files/emmc/pdf/Financing%20Report-acc_en.pdf. [28]

Ministry of Environmental Protection, Eco Traders Ltd. and Ricardo Energy and Environment (2015), *Assessment Of Greenhouse Gas Emission Reduction Potential And Recommended National Target For Israel*, Inter-ministerial Committee for the Formulation of the National Greenhouse Gas Reduction Target. [11]

New York University (2008), *The Effects of Inclusionary Zoning on Local Housing Markets: Lessons from the San Francisco, Washington DC and Suburban Boston Areas*, http://furmancenter.nyu.edu/publications/index.html (accessed on 23 May 2019). [66]

OECD (2019), *Accelerating Climate Action: Refocusing Policies through a Well-being Lens*, OECD Publishing, Paris, https://dx.doi.org/10.1787/2f4c8c9a-en. [2]

OECD (2019), *Information on Residency for tax purposes - Israel*, https://www.oecd.org/tax/automatic-exchange/crs-implementation-and-assistance/tax-residency/Israel-Residency.pdf (accessed on 13 March 2020). [64]

OECD (2019), *Making Decentralisation Work: A Handbook for Policy-Makers*, OECD Multi-level Governance Studies, OECD Publishing, Paris, https://dx.doi.org/10.1787/g2g9faa7-en. [88]

OECD (2018), *Automatic Exchange - Organisation for Economic Co-operation and Development*, https://www.oecd.org/tax/automatic-exchange/ (accessed on 13 March 2020). [65]

OECD (2018), "OECD Economic Surveys: Israel", https://www.oecd-ilibrary.org/docserver/eco_surveys-isr-2018-en.pdf?expires=1583772521&id=id&accname=ocid84004878&checksum=71111436997298176DD167D3630AA6C1 (accessed on 9 March 2020). [60]

OECD (2018), *OECD Economic Surveys: Israel 2018*, OECD Publishing, Paris, https://dx.doi.org/10.1787/eco_surveys-isr-2018-en. [9]

OECD (2018), *Rethinking Urban Sprawl: Moving Towards Sustainable Cities*, OECD Publishing, Paris, https://dx.doi.org/10.1787/9789264189881-en. [4]

OECD (2017), "Spatial Planning and Policy in Israel - The Cases of Netanya and Umm al-Fahm", https://www.oecd-ilibrary.org/docserver/9789264277366-en.pdf?expires=1573429460&id=id&accname=ocid84004878&checksum=E4F69821AC4C91CB748B6CEFEDFCCC5C (accessed on 13 November 2019). [38]

OECD (2017), *Spatial Planning and Policy in Israel: The Cases of Netanya and Umm al-Fahm*, OECD Publishing, Paris, https://dx.doi.org/10.1787/9789264277366-en. [6]

OECD (2016), *OECD Territorial Reviews: The Metropolitan Region of Rotterdam-The Hague, Netherlands*, OECD Publishing, Paris, https://www.oecd-ilibrary.org/docserver/9789264249387-en.pdf?expires=1583750063&id=id&accname=ocid84004878&checksum=E3BC445E10DFB0D6C1FB7CE5700DFABE (accessed on 9 March 2020). [73]

OECD (2015), *OECD Territorial Reviews: Valle de México, Mexico*, OECD Territorial Reviews, OECD Publishing, Paris, https://dx.doi.org/10.1787/9789264245174-en. [34]

OECD (2014), "Compact city policies: Korea - Towards sustainable and inclusive growth", https://www.oecd-ilibrary.org/docserver/9789264225503-en.pdf?expires=1563376861&id=id&accname=ocid84004878&checksum=7C0E08BB137FAAAF3CB460DD8C00BC03 (accessed on 17 July 2019). [42]

OECD (2012), *Compact City Policies: A Comparative Assessment*, http://www.oecd.org/regional/compactcity (accessed on 7 June 2019). [35]

OECD (2011), *OECD Economic Survey: Israel 2011*, OECD, Paris, https://www.oecd-ilibrary.org/docserver/eco_surveys-isr-2011-en.pdf?expires=1583157123&id=id&accname=ocid84004878&checksum=4B176C6C5ECC1DB03B375DC9C38A0288 (accessed on 2 March 2020). [59]

OECD/ITF (2018), *Policy Directions for Establishing a Metropolitan Transport Authority for Korea's Capital Region*, http://www.itf-oecd.org (accessed on 20 March 2019). [72]

OECD/ITF (2017), "Strategic Infrastructure Planning: International Best Practice"*, Case-Specific Policy Analysis series*, OECD/ITF, Paris, https://www.oecd-ilibrary.org/docserver/4142787d-en.pdf?expires=1532006152&id=id&accname=ocid84004878&checksum=B206309A7D0CCA9EF670517C0B6CEE35 (accessed on 19 July 2018). [39]

OECD/The World Bank/UN Environment (2018), *Financing Climate Futures: Rethinking Infrastructure*, OECD Publishing, Paris, https://dx.doi.org/10.1787/9789264308114-en. [19]

Pearlmutter, D., C. Freidin and N. Huberman (2007), "Alternative materials for desert buildings: A comparative life cycle energy analysis", *Building Research and Information*, Vol. 35/2, pp. 144-155, http://dx.doi.org/10.1080/09613210600980309. [14]

Rogers, K., A. Jaluzot and C. Neilan (2012), *Green benefits in Victoria Business Improvement District.* [81]

S&P Global Rating (2019), *Public System Finance Review: Israeli Municipalities*, S&P Ratings Direct, https://www.maalot.co.il/Publications/SR20190123152558.pdf. [22]

Streicher, K. et al. (2020), "Cost-effectiveness of large-scale deep energy retrofit packages for residential buildings under different economic assessment approaches", *Energy and Buildings*, Vol. 215, p. 109870, http://dx.doi.org/10.1016/j.enbuild.2020.109870. [31]

Tel Aviv-Yafo Municipality Environment and Sustainability Authority (2018), "A Report on the Environment and Sustainability in the City of Tel Aviv-Yafo", https://www.tel-aviv.gov.il/Residents/Environment/Documents/%D7%93%D7%95%D7%97%20%D7%A1%D7%91%D7%99%D7%91%D7%94%20%D7%95%D7%A7%D7%99%D7%99%D7%9E%D7%95%D7%AA%20%D7%91%D7%A2%D7%99%D7%A8%20%D7%AA%D7%9C%20%D7%90%D7%91%D7%99%D7%91%20%D7%99%D7%A4%D7%95%20-%20%D (accessed on 29 November 2019). [53]

The Mersey Forest et al. (2018), *The green infrastructure valuation toolkit*, https://www.merseyforest.org.uk/services/gi-val/ (accessed on 13 November 2019). [87]

The World Bank (2019), *Betterment Levies | Urban Regeneration*, https://urban-regeneration.worldbank.org/node/15 (accessed on 22 July 2019). [77]

Trinomics and IUCN (2019), "Approaches to financing nature-based solutions in cities", https://oppla.eu/sites/default/files/uploads/working-documentfinancing-nbs-cities.pdf (accessed on 13 November 2019). [86]

UCL Urban Lab and Engineers Exchange (2014), *Demolition or Refurbishment for Social Housing?*, University College London, http://www.engineering.ucl.ac.uk/engineering-exchange/files/2014/10/Report-Refurbishment-Demolition-Social-Housing.pdf. [24]

UK GBC (2013), *Retrofit Incentives: Boosting uptake of energy efficiency measures*, UK Green Building Council, https://www.ukgbc.org/sites/default/files/130705%2520Retrofit%2520Incentives%2520Task%2520Group%2520-%2520Report%2520FINAL_1.pdf. [23]

UK Government (2014), *Community Infrastructure Levy*, https://www.gov.uk/guidance/community-infrastructure-levy (accessed on 6 December 2019). [90]

Vartholomaios, A. (2013), *The green space factor as a tool for regulating the urban microclimate in vegetation-deprived Greek cities*, https://www.researchgate.net/publication/266402824_The_green_space_factor_as_a_tool_for_regulating_the_urban_microclimate_in_vegetation-deprived_Greek_cities (accessed on 25 March 2019). [83]

WorldGBC (2019), *Bringing embodied carbon upfront*, World Green Building Council, London, https://www.worldgbc.org/bringing-embodied-carbon-upfront-report-webform. [3]

WorldGBC (2013), *The Business Case for Green Building: A Review of the Costs and Benefits for Developers, Investors and Occupants*, World Green Building Council, https://www.worldgbc.org/news-media/business-case-green-building-review-costs-and-benefits-developers-investors-and-occupants. [13]

WorldGBC and European Commission (2018), *Creating an Energy Efficient Mortgage for Europe: Towards a new market standard*, World Green Building Council, https://www.worldgbc.org/sites/default/files/Creating%20an%20Energy%20Efficient%20Mortgage%20for%20Europe%20-%20Towards%20a%20New%20Market%20Standard%20-%20Web.pdf. [21]

Notes

[1] https://www.newyorker.com/news/news-desk/israels-housing-protest

[2] https://www.timesofisrael.com/states-inability-to-hammer-out-housing-crisis-fix-leaves-many-out-in-the-cold/

[3] Israel is divided into six districts: Haifa District, Jerusalem District, Tel Aviv District, Central District, Northern District, and Southern District.

[4] https://www.timesofisrael.com/states-inability-to-hammer-out-housing-crisis-fix-leaves-many-out-in-the-cold/

[5] https://new.usgbc.org/press/benefits-of-green-building

[6] What the specifications of the house were

[7] https://www.designingbuildings.co.uk/wiki/Target_emission_rate_TER

[8]https://energywatch-inc.com/breaking-new-york-city-council-passes-first-of-its-kind-ghg-emissions-cap-for-buildings/

[9] http://www.oecd.org/gov/ethics/gpp-procurement-Netherlands.pdf

[10] https://europa.eu/investeu/projects/sustainable-social-housing_en

[11] https://www.euractiv.com/section/energy-environment/news/more-banks-join-eu-backed-pilot-scheme-for-green-mortgages/

[12] External benefits includes avoided emissions and the value of peak hour savings.

[13] https://www.straitstimes.com/singapore/environment/new-green-lease-guide-launched-for-commercial-landlords-and-tenants

[14] 30% is the typical threshold for affordable housing (Center for Neighborhood Technology, 2019[12])

[15] https://thehouseofhopecdc.org/

[16] https://warwickpost.com/fair-house-renovation-creates-10-affordable-housing-apartments/

[17] https://energy-cities.eu/best-practice/the-brussels-green-loan-scheme/

[18] https://www.haaretz.com/.premium-fast-track-to-urban-sprawl-1.5292839

[19] An urban core consists of a high-density cluster of contiguous grid cells of 1 km^2 with a density of at least 1,500 inhabitants per km^2 and where gaps in the high-density cluster are filled using the majority rule iteratively. The majority rule means that if at least five out of the eight cells surrounding a cell belong to the same high-density cluster the cell will be added. This is repeated until no more cells are added.

[20] https://en.globes.co.il/en/article-denser-urban-construction-approved-1001296329

[21] In addition to the Israel government's National Master Plan 35, and the regional District Master Plans, each municipality is supposed to develop their own plans, e.g. the Local Comprehensive Plan or Local Master Plan.

[22] Main legislative body of the Israeli government

[23] According to Tel Aviv's Sustainable Planning and Energy department, these seven neighbourhoods meet a wide range of sustainability goals and integrated infrastructure, whereas they are yet not net-zero.

[24] Information from Tel Aviv Municipality (email exchanges)

[25] 3,000 in the entire country, as of 2016 (Haaretz, 2016[61])

[26] According to the Israel Planning Administration, the NMP is to be replaced by a new mechanism that is being developed (Israel Planning Administration, 2020[8])

[27] Green infrastructure, on the other hand, can be defined as an ensemble of green areas embedded in the built environment.

[28] Estimations are based on results from (Herzog, Shalabna and Maor, 2017[80]), calculating Israel's electricity consumption for air conditioning as a function of temperature.

[29] Estimated social costs in terms of impacts on health, as well as on buildings envelops, and crops (Rogers, Jaluzot and Neilan, 2012[81])

[30] Carbon sequestration benefits are monetized by multiplying the tonnes of carbon stored by the non-traded price of carbon (Rogers, Jaluzot and Neilan, 2012[81])

[31] As of 2011, the North West England is no more compulsory, it has been set as "guidance"

[32] Still under construction

[33] Put in place in 2016

4 Policies for a sustainable transport sector in Israel

This chapter discusses how Israel can both mitigate its (still increasing) emissions from the transport sector and improve its population's well-being, notably by improving accessibility to opportunities (e.g., jobs, services, education, health facilities, etc.). After presenting the state of play, the chapter examines how improving taxation can limit emissions from private vehicles. It then highlights the need to improve road management: re-allocating and re-designing road space to promote accessibility and safety, and using tools (e.g. parking regulations, congestion charging) to use road space more efficiently. The chapter then examines how accessibility-based planning and appraisal frameworks can make public and active transport attractive alternatives to private cars and help fund infrastructure for these modes. It finally focuses on adapting governance and developing fully functional metropolitan transport authorities.

In Brief

Key findings and recommendations

The transport sector is the second largest emitter of GHG emissions in Israel and its emissions have been increasing, driven by population growth and the expansion of car ownership within the population. Recommendations for climate mitigation policies in the transport sector in Israel are:

Align the taxation of private car use with its environmental damages and external costs

Fuel and car taxation are high in Israel relative to international standards. However, it can be better aligned with GHG emissions, environmental and social damage (air pollution, congestion, noise, road wear), without substantially increasing the tax burden. Three priorities are:

- Align fuel taxation according to the environmental damage of combustion. Phase–out the tax benefits for diesel consumption (worth 0.28% of GDP in 2018).
- Regularly update the car purchase tax (already aligned with external costs), to maintain environmental benefits and limit erosion of the tax base.
- Consider the long-term replacement of fuel tax by distance and place based taxation, which can vary depending on vehicle characteristics.

Manage road space and prioritise public and active transport modes

- Re-allocate and re-design roads to create a new user hierarchy where sustainable (i.e. low carbon, low space intensive modes) are prioritised over individual cars. Adopting a "Complete Streets" approach to road and project design that aims at safely balancing space between a diverse range of users and activities is also necessary.
- A number of tools can help to improve the use and management of road space, but should be inscribed in the overall strategy to re-order user priorities and enhance accessibility:
    - Make use of parking fees and regulations which are aligned with the new user hierarchy (e.g. zoning indexed to public transport availability and city area). Liberated parking space can be used to promote active modes (e.g. with larger sidewalks and bicycle lanes).
    - Congestion charging can effectively reduce traffic in big cities. Distance and time differentiated schemes target more precisely the social costs of driving and are thus more effective, more efficient and bring better opportunities for the population to adapt. If adopted, general distance-based taxation would in the long-run incorporate congestion charges in place, as in this scheme driving through more central and congested areas could be taxed more severely.
- In parallel, alternatives to private car journeys should be promoted and targeted compensatory measures should be considered for population disproportionally affected by new policies. A focus on revenue recycling can enhance public support for policy changes.

Focus on accessibility instead of mobility to unlock important opportunities

- Use accessibility indicators to plan mobility systems and explicitly link land-use and housing decisions with transport accessibility criteria.

- Develop appraisal methodologies that mainstream accessibility criteria. This will accelerate the implementation of the Strategic Plan for the Development of Public Transportation, allocating efficiently dedicated funds and steering more investment for public and active modes.

Widen financial capacity to ensure sustainable transport budgets

- Fares need to help optimise public transport services and cover a substantial proportion of the system's operational costs. The implementation of on-peak and off-peak tariffs can help limiting crowding in public transport.
- Overall, a balance needs to be found between financial equilibrium and affordable transport. This can be done by keeping fares close to levels where operational costs are recouped and fares optimise usage. Targeted subsidies can then be modulated according to people's family income in order to reduce vulnerabilities.
- Funding sources for investment in transport can be enlarged by exploring land value capture mechanisms, levying new taxes on businesses, and channelling of charges on private vehicles, in addition to fare box revenue and general transfers from the central government. This can help ensure covering maintenance, expansion, improvement and regulation of transport, in addition to operational costs.

Devolve responsibility, develop capacity and improve coherence

The regulation of public transport in Israel is led by the central government. This presents shortcomings as local level governments tend to better placed to address local particular transport needs.

- Shift capacity and responsibility to the local level within a framework that enables (or requires) the creation of Metropolitan Transport Authorities (MTAs) to provide responsiveness while avoiding over- fragmentation of responsibilities. It would also allow building planning and regulatory capacity inside the public sector (another limitation of the current model). This is particularly needed in the context of fast evolving transport services and the need to adopt a Mobility as a Service (MaaS) approach.
- Develop fully functioning MTAs that have: defined responsibilities and formal authority with legal backing; secure financial and technical capacity; strategic level planning responsibilities; and predominant municipal representation in their governance structure (e.g. board of directors); and responsibilities beyond public transport (e.g. active modes, road management, safety).

Create a national policy for metropolitan and urban transport to: guide local policy and investment towards climate and well-being goals, standardise local planning tools, and bridge technical capacity gaps across territories.

4.1. Introduction

Making up 23% of GHG emissions in 2016 (the second emitter behind energy industries),[1] the transport sector appears as a major challenge for climate change mitigation policies in Israel. The high increase in transport emissions (+12% between 2011 and 2016) is the result of deep societal changes, including rising living standards that increased investment in durable goods and more particularly to buy private vehicles. Slowing and reverting the growth of transport emissions entails structural changes, which include the development of palatable transport alternatives that would reduce people's dependence on private vehicles and, when private cars are needed, the renewal of the private vehicle fleet.

The Israel government designed a National Plan for Transport in 2015, which is used as a basis to reach the Paris Agreement goals (a 26% reduction of GHG emissions per capita by 2030 relative to their level in

2005). This plan sets as an objective for 2030 a 20% reduction in vehicle-kilometres travelled, as compared to a business-as-usual (BAU) situation. However, such scenario does not entail a net decrease of the distance travelled by car relative to the current situation: the plan consists in limiting the increase of this value.[2] The development of public transport in metropolitan areas and for intercity journeys is envisaged as the main driver that would allow reaching the car travel reduction objective. Beyond car travel reductions, in 2018, the Minister of Energy presented a plan which forecasted the ban of diesel and gasoline car imports in 2030, with the aim of shifting the transport sector towards technologies based on gas and alternative fuels (this plan has not yet been presented in Parliament).

Policies leveraging synergies between climate change mitigation and other well-being objectives have the potential to accelerate climate action. The performance of the transport sector should be assessed considering its capacity to reach the following goals: enhancing physical accessibility, ensuring affordable services, safety and security, reducing air pollution and noises, associated risks and habitat damages, and limiting climate change (OECD, 2019[1]).

This chapter argues that efficient climate policies in the transport sector should both reduce the need for journeys by private vehicles and the emissions from each vehicle when needed. Policies should focus on providing accessibility, which means easing the capacity to reach destinations for goods, services and opportunities instead of only enhancing physical mobility (Litman, 2019[2]). For instance, (Suhoy and Sofer, 2019[3]) measured relative accessibility *via* public transport to workplaces using detailed locality data in Israel. They identified notable gaps, as the number of job localities only accessible by private vehicles is by far higher than the number of job localities accessible by public transport.[3] Developing sustainable transport modes such as cycling, walking and public transport is crucial for the transition to a low carbon economy. Shortening the distance between people and their needs (goods, services and job and leisure opportunities) would also allow to significantly reduce emissions from the transport sector. However, enhancing accessibility in order to reach transport objectives requires policies that go beyond the transport sector and also address the housing sector, spatial planning and labour policies (see also previous chapter).

This chapter examines how the transport sector can contribute to Israel's climate change mitigation objectives for 2025 and 2030. It focuses on surface transport and the need to reduce reliance on private vehicles, which account for 90% of all the distance travelled by motorised modes in Israel (OECD, 2016[4]) and more than half of emissions (Tamir et al., 2015[5]). Section 4.2 introduces the general context of the transport sector in Israel. Section 4.3 points out the necessity of aligning taxes on fuels and vehicles to external costs in order to reduce transport emissions. Section 4.4 explores the opportunities provided by a better management of road space that prioritises public and active transport modes as opposed to private cars. Section 4.5 shows that these measures need to go hand in hand with strong investment on public and active transport to make it more attractive. It highlights the need for developing appraisal methodologies that incorporate accessibility as a central criteria to investment decisions, and make in this way a strong case for public and active transport modes. It also emphasises the need to increase the funding sources for transport. Finally, it also discusses the need to adapt the governance for transport, increasing the role of local authorities, while setting up metropolitan transport authorities and developing a national policy for urban and metropolitan transport. It also emphasises the need for improved regulation and integrated spatial planning, that goes beyond the transport system, can help scale up climate ambition in the transport sector.

4.2. Context: road transport in Israel

Emissions from transport have been steadily rising in Israel for more than a decade, increasing by 12% over the five-year period 2011-2016 and by 24% between 2006 and 2016.[4] This has been mainly driven by the large population growth occurring in the same periods (over 10% and 21% respectively), but also by the increasing share of car ownership. Although the number of private cars per person is low relative to other OECD countries (311 passenger cars per 1000 inhabitants in 2015, according to the OECD-ITF, compared to 463 in average in OECD countries)[5], this share increased in Israel by 30% between 2010 and 2015.[6] Cars are also used intensively and Israel has one of the highest number of kilometres per vehicle in the OECD due to an increased dependence on private car journey in many Israelis' daily life.[7]

Private cars are crucial for the mobility of passengers in Israel, notably because of the poor state of the public transport, which only account for 22% of commuting (Bleikh, 2018[6]). A high and increasing share of workers are commuting outside their areas of residence, up by 10 percentage points between 1990 and 2016 (from 43.9% to 53.9%). Moreover, an increasing share of these workers are using their private cars, which accounted for 60% of journeys to the workplace (Bleikh, 2018[6]).

Local spatial planning is also partly responsible for high transport emissions. In Netanya, for instance the city fabric is discontinuous, due to new neighbourhoods being built far from the city centre and commercial areas, increasing the dependence on private vehicles. The situation is likely to be worsened by new urban developments if not carefully designed (also see chapter 3 on the residential sector).

The rapidly growing demand for housing, mainly due to high population growth of over 1.96% per year between 2009 and 2018,[8] has led to an increasing number of new housing projects. The government will build 1.5 million homes by 2040. As the development of large housing projects is easier in peripheral areas (because the land is state-owned) and makes it easier to keep pace with the growing housing demand, there is a risk that, without legal requirement to make employment and services accessible from housing developments by public transport, the city will continue to expand in a way that fosters car dependency. This importantly hinders all climate change mitigation efforts in the transport sector.

Perhaps even more significant than its climate effects, transport in Israel has many other detrimental effects on well-being. As transport infrastructures did not adapt to the upsurge of car ownership, congestion and air pollution stand as major issues in Israel. In 2015, PM2.5 caused the death of more than 2 000 people, according to the Global Burden of Disease database, and the number of people exposed to this pollution have been increasing (Environment and Health Fund and Ministry of Health, 2017[7]). A government-commissioned experts estimated that the total cost of car use to the Israeli economy up to 6% of its GDP (Israeli Tax Authority et al., 2008[8]), including 2% due to the damages of air pollution to health and ecosystem and 2% due to congestion cost (this number was confirmed by (Trajtenberg et al., 2018[9])).[9] This figure, relatively high in international standards, is due to the fact that Israel has the highest road traffic density per network length in the OECD by far (3.5 time the OECD average). Other externalities (accidents due to traffic, noise, the occupation of public space by free parking places for private vehicles and infrastructure building and maintenance costs) add up to the cost of private vehicle use in Israel and account in total to 2% of GDP, according to the Israeli Tax Authority. As a comparison, the external costs of road transport in EU countries in 2016 amount for 4% of their GDP, with accidents being the highest external cost (European Commission, 2019[10]).

Pricing policies for transport (i.e. fuel and car purchase taxes), which reflect the external costs of private car use, can contribute to a reduction of GHG emissions. In the case of Israel, where alternatives to private cars are often limited and tax rates are already high, relative to international standards, a strong increase of the average taxation would probably hurt households' purchase power without decreasing significantly car use. In the longer-run, shifting the car purchase tax towards a distance-based taxation would allow more accurate pricing of external costs and thus would be economically more efficient. In the short-run, in addition to adjusting the existing taxes, implementing congestion charges in big cities has the potential to both mitigate GHG emissions and improve air quality; the social outcomes should be carefully assessed and anticipated in order to gain public acceptability. The deployment of public transport and facilities for active transport modes (cycling and walking) would allow for much stronger decrease of GHG emissions, and government needs to scale up Israel's transport plans. Finally, the impact of transport policies on climate and well-being can be enhanced if they are implemented in parallel with an integrated spatial planning that enforces accessibility to goods, services and opportunities.

4.3. Limiting private cars' emissions through a consistent pricing policy on fuels and vehicles

Taxes on fuels and vehicles in Israel are already high relative to other countries but do not properly reflect the external costs of vehicle use on climate, environment, health and, more generally well-being. An appropriate tax policy on fuels and vehicles has the potential to reduce emissions from the most emitting vehicles without increasing the average fiscal burden on citizens.

4.3.1. Israel has high effective carbon rates but the prices across different fuels are misaligned with climate and other well-being objectives

Israel taxation on fossil fuels for road transport is high relative to other OECD countries. The OECD report "Taxing Energy Use" (OECD, 2019[11]) shows that Israel has the highest effective carbon price on road emissions among 44 OECD and G20 countries (more than EUR 280/tCO2, while the median rate is around EUR 160/tCO2). As Israel does not have an explicit carbon tax, this high price is due to high excise taxes on fuels for transport. The level of taxation is also higher than the highest estimates, in other countries, of the full range of external costs, including GHG emissions, congestion, noise, accidents and local air pollution. While the excise tax amounts to NIS 2.4 per litre for diesel and NIS 3.1 per litre for gasoline (see Table 4.1), the highest estimates of marginal costs in France and the United Kingdom do not exceed ILS 1.37 per litre (equivalent EUR 0.35 per litre)[10] (OECD, 2019[11]).

Whatever the level, the price differential between fuels however, should be aligned with their different social costs, including their related GHG emissions. Policies need to give incentives to drivers to choose greener vehicles and to reduce journeys in vehicles running on fossil fuels. Putting the right price signal on fossil fuels in the transport sector would reduce the use of the most emitting vehicles; for the owners of those vehicles, it would limit unnecessary journeys and foster car-sharing and public transport use, which only accounts for 20% of daily journeys so far (Trajtenberg et al., 2018[9]) This could also create new options for new transport alternatives such as shared mobility services and car-pooling.

Although the average taxation rate on fuels is high, the different excise tax rates between fuels do not provide the right price signals on their external costs on climate and air pollution. As a consequence, drivers' choices of vehicles will not be steered towards greener vehicles. Table 4.1 shows the different excise tax tariffs for each fuel as well as their estimated emissions of GHG. A striking example of this misalignment is the higher tax rate on gasoline relative to diesel, although it emits less CO_2 per volume consumed (OECD, 2016[4]). The lower tax rate for diesel fuel is even less justified when pollutants other than GHG are taken into consideration, since diesel vehicles tend to emit much more particulate matter and nitrogen oxides (OECD, 2016[4]). Finally, there is no argument, from an environmental point of view, for applying a much lower rate on the local production of biodiesel than on imported biodiesel.

LPG and natural gas taxation is also particularly low relative to other fuels. It is taxed about 30 times less than gasoline although it emits two thirds of the CO_2 equivalent from petrol. Natural gas that can be used for transport, and more particularly trucks (CNG and LNG) has an excise tax of ILS 17 per ton, which is equivalent of EUR 1.90 per ton of CO2eq (with the perspective of increasing the excise rate to 1,400 per ton within a period of eight years). The share of vehicles running with alternative fuels (gas and electricity) only amounted to 0.8% of the car fleet in 2015, but the discovery of a new source of gas by Israel will lead to the development of gas-powered vehicles. Although it is not carbon neutral, LPG and natural gas can be considered a useful transition fuel to go towards the low-carbon economy, as other modes (and more particular EVs) require heavy investment that are hard to implement fully in the short term. However, policies enhancing the use of LPG and natural gas in transport should be made on a clear assessment of the costs and benefits, including for public health and climate, as a recent study showed that gas-motored trucks emit much more NOx than diesel (Vermeulen, 2019[12]).

Table 4.1. Excise tax rate and CO_2 equivalent emissions per fuel

Fuel type	Excise tax tariff (per 1000 litre)	Emission factor of GHG emissions (per litre)	Effective carbon rates (per ton of CO2e)**
Diesel fuel	ILS 2,942.45	2.69 kgCO2eq	EUR 253.08
Gasoline	ILS 3,071.10	2.32-2.20 kgCO2eq	EUR 310.73
LPG	ILS 119.6*	1.52 kgCO2eq	
CNG	ILS 17.12 per 1000kg	0.44 kgCO2eq	EUR 1.90
LNG	ILS 17.12 per 1000kg	1.15 kgCO2eq	EUR 1.90
Biodiesel - import	ILS 2,942.45	2.59 kgCO2eq	
Biodiesel – local production	ILS 974.32	2.59 kgCO2eq	

Sources: Israel Tax Authority, and Defra conversion factors, 2019.
* IEA quarterly statistics (International Energy Agency, 2019[13]).
** Taxing Energy Use 2019: Using Taxes for Climate Action, OECD Publishing.

Aligning the excise tax rates to carbon emissions would be a first step towards a greener taxation of fuels. However it is important that, this alignment is not made by simply reducing the gasoline tax rate. This would be counterproductive concerning the wider objective of reducing fuel combustion since it entails a decrease in fuel prices for 96% of private vehicles. An alternative, more palatable from an environmental point of view, is to make the alignment upward, increasing diesel and biodiesel taxation. This increase in diesel prices would affect mostly users of taxis, buses and trucks, since 67% of their fleet consists of diesel-fuelled vehicles. Increased resort to the existing supports for the renewal of these vehicles might therefore be needed and should be anticipated in budget. Distributional and sectoral effects of this policy should also be assessed in order to calibrate other enabling and compensating measures.

Another way to make fuel taxation more efficient would be to phase out tax advantages linked to diesel consumption. The *Excise Tax on Fuel Order* instituted in 2005 tax rebates on diesel for buses, taxis, fishing boats and working vehicles (like tractors for agriculture). In 2018, these tax expenditures amounted to ILS 3.6 billion (0.28% of GDP) and accounted for the bulk of support to fossil fuels in Israel (OECD, 2018[14]). Phasing out such support to working vehicles would reduce the incentives for wasted consumption of diesel, which causes serious pollution. It would also increase incentives for fleet renewal and penetration of cleaner technologies in these segment of the vehicle fleet. While this also holds in the case of vehicles dedicated to public transport services, detrimental effects on different population groups (due to likely fare increases) should be assessed and where necessary compensated (e.g. via targeted subsidies-see below). Putting incentives for cleaner public transport or conditioning tender for public transport to environmental conditions can also be considered.

Phasing out this support to fuel consumption would create fiscal space to reduce the public debt or increase other subsidies or expenses; it would also increase the incentives to invest in less fuel-intensive vehicles. Government could use a part of the savings on fossil fuel subsidies to curb its potential detrimental effect by redistributing revenues to the sectors concerned. More particularly, it could be used to implement measures that would enable and facilitate the transition of the sector towards more sustainable modes of transport and production. In the transport sector, further support to the renewal of the bus and taxi fleets is an option, as they account for a substantial share of GHG emissions in the transport sector (around 15% in 2015 according to (Tamir et al., 2015[5])). Channelling new resources to public transport investment is also an option. For instance, Ile-de-France Mobilités, the metropolitan transport authority in charge of the Paris Region has been granted since 2016 a percentage of the revenue that comes from the internal tax on energy products (petrol and diesel) that are sold in the Paris region; this percentage, is used for improving the public transport network (ITF, 2018[15]).

In the longer-run, fuel taxation could be gradually substituted by a distance-based tax (see section 0).

4.3.2. Making the car fleet more sustainable: finding the right policy mix

Israel is putting the most polluting vehicles out of the market with standards and regulations

Most of the policies aiming at reducing emissions from private vehicles in Israel are focused on controlling the car fleet quality with standards and regulations, which forbid the sale or circulation of vehicles emitting the most GHGs, and pollutant gases by kilometre travelled. Standards and regulations for improving vehicle technology have been the cornerstone of environmental policies in the transport sector for a long time. Israel has been following European standards (Euro 4, 5 and 6 standards) since the mid-1990s and, since March 2006, gasoline motored vehicles have been required to undergo stringent emission checks. In 2012, standards were reinforced and roadside spot checks were implemented in 2013. If a vehicle fails to pass the roadside test, the owner has to pay a fine or make the required reparation. Failure to pass the annual emission check also prevents the renewal of the car licence.

Moreover, in October 2018, the Ministry of Energy presented a plan against pollution which included the phasing out of fossil fuels in the transport sector and the deployment of electric vehicles and trucks powered by gas (Compressed Natural Gas). A ban against the import of vehicles powered by diesel or gasoline will also be implemented in 2030 according to the plan, while the deployment of electric vehicles will be gradual (27,000 vehicles are expected to be sold in 2022, 177,000 by 2025, 665,000 in 2028 and 1.4 million by 2030). This plan has not been presented to Knesset yet.

Several Israeli cities also implemented Low Emission Zones (LEZ) to limit air pollution, particularly from diesel cars. One was initiated in 2018 in Haifa. In a first phase heavy diesel vehicles were banned from the area. The prohibition was then extended to light commercial vehicles; another LEZ was introduced in January 2020 in Jerusalem. Past experiments in other cities, like in Berlin, London or Copenhagen show that such policies have been effective in reducing the number of older and more polluting vehicles, incentivising the purchase of vehicles that are cleaner. The LEZs in Haifa is expected to reduce vehicular emissions by 20%, while the LEZ in Jerusalem is expected to reduce vehicle related CO_2 emissions by 8%, NOx emissions by 55% and PM by 30%.[11]

LEZ in Israel have been implemented gradually, providing a clear signal easy to anticipate. However, it is important that they do not have detrimental impacts on vulnerable population's well-being, as those might have some difficulties switching for compliant vehicles, more particularly when light vehicles would be covered. Coping with these issues would entail improving public transport service and infrastructure for walking and cycling, as well as a communication strategy for vulnerable groups, as suggested by consultation groups working on the ultra-low emission zone in London.[12]

Regulation (car standards and LEZ) have been efficient in renewing and greening the car fleet and providing a clear signal for people and car constructors. It succeeded at institutionalising basic standards and it contributed to the improvement of air quality in city centres: between 2000 and 2017, NOx concentration in the commercial centre of Tel Aviv was reduced by 63%, SO2 concentration by 79% and CO concentration by 84%.[13]

In theory, this type of regulation is not as efficient as emission taxation. First, it has no effect on the use of vehicles that comply with standards outside use in the given area where the LEZ is established.. Israel has the second highest mileage per vehicle in OECD countries so it is important to implement tools that directly tackle excessive use. Moreover, it does not spur innovation for building vehicles that are more efficient than required by the standards used to restrict access to the area where the LEZ is implemented, as opposed to an emission tax. Nonetheless, LEZs have proven to provide a very visible incentive to comply with environmental standards, as they are generally set in areas that are of particular interest for passenger or freight vehicles to travel to or through. This can help reinforce signals provided by fuel taxation, which while in theory more efficient might be more diluted as benefits are distributed through time. In addition LEZs target pollution, which depend on concentration and exposure (which fuel taxes do not account for). It is important though to regularly update standards used to restrict access to the selected area. As congestion charges are increasingly considered in Israel (see Section 4.4.2), existing LEZ could be integrated to such scheme and transformed into charging zones with minimum standards (i.e. that do not allow the most polluting vehicles but levy a congestion charge on all other vehicles). This is the case of the "Area C" scheme in Milan (ITF-OECD, 2017[16]).

The car purchase tax can be improved to better reflect external costs of car use

The past reform of the car purchase tax contributed to a greener tax fleet, but also to an increase of overall emissions

The car purchase tax in Israel has historically been high: in 2009, it amounted to 95% of the purchase value for private cars (nearly doubling the price paid by consumers) and to 75% for commercial vehicles. It is therefore one of the highest among the OECD countries. As a result, private car ownership is relatively low among the population (319 passenger cars for 1.000 residents in 2016 compared to 417 in the United States, 478 in Greece and 548 in Germany). In 2005, the car purchase tax rate was decreased permanently for light-duty vehicles with the aim of incentivising the renewal of the fleet.

In 2009, Israel initiated a Green Tax Reform that consisted in a modulation (based on 15 grade standards) of the car purchase tax according to the externalities of vehicles use (OECD, 2016[4]). The Israeli government assembled an inter-ministerial commission that estimated the external effects of different ranges of vehicles on: air and water pollution, congestion, accidents, global warming, noise, infrastructure and land use. Car models were classified in 15 different categories, all of them with a specific car purchase tax rate. At the end, the effective purchase tax rate amounted to a rate between 10% and 83% in 2014, with an average at 60.6% and most of the car sales having a rate between 54% and 67%. The Green Tax Reform therefore decreased substantially the average car purchase tax (from 95% in 2009 to 60.6% in 2014).

In parallel with these changes, Israel implemented in 2007 a scrapping scheme that offered ILS 3 000 (EUR 550 in 2007) for the disposal of vehicles older than 20 years (3% of the fleet in 2007). This scheme was renewed in 2013 and had a huge unexpected success. As ILS 5 million was allocated yearly to this scheme for the 2013-2017 period, the whole budget for 2013 was spent in less than a day.

Overall, the combination of a more stringent regulation on vehicle emissions (higher standards, implementation of low-emission zones in metropolis, more stringent performance tests for vehicles –see previous section), the scrapping scheme and the Green Tax Reform allowed for a strong renewal of the car fleet. The introduction of new vehicles compliant with more stringent environmental standards and with better safety equipment, resulted in a safer and less emitting fleet. Casualties from traffic accidents decreased between 2005 and 2017 by 39% in Haifa, by 34% in Tel Aviv and by 22% in Jerusalem.[14] In particular, the sales of vehicles with smaller engines, which are in general the less emitting, increased. While vehicles with engines below 1300 cubic centimetres (cc) amounted to less than 5% of imports in 2010, they made up to 25% of car sales in 2014 (OECD, 2016[4]).

As this reform resulted in a decrease of the car purchase tax for most car models, it had a mixed aggregate effect on environmental outcomes. On the one hand, it improved cars environmental performance and led to a long term decrease of the average pollution per vehicle. Integrating the many different pollutants in the tax basis allowed to decrease the CO_2 emissions per car without increasing air pollutants like NOx and PM, unlike reforms in other countries such as Ireland, which reform fostered the sale of diesel cars (Ryan et al., 2018[17]). On the other hand by decreasing the final prices of cars, the reform contributed to an increase in car ownership in Israel, exacerbating related issues like congestion or infrastructure erosion. The net effect of the reform was also an increase in total emissions, including GHG emissions (OECD, 2016[4]): even though the average vehicle emitted less pollutants per kilometre, more cars on the market increased the total number of kilometres driven, which largely offset positive effects on climate. The reform also had detrimental effects on other well-being dimensions. The increase of the number of cars due to the reform exacerbated congestion and its related nuisance (time loss, noise, pollution). The number of vehicles increased by 17% between 2013 and 2016.[15]

The increased number of cleaner vehicles may also reduce government revenue. As people bought less vehicles at higher rate of taxation (i.e. the most polluting ones), the total tax revenues decreased.[16] A frequent revision of grade standards that are used to set the tax rate should therefore avoid a decrease of average tax rates and the relating tax revenue. It would also improve the fleet in a dynamic way that takes into account technological progress.

Improving the current car purchase tax

Even when the Green tax reform in Israel may have had some detrimental effects (see previous section), the car purchase tax has many benefits. Israel was the first country that fully integrated the different externalities of cars into its car taxation and succeeded to reduce the emissions per car (OECD, 2016[4]). Moreover, the tax rates are high and this has contributed to maintaining a car ownership rate that is low relative to other countries. Phasing-out the car purchase tax without compensating with the increase of other types or car taxation would have the direct effect of incentivising car use and worsen the detrimental effects described above. Finally, a car purchase tax can be useful to price the external costs of resource use for car construction, in case it cannot be done upstream in the supply chain. This possibility could be explored by the Israeli authorities.

In the short term, the car purchase tax can be improved so that, together with fuel taxation, it builds a system that provides a good price signal on both the purchase and the use of cars. As fuel taxation, aligned with carbon emissions (as described in Section 4.3.1) would price the climate effect due to car use, the car purchase tax would shift consumption choices towards greener vehicles. Their interactions should be carefully assessed in order to provide a consistent price signal.

In order to maintain its environmental benefits, it is important that the car purchase tax is regularly updated. If categories and rates are not revised, regular technology would be priced at the same level as cutting-edge technology and there is a risk that a boost of car ownership would lock-in people in a car-driven system. It would also limit the erosion of the tax base due to the increased acquisition of greener vehicles. Moreover, the car purchase tax should not lose its environmental objectives at the expense of other social objectives. A recent project to increase electric vehicle taxation from 10% to 30%[17] was announced by the tax authority to fight deficit. Such reform would blur the tax signal that favours the acquisition of less polluting vehicles.[18] Other types of tax reforms, based on increasing income tax more that consumption taxes, would be both more efficient from an environmental point of view and better targeted from a distributional point of view.

In the longer term, a distance-based taxation (see Section 0) could be implemented. This would mainly replace fuel taxation but could, in the same way as a fuel tax, support the price signals provided by the differentiation of the purchase tax on cars during a transition period until the fleet is entirely or in its majority electric. Such a scheme would price at a higher rate kilometres driven by more polluting vehicles, in addition to differentiating rates based on time and place (depending on the intensity and saturation of road space). In this way it could reinforce the purchasing tax effect on the choice of cleaner vehicles. The rates can be defined following the same evaluation grid used for the car purchase tax. As a distance-based taxation is gradually phased-in, the car purchase tax can be gradually revised to find the optimal combination between a price signal at the moment of the car purchase and one throughout its use. As the fleet becomes increasingly electric, the transition towards distance-based taxation can ensure that other externalities (e.g. space consumption, infrastructure damage) are accounted for-since in any case GHG and pollution emissions will be progressively reduced as an external cost-, while also allowing maintenance of stable tax revenues.

Subsidies to public servants' car fleet should be phased out

The public sector in Israel had more than 800.000 employees in 2018.[19] Most of them, due to wage agreements, benefited from special treatment for their vehicles. This encourages the use of private cars, covering a large part of their car expenses and including free parking, even though it is for private use.

The National Plan to Reduce Air pollution considers a bulk of policies aiming at shifting private car use towards greener transportation like public transport or biking. Phasing-out the specific benefits for car use in the public sector would undoubtedly be a first step. However, the distributive impact of such measures should be carefully assessed, as the latter should not result in a decrease of purchasing power for public servants that would make useful professions less attractive. Instead, the government revenue once used for subsidising the car fleet could be recycled into public sector wages, and a part could be used to encourage greener transport when it is a feasible option (specific subsidies for employees that use public transport, for instance). This would also facilitate negotiations with workers' representative and make the phasing-out of car use subsidies more acceptable.

Subsidising less polluting vehicles like EVs is not the right answer to improve overall transport and well-being conditions in Israel

If well-designed, the combination of a fuel tax and a car purchase tax reflecting the externalities of car use should provide the appropriate signal in favour of EVs, and there is no need for adding another instrument to incentivise their purchase. It is important to carefully assess the potential reduction of taxation for greener vehicles like electric or hydrogen vehicles, as it may accelerate the increase of car ownership in Israel, worsening congestion and still causing emissions (e.g. electricity production, tyre and break wear) which are not always accounted for. Yet, EVs can also be a major (low-cost) source of flexibility, improving the integration of renewables and the efficiency of the power system (Chapter 2). Overall, if well designed, the modulation of the car purchase tax and the fuel tax should provide enough a signal to stir transport choices and adding a tool could only blur this signal.

Several experiences show how subsidies or preferential tax treatment might increase car ownership and their amenities, and more specifically congestion, which is already a major issue in Israel. Norway has been encouraging EVs since the 1990s by providing registration tax exemption, free public parking, a reduction in the annual circulation tax, a reduction of company car tax and a road toll and a ferry charge exemptions; moreover, EVs have been authorised on bus lanes since 2005. This policy package was successful in increasing the share of electric vehicles, in 2018, Norway was by far the first market for electric cars, which accounted for 46% of all new car sales (IEA, 2019[18]). However, this also resulted in an increased congestion for buses that might have discouraged the use of public transport.

The environmental effects of such policy is also questionable. France introduced a "feebate" policy, including fees and rebates, for car purchase in 2008, which consisted in a rebate for low-emitting cars and a fee for high-emitting cars. This measure finally resulted in an increased number of car sales and a negative environmental outcome (D'haultfoeuille, Givord and Boutin, 2013[19]).

There might also be mitigated effects on air quality. Although the electrification of private vehicles would limit exhaust emissions of particulate matters and NOx, EVs may have less impact that expected on air quality, as they weight much more, and hence emit more particulate matters outside the exhaust system than internal combustion engine vehicles, accounting non-exhaust emissions such as tyre wear, brake wear, road surface wear and resuspension of road dust (that altogether make up 85% of PM2.5 and 90%

of PM10 emissions from traffic) (Timmers and Achten, 2016[20]). This makes the case for more stringent regulation for these particular emissions, which have not decreased in Israel since 2000 at least.

The climate effect of putting incentives for EVs should be carefully assessed. There might be supplementary emissions by an increased energy consumption. The effect of an increased number of electric vehicles on climate depends on the energy sources of electricity generation. In Israel, electricity is mainly produced from natural gas (66% in 2018, according to IEA) and coal (30%), renewable energies making up less than 3% of total electricity generation (see the chapter on electricity). The share of natural gas is likely to grow to replace coal in the coming years, as both the Ministry of Environment Protection and the Ministry of Energy include a complete coal phase-out by 2030. Final government decision is still pending (EcoTraders, 2019[21]).

Finally, higher penetration of EVs without curbing the expansion of car ownership in Israel would not allow the country to reach its climate goals. A simulation shows that a policy that increases the share of low-emitting vehicles but fails to dampen the current increase of car ownership would fall short of climate objectives (see Box 4.2). It would certainly reduce emissions relative to the government's BAU scenario but the achievement of objectives rely on a limited increase of cars. If car ownership follows the same pathway than the current one (around +5% per year according to the Statistical Yearbook of Israel), climate objectives are impossible to reach, even with 25% of modal shift towards public transport or active modes. Israel would also fail to significantly reduce private car mileage, which is the objective of the National Plan for Transport to reach for the Israeli contribution for the Paris Agreement. Taking this into account, is important when planning investments in supporting infrastructure for electrification (e.g. charging stations), since the location and type of infrastructure needed will be different if it is to be compatible with high shares of shared rather than private mobility (Goetz, 2017[22]).

As a conclusion, policies supporting low-emitting vehicles should be carefully designed to avoid off-setting efforts to control an increase in the stock of cars. Setting the right standards to support their uptake but regularly updating them is key to limit the increase of car sales to a level that does not undermine climate objectives or worsen congestion. Vehicles' weight, a driver for non-exhaust emissions, should be integrated in policy design. As the increase of car ownership might be difficult to curb, measures that limit the use of individual cars (including by better managing road space), and foster shared trips and high-occupancy, in parallel to policies that fosters the penetration of cleaner vehicles (see Sections 4.4 and 4.5) are needed. Fostering high occupancy will also be particularly important to meeting climate goals in the light of potential penetration of automated vehicles, which will probably tend to be larger (Fulton et al., 2017[23]).

Box 4.1. Estimating the effect of an increased growth in the car fleet on climate objectives in Israel

Comparing climate scenarios for emissions from passenger vehicles

We are comparing different mitigation scenarios to asses, under certain assumptions, the impact of a subsidy to low and zero emission vehicle that would improve the car fleet, but also increase the total number of passenger vehicles.

This estimation compares different scenarios that were built in consistency with the hypothesis the Israeli Ministry took to assess the reduction potential of each sector in Israel in 2015 (Tamir et al., 2015[5]). As they do not aim to reflect directly reality, these scenarios provide a schematic assessment of what would happen if some policies were implemented in a certain context.

- **The BAU scenario**, defined in (Tamir et al., 2015[5]), considers a scenario where the numbers of car increases by 2.38% each year and the share of petrol-motored vehicles slightly decreases (from 95% in 2013 to 77% in 2030), mostly at the benefits of diesel-motored vehicles (from 3.4% to 15% in the same period).
- **The mitigation scenario**[20] is based on the assumptions on mitigations measures made in (Tamir et al., 2015[5]), including major technological innovations and the penetration of more efficient vehicles and fuels. More importantly, this scenario assumes a modal shift from private cars to public transport, walking or cycling of 25%, meaning that 25% of the kilometres driven by private cars would be replaced by more sustainable transport modes. This is reflected in a decrease in the average mileage for each car, but not in the total number of cars, which follows the same path as the BAU scenario.[21]
- **The greening scenario** has similar assumptions as the mitigation scenario and includes the same mitigation measures (technological innovation, same decrease of annual average mileage due to modal shift). It also adds-up a policy that increases the share of electric vehicles and LPG-motored vehicles (respectively 15% and 5% of the car fleet in 2030), but also the total car fleet. The car fleet increases by 2.38% per year between 2013 and 2020, following the same path as other scenarios, and by 5% per year between 2020 and 2030 due to the new policy. This latest figure was chosen in accordance with later trends in car ownership and should therefore be considered as a conservative hypothesis. The purpose of this scenario is to estimate the effect of a policy implemented in 2020 that would both reduce average emissions per vehicle and increase the car fleet.

The results, presented in Figure 4.1 and Figure 4.2, show that a greening scenario does not reach the same level of mitigation than a full mitigation scenario. This means that climate objectives are harder to reach if the deployment of low or zero emission vehicles increases the total number of vehicles. More specifically, the mitigation scenario would decrease CO_2 emissions by 33% relative to a BAU scenario and a greening scenario would only reduce them by 22%.

More strikingly, the greening scenario falls short of the transport sector objective set in Israel NDCs which consisted in the decrease by 20% of car mileage relative to a BAU scenario. If the mitigation scenario succeeds at decreasing private car mileage by 25% (as initially considered), the greening scenario reduces total private car mileage by only 5%. The reduction is driven by a modal shift towards more sustainable transport that decreased the average mileage for each car. But this effect was largely offset by the increase of car ownership.

Figure 4.1. Impact assessment of policy scenarios on CO_2 emissions from private cars

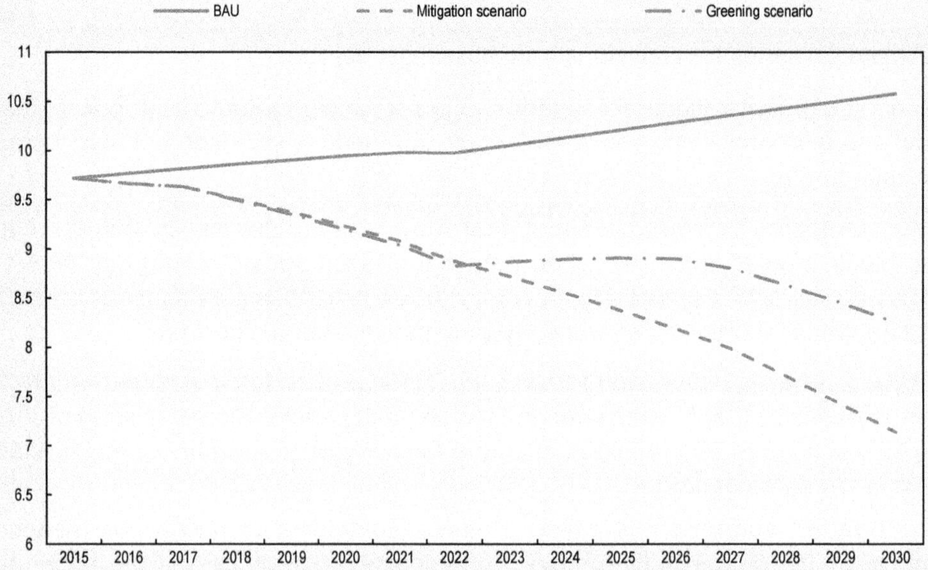

StatLink https://doi.org/10.1787/888934156162

Source: Authors calculations using data and assumptions from (Tamir et al., 2015[5]).

Figure 4.2. Impact assessment of policy scenarios on private car mileage

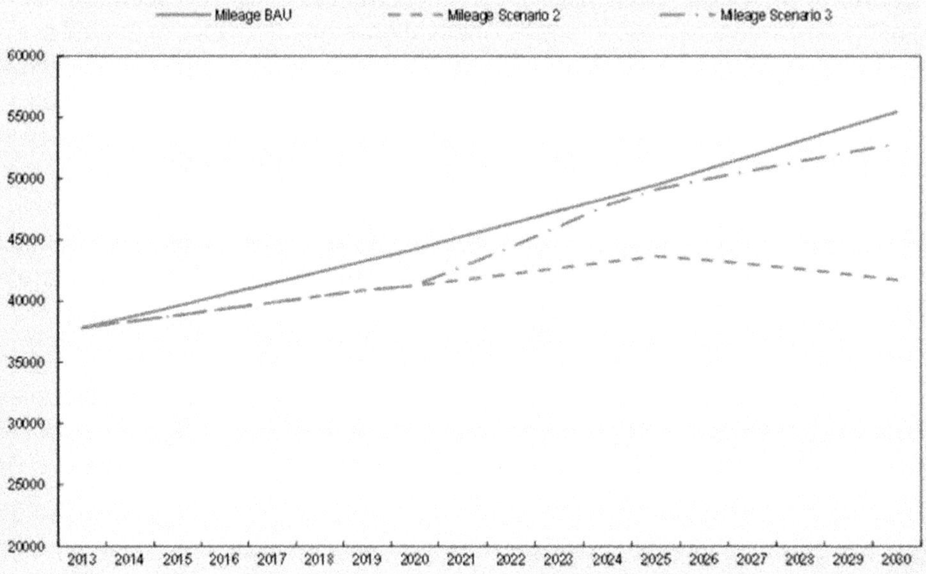

StatLink https://doi.org/10.1787/888934156181

Source: Authors calculations using data and assumptions from (Tamir et al., 2015[5]).

4.3.3. Considering a distance-based taxation in the long term

In the longer term, a distance-based taxation would efficiently replace the fuel tax, as well as congestion charges (see Section 4.4.2). The transition should be carefully monitored in order to avoid a shock on public finance.

The externalities of transport use have many different drivers (see Figure 4.3). Some of them are dependent on fuel use and type (like GHG emissions), others on combined factors: the impact of driving on exhaust pollution, for instance, differs, according to the car quality, its use intensity and the place it is used (such as road and infrastructure wear, occupation of free parking) (van Dender, 2019[24]). As for the effect of vehicle use on congestion, which stands for 27% of estimated costs from transport usage according to (van Essen et al., 2019[25]), it depends on the size of the car and the timing of its use. The relations between externalities are therefore complex and taxing them appears as a challenge.

Figure 4.3. External costs, drivers of external costs and tax instruments

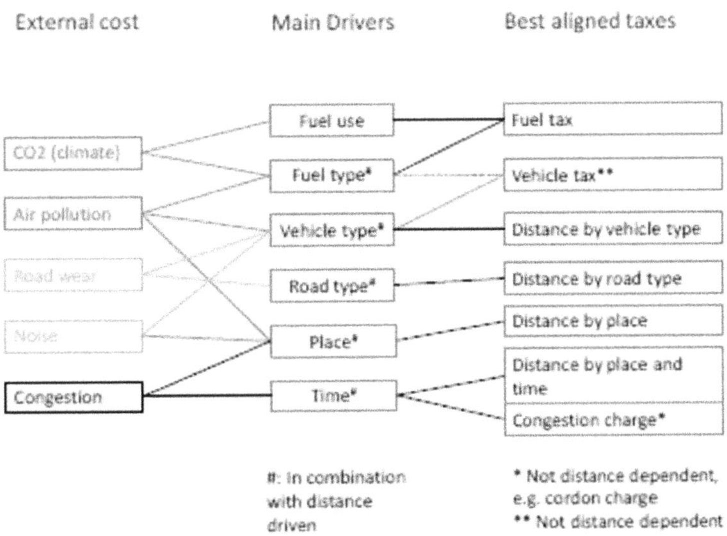

Source: Van Dender (2019).

Existing taxes on transport in Israel fail to reflect correctly the different externalities of transport use. While fuel taxation can reflect the effect on climate, it fails to price precisely the effect that fuel combustion has on local air quality, as it strongly depends on the vehicle quality, but also, for instance, on the initial pollutant concentration, hence on other people's use.

On the other hand, vehicle taxation, which is calibrated in order to reflect the average costs of car use does not account for the intensive use of each car. Reducing car use is a prominent lever for reducing GHG emissions from transport in Israel, as the country has the second highest mileage per car in the whole OECD (17,700 vehicle-km per road motor vehicles-see Figure 4.4) after the United States of America although population density is more than ten times lower in the latter.[22] As car taxation fails to put a price on every kilometre driven, it does not reduce unnecessary trips and has a limited effect in reducing pollution. Nor does it foster car sharing, while 80% of Israelis drive alone (Trajtenberg et al., 2018[9]).

Figure 4.4. Vehicle use intensity per year in thousands of kilometre per road motor vehicle across OECD countries (in thousands vehicle-km per road motor vehicle)

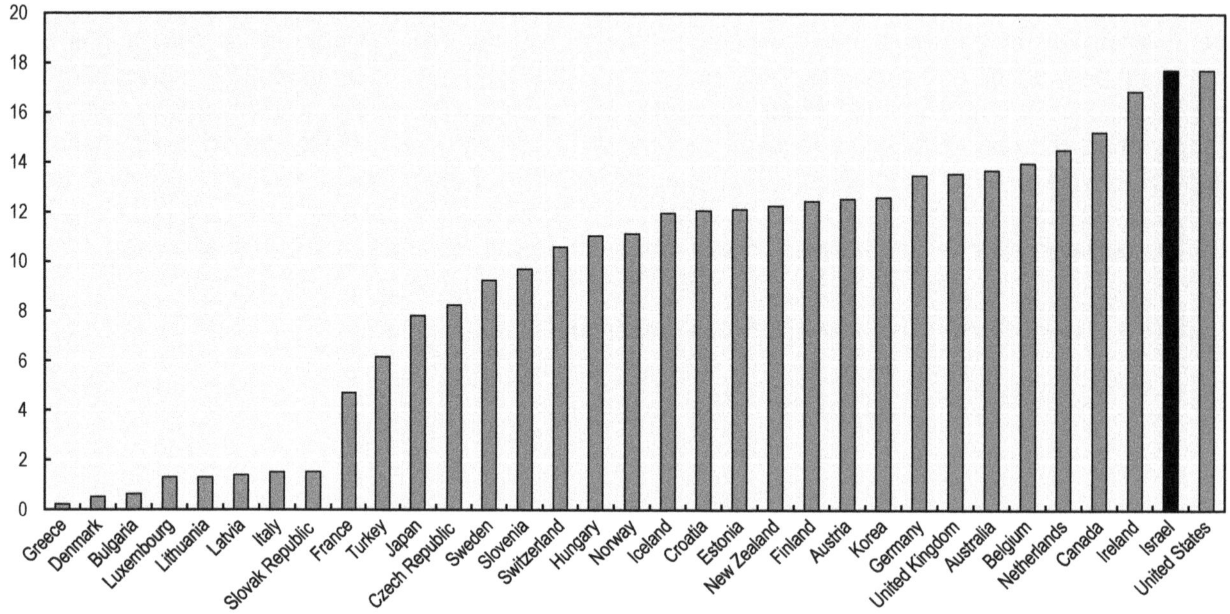

Note: the year is 2015 or the latest data available.
Source: OECD-ITF.

StatLink https://doi.org/10.1787/888934156200

A tax proportional to the distance driven has the advantage of being suited to integrating many externalities linked to transport, such as noise, road wear, congestion and air pollution, which are often proportional to car use (Figure 4.3). Implementing such taxation, with a modulation by vehicle type that applies a higher rates for more polluting models, constitutes a good option to supplement fuel taxes.

This type of tax relates the price paid more closely to actual pollution than the car purchase tax by pricing both vehicle use and equipment choices. In order to reflect a broader range of externalities, congestion charges can be integrated by applying higher rates in case of congestion. As the purchase tax has however the advantage of providing an immediate price signal at the point of decision to purchase, the complete phase-out of this tax could result in accelerating car ownership, and deteriorating the tax base. Thus, an optimal combination of these taxes should be assessed.

The development in electronic metering technologies and its diffusion in the car fleet will probably reduce these costs of implementation. Finally, recent technology developments using GPS allow for a modulation of this tax according to the place and the moment of driving, and would then contribute to a broader internalisation of costs, including congestion (van Dender, 2019[24]).

Action in the short term would consist in implementing congestion charges in metropolis based on the distance driven. In the longer term, those schemes could be transformed into a national distance-based taxation by being expanded to the whole country and modulated according to vehicles characteristics (higher rates would be applied to more polluting vehicles) and to congestion.

Distributive effects of combining the car purchase tax with a distance-based taxation can be important. It would benefit households and firms that do not use much their vehicle or use it for short distances, and would negatively affect long commuters. Targeted compensatory measures can be considered but an efficient public transport network would be the best policy tool to smooth the transition (see section 4.5).

4.4. Improving road management and allocation will be key for lowering GHG emissions and enhancing life quality

4.4.1. Rethinking road management to increase the use of sustainable modes

Generating an efficient use of road space needs to be a priority for transport systems in Israel. Thus, transport modes that generate higher social benefits and lower GHG emissions and other social costs, relative to the road space they consume (e.g. walking, cycling, public transport and other forms of shared-trip services), need to be prioritised. Making an efficient use of road space will also require that the demand for the use of this infrastructure is managed to avoid congestion; which in addition to generating time and other economic losses exacerbates traffic noise and emissions of gaseous pollutants, greenhouse gases and particles (Crozet and Mercier, 2018[26]). Rethinking road allocation is also an opportunity to incorporate new transport modes (e.g. electric scooter often known as micro-mobility), which have a strong case in the light of road space allocation that prioritises low-carbon and space efficient modes (OECD, 2019[1]). Having dedicated road space and specific regulation could avoid the negative impacts (e.g. accidents) from the expansion of these modes.

The allocation of road space in cities in a way that is coherent with sustainable goals (including climate) is particularly important since public space (and road space as part of this) is scarce in these territories, especially as they grow. A number of cities worldwide, like Paris and Copenhagen, have for this reason engaged in plans and projects that reallocate road-space from cars to other users. Israel authorities could use international guidelines as a reference to rethink road allocation in existing urban areas as well as in new neighbourhoods being planned. For instance the Institute for Transportation and Development Policy (ITDP, 2016[27]) explicitly establishes the following hierarchy of users: 1) pedestrian access; 2) non-motorised vehicles movement and parking; 3) public transport; 4) non-motorised goods carriers; 5) freight movement; 6) taxi services/car-pooling/car-sharing; 7) private motor vehicle movement; 8) private motor vehicle parking.

A "Complete Streets" approach should also be adopted so that transport projects planned are embedded in a holistic strategy for reconfiguring street design and public space. Complete Streets refers to a design that aims at safely balancing space between a diverse range of users and activities, such as walking, cycling, public transport, private vehicles, commercial activities and residential areas (Litman, 2015[28]). Although there is no singular design prescription, main elements of this approach include prioritisation of space for the pedestrian environment (i.e. sidewalks, crosswalks), implementing traffic calming measures, bicycle accommodation (i.e. protected or dedicated bicycle lanes) and dedicated space for public transport (i.e. BRT, transit signal priority, bus shelters). The new approach to road design and allocation should also incorporate safety considerations and be aligned with a safe system approach, i.e. the principle that errors will happen but traffic fatalities and serious injuries should not be inevitable. Therefore the system of roads should be designed so that human error does not result in serious or fatal injuries (Lockard et al., 2018[29]), As put by (Lockard et al., 2018[29]) "[s]afety and the environment converge when it comes to land use".

Introducing well-tailored parking policies will also be needed for efficiently managing road space. International evidence has demonstrated that the parking space required could be reduced by 10-30% with efficient parking policies, and these could also reduce general vehicle traffic (Litman, 2018[30]). Providing easy and cheap access to on-street parking incentivises car use and contributes additionally to congestion, since a part of the time of the travel is often dedicated to cruising for parking.

On-street parking is nearly free in Israel, thus there is wide room for manoeuvre in making use of parking fees and parking restrictions. The requirement for employers to provide free parking commodities to their employees in wage agreements could be reconsidered for instance. An option is to replace this advantage by an increase in wages, possibly with a bonus for employees using commuting modes other than private cars (e.g. public transport).

More generally, authorities could introduce different pricing zones to provide incentives to increase or decrease the availability and occupation of parking in diverse areas and for different time periods. In Lisbon, for example three parking pricing zones exist. Zoning is determined according to the availability of public transport services and to the density of parking sought for in the different areas. Red areas correspond to main transport corridors. In these areas relatively high parking prices and lower maximum parking duration limits (maximum 2 hours) are implemented. Contrastingly, in green zones, where there is relatively low public transport availability and where parking space is less scarce, parking prices are the lowest and time limits are larger (maximum 4 hours). Yellow areas are central areas of the cities that while not a transport corridor, have a relatively high availability of public transport. In these areas the price of parking is not as high as in red zones but still significantly higher than in green zones and the maximum time allowed for on-street parking is 4 hours (Lisboa, 2018[31]); (ELTIS, 2014[32]).

Copenhagen also has a three zone parking scheme that has the objective of discouraging car usage while promoting active transport modes such as biking in the city centre; parking prices in peripheral areas of the city are lower (Kodransky and Hermann, 2011[33]). Similarly, in Strasbourg a concentric three-zones parking pricing scheme imposes higher parking prices as well as lesser parking times on the city centre, as compared to the peripheries of the city. This policy has gone in hand with a replacement of on-street parking spaces in the city centre for cycling lanes and tram ways. This policy bundle seeks to reduce car usage on the city centre, as well as to concentrate long-term parking needs to park-and ride and other off-street parking facilities in more residential areas on the outskirts of the city (Paul-Dubois-Taine, 2013[34]). Cities in Israel could create a similar dynamics as various public transport projects will be developed in the short term. Israel could also opt for introducing smart parking meters with real-time fare adjustments, which in San Francisco for instance, have increased the effectiveness of variable-rate on-street parking pricing (OECD, 2015[35]).

Governments can also promote a more efficient use of private cars through incentivising off-peak commuting and shared trips. In Israel, the Ministry of Finance and the Ministry of transport are driving together a pilot project to reduce the congestion in Tel Aviv and increase the vehicle occupancy rate (as 80% of Israelis drive alone (Trajtenberg et al., 2018[9])). This scheme includes compensation for 100,000 volunteers travelling off-peak hours and a joint work with employers to foster shared journeys or teleworking (EcoTraders, 2019[36]). Enlarging collaboration with employers to upscale these type of projects will be important. While public funds channelled to this type of programmes should be assessed in the wider context of potential alternative investment for expanding and improving the public and active transport infrastructure, it is important that active policy increases vehicle occupancy, especially in the light of the development of automated cars (which will tend to be larger) (as discussed in Section 4.3.2).

Policies that improve road management (see below) can be effective for incentivising walking and cycling. An OECD study shows that the implementation of a congestion charge in Milan increased daily bike-sharing use by 5.8%, and extending the charging system to early evening increased bike-sharing by 12% in this time window. The main driver of this shift to greener transport mode is the decline of road congestion, which created safer conditions for bike use (Cornago, Dimitropoulos and Oueslati, 2019[37]).

4.4.2. Implementing congestion charging schemes in the short term

Congestion in Israel is a central issue for people's well-being and the country's economy and is a prominent issue in all the country's big cities. Israel has, by far, the highest driving distance per kilometre of network of all OECD countries (see Figure 4.5) (OECD, 2015[35]). Traffic congestion causes an average loss of 60 minutes per road-user per day (IMF, 2018[38]) and (Trajtenberg et al., 2018[9]) estimates that the costs for the Israeli economy account for 2% of GDP (including the cost of extra gasoline lost in traffic jams and the value of time lost due to congestion), in contrast with 1% of the GDP in the European Union (Casullo et al., 2019[39]). It also brings other nuisances for residents, like a concentration of air pollutants and noise.

Figure 4.5. Road traffic density per network length, 2014 or latest available year

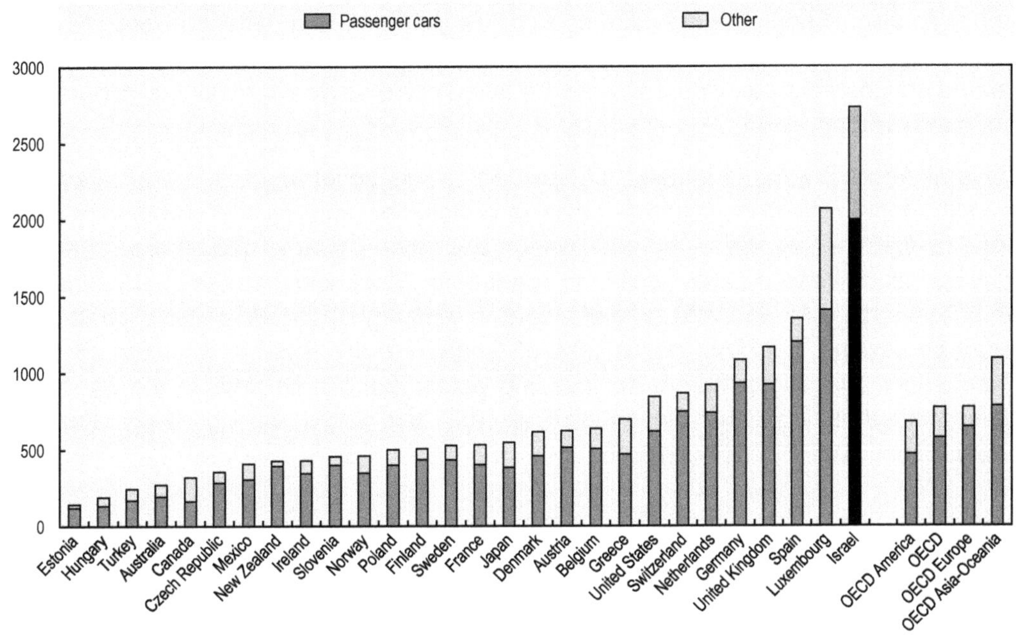

Note: from (OECD, 2015[35]).
Source: Eurostat (2015), Transport Statistics (database); North American Transportation Statistics (2015), Statistics Online Database; UNECE (2015), "Transport", UNECE Statistical
Database; and national sources.

StatLink https://doi.org/10.1787/888934156219

With no specific measure taken to tackle congestion, this issue is likely to worsen as both car ownership and population grow. As stated above, the National Plan for Transport, a public transport plan designed by the government to reduce GHG emissions from transport and to reach the Paris Agreement goals, has the objective of limiting car mileage to 44.4 million vehicle-km, which is still higher than the 43.9 million vehicle-km in 2016. In this context, even compliance which such a plan will entail an increase in car use and thus very probably a further increase in congestion.

Further road expansion is unlikely to solve this issue, partly because there is a physical limit to expand roads. Adding road capacity also encourages movements by car, and, in the end, this induced demand might completely offset the congestion-reducing effect of a supplementary road capacity (see also Section 4.5.3) (IMF, 2018[38]) (Hymel, Small and Dender, 2010[40]).

Implementing congestion charging schemes in Israel's big cities can be an effective solution in the short term. Congestion charging would have the advantage of pricing congestion explicitly and thus helping cope with a number of its negative externalities, reducing the numbers of vehicles that crowd the city centres. Past experiences in other metropoles have shown that the implementation of a charging toll immediately decreased traffic around the cordon by 20% in average and up to 60% in some arterial roads in the case of Stockholm (Eliasson, 2014[41]). The effect declines in the longer term but remains substantial (Börjesson and Kristoffersson, 2017[42]). For this reason, although road pricing schemes are not yet widely used, cities considering implementing such schemes are growing in number (ITF, 2019[43]). While using different types of pricing options, cities like London, Milan, Stockholm, and Singapore have congestion charging schemes that cover whole areas of their cities.

In Israel, the idea of implementing such scheme has been under examination since 2008. The Ministry of Finance brought for approval in the 2020 budget a congestion charge in the city of Tel Aviv, where 60% of the nation's congestion costs are concentrated. The scheme is expected to become operational in 2021.In the longer-term, as discussed in the previous section, transitioning to a distance-based taxation scheme (differentiated by type of vehicle, time and space) would be most effective. In this case driving through more central and congested areas would already be taxed more severely, making a separate congestion charging scheme redundant.

There are several different ways to shape a congestion charge scheme, presented in Table 4.2. Ideally, the amount paid should reflect the external costs of congestion paid by the community and therefore, ideally, depend on the time and use of the car. London and Milan implemented an area charge, which is a charge for driving into or within an area, while the scheme for Stockholm has the characteristics of cordon charging, which is a charge for each crossing of a cordon (although there are a maximum number of times that a user can be charged per day). In the case of Singapore, the scheme is a combination of cordon charging and corridor charging (Charges for passing points along a corridor in a city), currently using electronic differentiated pricing. Other places like California, and Seoul, among others, apply road tolls to particular corridors only. (OECD/ITF, 2019[44]).

Table 4.2. Options for differentiating road pricing systems

Type*	Main characteristics	Options		
		Scheme coverage	Fixed or variable charges	Other considerations
Cordon charging	Charge for each crossing of a cordon delimiting the charging zone in a city	Location and size of cordon	time of day day of the week number of trips vehicle type direction of travel	Exemptions Concessions Frequency of revising prices
Area charging	Daily charge for driving into or within a defined area but no additional charge for crossing cordon more than once	Size and location of area/s	time of day day of the week vehicle type distance travelled	
Corridor charging	Charges for passing points along a corridor in a city	Number and location of charging points	time of day day of the week number of trips vehicle type direction of travel	
Variable tolls	Peak charges for already tolled highways and bridges	Local, Regional, National (dependent on toll network)	time of day day of the week vehicle type distance travelled	
Tolled lanes	Tolled lane on un-tolled road segment, often discounted/exempt for high occupancy vehicles	Number and location of charging points	time of day day of the week vehicle type vehicle occupancy	
Electronic time, distance and place-based charging	Uses transponders to enable charging of any use of the entire road network or a specified part of the network.	Local, Regional, National, specifically congested routes	time of day day of the week vehicle type distance travelled	

Source: (ITF-OECD, 2018[45]).

Cordon and area charges fail to effectively price the external costs of congestion. Contrastingly the ideal congestion charge scheme should be designed as a distance-based taxation i.e. modulated according to the real-time congestion pattern, hence the time and place of the driving (see *supra*). Founding taxation on the basis of crossing a line fails to mandate the right incentives to drivers who have no reason to limit their driving once the line is crossed. The potential mitigation effect is therefore weaker than in the case of a charging system based on the distance driven. It is even weaker in cases the charge is paid only once a day. Moreover, cordon and area charges should be carefully designed and regularly updated to avoid bottlenecks effects at the limit of the charged zone, as congestion can displace in another area.

As highlighted in Section 0, distance-based taxation is an efficient tool to capture a broad number of externalities from car use: congestion charges can approach such scheme, applying the concept to a certain zone. A distance-based charging rate depends on real-time congestion inside the city, as in Singapore, integrates most external costs of congestion and appears as the most efficient system. In addition it provides a larger scope for adapting behaviour (e.g. shifting to off-peak travel appears as an option in addition to modal shift). In this case, no trip would be left unpriced and short trips would not be overcharged because the driver crossed a certain line. This requires that few exemptions should be allowed for private vehicles (for residents or taxis for instance), even though they might improve public acceptance, in order to implement the proper incentives.

This rate can also depend on the vehicle size. A usual method to estimate the charging rate is to estimate and price the time loss in traffic and consider the marginal cost of a supplementary car in the traffic. The UK Department for transport, estimates the marginal external cost of congestion from GBP 0.01 per vehicle km in rural area motorways to GBP 0.692 in 2015 (2010 prices[23]), adding up costs of time loss in congestion as well as operating costs.[24]

Needless to say, some precision of the scheme can be forgone at the benefit of clarity, as a high degree of differentiation is not always readable for drivers and car owners. Unclear schemes would make users less reactive to the price signal and would increase oppositions to the scheme. The differentiation should thus be made simple and clear In the case of Stockholm, traffic volumes decreased by 20-25% during the trial period of a congestion charge and the system gathered general support in a referendum, with a simpler system based on a cordon charge. Peak and off-peak prices are nonetheless an important feature of the scheme.

Following track of vehicles moves in the concerned zones is necessary when implementing a congestion charge; modulating it according to time and place requires some higher level of technology. Using GPS technology seems feasible, as long as privacy issues are carefully managed. (OECD/ITF, 2019[44]).

4.4.3. Gaining public support

Policies aiming at better managing roads will change the relative prices for transport users, namely making car use more expensive (ideally where and when it causes the highest external costs). Gaining public acceptability is challenging but crucial to make these type of measures more perennial and less dependent on political cycles. Guaranteeing access through alternative modes of transport is an important part of gaining public acceptability. This is also necessary to make the policy cost-effective, since only in this way can the new pricing trigger behavioural change instead of only imposing economic burden on segments of the population. In any case, careful assessment of negative distributional impacts is necessary to ensure that no group is overburdened as well as to prevent relevant opposition.

Congestion charges for instance may have some distributional impacts that should not be overlooked, as they increase the cost of private transport and may therefore deteriorate households' purchasing power. (OECD/ITF, 2019[44]) In Israel, total private vehicle expenses constitute 15% of income for households' in the lowest decile, while only 9% of income of households in the highest decile.[25] This means that the implementation of a new charge could potentially be regressive. Even though the modulation of the taxation by time or distance has the potential to alleviate this effect, this is far from certain and should be assessed, as this depends on the possibility for people to change their daily commute and other trips.

Beside, differentiating zones inside the city might have an impact on housing prices, especially for instance if charging zones coincide with places concentrating jobs and thus make living in the area even more advantageous (since one could walk or bike instead of commuting by car). This could push poorer households out of the city centres and benefit people owning real estate in the charging zones. This effect on property prices inside the zones would probably be exacerbated if residents are exempted from charges and enjoy free on-street parking. The negative impact on commuters from outside the centre can also be significantly alleviated if commuting from outside is made easier, by the presence of accessible and good quality public transport as well alternative transport modes (biking, walking) to car use.

Strategies and policies adopted in Israel to reach climate and other well-being goals by improving road management should be carefully assessed in order to anticipate potential problems and ways to compensate for this and improve the acceptability of measures. Mattioli et al. (2017[46]) proposes to build a vulnerability index assessing three dimensions of vulnerability (cost burden of energy expenditures, households' sensitivity, defined with their income, and their adaptive capacity, defined as access to jobs and selected services). Results are used to identify vulnerability to increases in fuel prices spatially across London, but the index could be used to assess other policies such as road pricing. The vulnerability index takes into account for each neighbourhood the cost burden of a measure for the population (as a share of income), their adaptive capacity and the access to jobs and selected services. The result showed that, in London, while the urban core tends to be less vulnerable to increases in fuel prices according to the vulnerability index, there are pockets of the city where there is very high vulnerability. The findings underline the need to assess policy effects with the use of disaggregated information rather than focusing on average users. They also highlight the importance of going beyond analysis of vertical equity (i.e. distributional impacts across income groups) to account for the wider context (e.g. access to alternatives) that places, or not, different population in a situation of vulnerability regarding a certain policy.

There is a strong case for improving the taxation of transport in Israel, as heavy congestion in the bigger cities is a known problem. The reform proposed above (in Section 2) consists in improving the alignment of fuel taxes with their carbon contents, which would automatically raise diesel taxation (when 96% of vehicles are fuelled with petrol). It also recommends allowing the purchase tax to react more easily to technological change, which will probably not increase significantly the average cost for transport for households. However, the implementation of a congestion charge will probably increase transport costs more significantly, since it would put a price on what used to be free (i.e. the use of road space in congested areas). New fiscal measures may meet opposition. In October 2019, the Israeli Minister of Transport, M. Smotrich, publicly asserted his opposition to the congestion charge in Tel Aviv, following the steps of his predecessor.

A first option to gain public acceptance would be to recycle the revenues, so that the measure would not appear as a way for the government to levy revenues (OECD/ITF, 2019[44]). (Marten and van Dender, 2019[47]) identifies several options countries took to use their revenues from carbon pricing, such as using it to change the tax system (shifting from an labour income based taxation to a pollution-based one), for inter-governmental transfers, transport-related spending, green and energy-related spending and compensation to energy users. While that does not mean the tax income should be earmarked,[26] a full disclosure of expenses allowed by the revenue could enhance the public acceptance for an increased tax burden.

In the case of Israel, there is a strong political case to recycle a large part of supplementary revenues in investments for transport (see section 4), even if the supplementary resources from congestion charges is likely to be low. A congestion charge entails heavy costs of monitoring and should not be expected to become a major source of revenue, nor should it be implemented with this objective as the main reason for doing so. For instance, the congestion charge and penalty charge notice fees (driving offences and parking fines) accounted for only 5% of TfL's 2013 budget. (ITF, 2018[15]) Even so, transparent revenue recycling enhances public acceptance. In addition, recycling revenues can also be used in the case of charges other than congestion (e.g. parking charges, and fuel and purchase taxes). Investment in public transport and active modes would facilitate the reduction of car use by making households able to find alternatives to private cars, making the new charges both more acceptable and more efficient for climate.

Taking into consideration that the development of alternatives is key to making private transport taxation efficient and accepted by society, the timing of the development and improvement of alternatives is crucial. It seems more efficient to develop public transport before, or at the same time as, the fiscal measures are introduced. In the short term, buses can be developed and have their quality and regularity improved, all the more if a congestion charge improves traffic in the city centres. The Mayor of London took this option, improved bus routes and put additional buses into services by the time the congestion charge was introduced. As a result, the majority of the 30% of car trips foregone by cars were replaced by bus trips. More structural works (light trains, metro) can be initiated for the long term (Transport for London, 2004[48]).

Gaining public support for a supplementary tax on transport can be tricky, more particularly in Israel where transport charges are already high and public transport quality is subject to strong criticism. Initial support is key and can be reached by involving stakeholders, targeted consultation efforts and a strict timeline for engagement (OECD/ITF, 2019[44]). The State government of New York is planning to introduce congestion pricing for Manhattan's central business district progressively, starting with taxis and for-hire vehicles. In Stockholm and Milan, the congestion charge was implemented after a referendum (in Stockholm, after an initial trial period) and the mayor of London had campaigned for it before being elected. However, experience showed that, once implemented, a congestion charge could reach a large political approval.

4.5. Public and active transport needs to be mainstreamed as an attractive alternative to private vehicles

In its National Transport Plan, designed in 2015, the Israeli government identified that modal shift from private car to sustainable transport modes presented the biggest mitigation potential in the transport sector. However, although the government has put a strong focus on public transport, further targeted efforts would scale up ambitions.

4.5.1. Israel made strong commitments to develop public transport

Public transport is key for Israel's climate mitigation strategy in the transport sector. Assessing emission reduction potential in every sector in 2015, the government identified in a report that modal shift from private car to more sustainable transport alternatives (public transport and cycling) had the biggest mitigation potential in the transport sector. This report assessed that Israel could reduce its transport emissions by 21% by 2030, -12% could be reached by behavioural responses due to better public transport infrastructure, the rest being largely from technological improvement of vehicles. This scenario considers that the development of public transportation would reduce car uses by 25% relative to a business as usual scenario.

The Israeli government chose to take a more conservative option than its report and set the objective of a 20% reduction of private car kilometres travailed by 2030. This amounts to an emission reduction of 2.2 million tons of CO_{2eq} relative to a business as usual scenario.

Accordingly, the government is developing a long-term strategy to boost public transport infrastructure investments with the Plan "Infrastructure 2030" and the *Strategic Plan for the Development of Public Transportation in Israel*. The latter, published by the Ministry of Transport in 2012, included an investment of ILS 250 billion over 25 years (around EUR 55 billion, taking 2012 exchange rates) to bridge the cumulative gap in public transportation infrastructure. It served as the basis for government to promote multi-year strategies and plans (until 2040-2050) for developing public transport in metropolitan areas and for Israel railways and allowed for specific infrastructure projects conceived to meet the national targets. The Ministry of Transport designed these plans and strategies in cooperation with local authorities. A particular focus was set on the expansion of public transport in metropolitan areas through the establishment of mass transit systems that use separate road space from private transportation, providing faster service over a larger area.

Israel's strategy to develop public transport includes:

- A 2040 strategy for Israel railways launched in 2017 and developed by both the Ministry of Transport and the Ministry of Finance. This strategy, coordinated and integrated in metropolitan mass transit systems, includes national routes with higher speeds and very few stops, as well as regional routes with more stops and broader coverage. Since 2018, a high-speed train has been operating between Jerusalem and Ben Gurion airport near Tel Aviv. The connexion between Ben Gurion and Tel Aviv was inaugurated in December 2019. As the number of train passengers has been increasing for more than a decade in Israel (from 12.7 million 2000 to 64.6 million in 2017),[27] due partly to an extension of the lines (+50% during the same period), the government aims to reach 250 million passengers in 2040.

- Public transport plans in the metropolitan areas of Tel Aviv, Jerusalem, Haifa and Be'er Sheva.

More particularly, the Tel Aviv mass transit plan, launched in 2016 by the government, aims to reach an objective of 40% of motorised trip by public transport, carrying 4 million passengers per day in 2040 (in 2016, public transport made up 20% of trips). As most of the public transport journeys are made by bus or suburban railways, the plan schedules the construction of metro lines, light train and bus rapid transit, the first light train run being due for 2021. This plan also has objectives for a better service, which implies an increased accessibility,[28] a broad coverage of the population and a higher average speed.

Israel's efforts to enhance the use of public transport has had some notable results, since trips in public transport have seen exponential growth for the last 30 years. Passenger train use has been increasing, going from 2.5 million passengers in 1990 to 12.7 million in 2000, 35.3 million in 2010 and 64.4 million in 2017 (see Figure 4.6). Bus use has also increased by 70% in 15 years. Moreover, important measures were implemented, like the Tel Aviv transport plan. A light train was opened in Jerusalem since 2011 and is expected to have all its five lines completed by 2024. The light train transports 130.000 people per day.

However, recourse to public transport is still very low relative to international standards. Perhaps surprisingly, therefore, half of the budget of the Strategic Plan is still unallocated. Further efforts are thus needed.

Figure 4.6. Public transport use in Israel

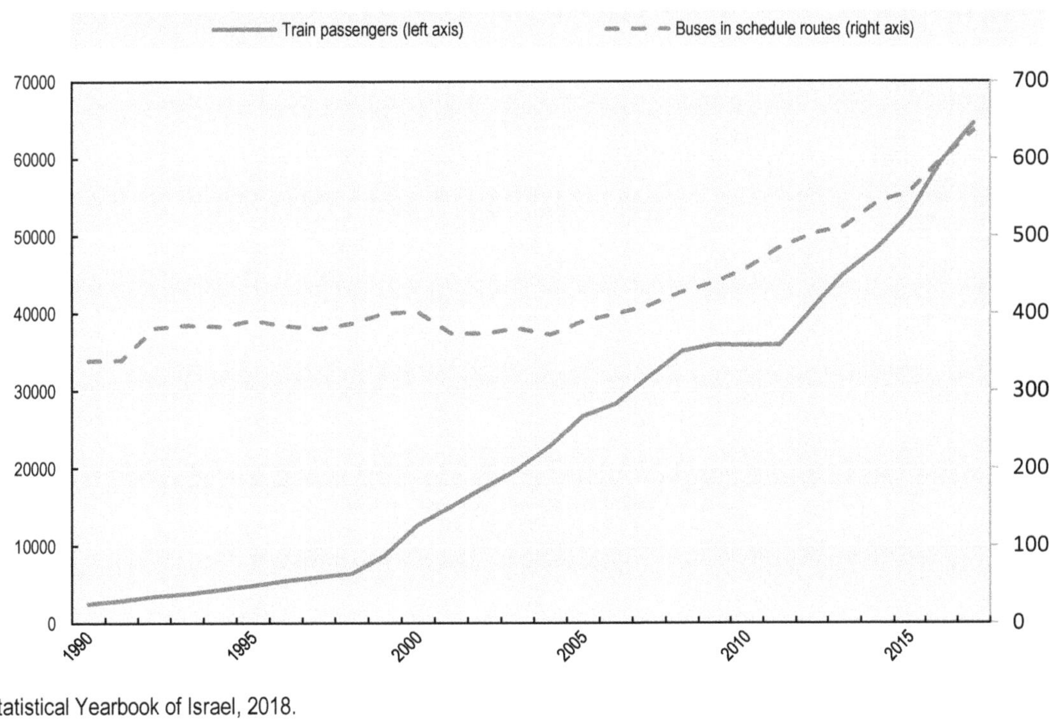

Source: Statistical Yearbook of Israel, 2018.

StatLink https://doi.org/10.1787/888934156238

4.5.2. Public transport and active modes in Israel have serious shortcomings

Public investment is particularly low in international terms. The IMF pointed out that the investment gap of Israel amounted to 20% relative to other countries, and that the level of investment for transport was particularly "inadequate" (IMF, 2018[38]). Figure 4.7 shows that this low investment also comes with a very low amount of public capital relative to other countries. Among 35 advanced economies, the average public capital stock amounts to 67% of GDP with average investment at 3.4%; as a contrast, these numbers are respectively 34% and 2.9% in Israel.

More particularly, public investment in transport is weak in Israel (1.3% in 2018), although the investment in public transport as a share of GDP has been notably enhanced (from 0.4% of GDP in 2014 to 0.7% in 2018, cf. Figure 4.8). The share of GDP allocated to investment in road infrastructures has been stable (around 0.6% of GDP between 2014 and 2018), although their use has escalated.

The share of workers performing activities outside of their residential areas increased by 10 percentage points between 1990 and 2016 (from 43.9% to 53.9%) and an increasing proportion of them are using their private cars. As a result the share of commuting journeys by car increased to 60% in 2016, compared to 31% in 1983 and 48% in 1995 (Bleikh, 2018[6]). In parallel, journeys to work have been increasing and the duration of journeys to work increased by nearly 30% for people working outside their localities between 2005 and 2017(see Figure 4.8), which reflects the relevant sprawl in cities (see previous chapter).

Figure 4.7. Public investment and public capital in Israel: Public capital stock and public investment, 2017

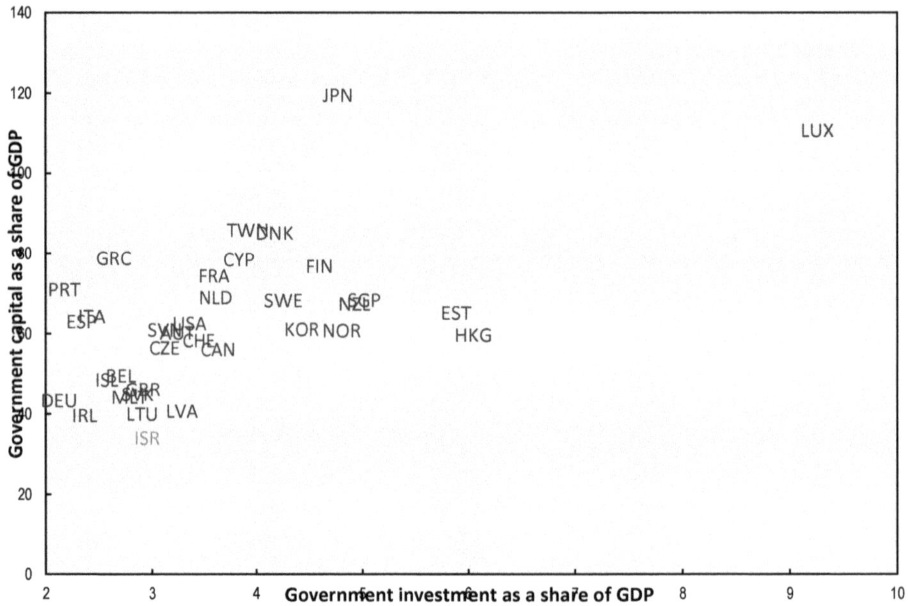

Source: IMF, *Investment and Capital Stock Dataset*, http://www.imf.org/external/np/fad/publicinvestment/.

StatLink https://doi.org/10.1787/888934156257

Figure 4.8. Evolution of the investments for transport and commuting in Israel

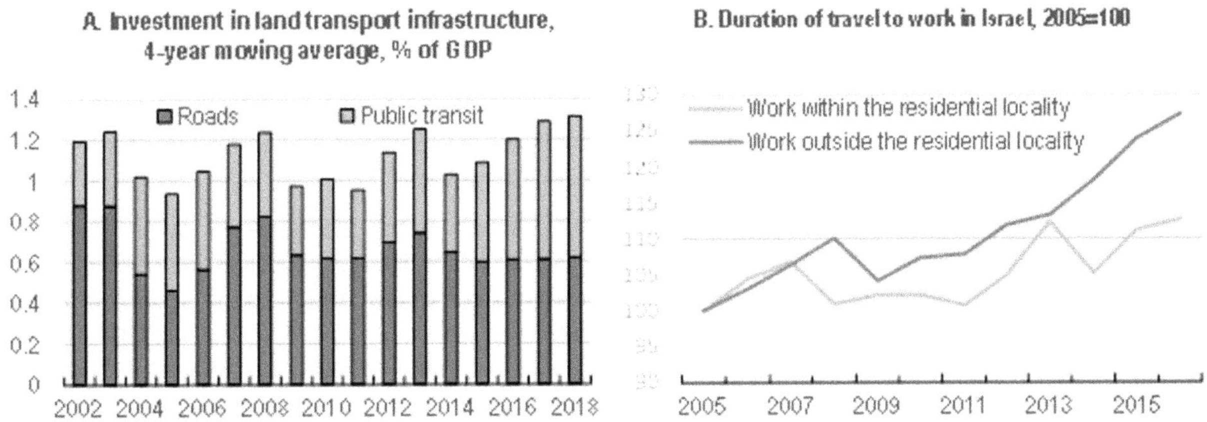

Source: Central Bureau of Statistics.

The public transport network is lagging behind commuting and general mobility patterns. First, public transport is unavailable, or has reduced frequency, during Shabbat (from Friday at sunset to Saturday after sunset) and Jewish holidays, which makes private vehicles indispensable for people traveling during these times. Besides, many employment sites are not accessible by public transport. (Suhoy and Sofer, 2019[3]) developed index that showed that the number of workplaces that can be reached by public transportation are less than half of the number of workplaces accessible by private vehicles, according to a majority of employees. This accessibility index is lower in peripheral localities, and particularly for Arab localities.

Furthermore, even where public transport is an option, it is not the first choice for most people for their daily journeys: as 92% of the population is connected to public transport, only 20% use them. As a result, most people using a bus do so because they cannot afford their own vehicle. Using a 2014 household survey, (Suhoy and Sofer, 2019[3]) show that employees with a low level of income and a relatively weak socioeconomic background are more inclined to use buses and employer-organised shuttles to go to work. It also shows that, although people have an accessible and regular bus service nearby, less than 35% of them would chose a bus to commute. Train seem to attract much more people than buses when available, however trains only makes up 2% of journeys to work, against 8% in other OECD countries (although this share has increased significantly in Israel).

Public transport limitations widen regional inequalities. Public transport accessibility is particularly low in peripheral areas (Suhoy and Sofer, 2019[3]), which increases the dependence on private transportation. In Jerusalem, Tel Aviv, Haifa and Be'er Sheva, around 50% of workers use their cars to go to work; in cities of less than 100.000 inhabitants, more than 60% do so, and 70% in rural areas (Bleikh, 2018[6]); the share of journeys by bus also decreases with the size of the city. The spatial differences in public transport accessibility have a strong social impact since access to public transport may define access to jobs. Even though private shuttles organised by employers flourish, they do not appear as a lasting satisfactory solution. A major issue is that such pattern may hinder competition and workers' capacity to change employer. Moreover, people need transport services to perform a number of activities beyond jobs.

Arab populations are particularly affected. This is linked to the fact that they live in peripheral areas: 73% of Arab Israelis live in localities with fewer than 100.000 inhabitants (against half of Jewish Israelis). Moreover, Arab localities are particularly underequipped, even compared with Jewish localities of similar size. Comparing Jewish and Arab localities with fewer than 50.000 inhabitants, (Bleikh, 2018[6]) shows that Arab localities resort much less (5% against 11% in Jewish localities) to public transport and much more to private shuttles (19% against 8%). A recent study by the Bank of Israel showed that, the quality of bus service in large Arab localities (more than 20.000 inhabitants), which concentrate half of Arab Israeli that do not live in mixed areas, is lower by about a third than the level in Jewish localities with similar characteristics (Bank of Israel, 2019[49]). This poor quality in public services hinders access to jobs in regions already suffering from high poverty rates (Gal, Madhala and Bleikh, 2017[50]).

Arabs living in Arab localities are also the less satisfied population with the conditions of roads and sidewalks. This makes the development of public transport, specifically buses, more difficult as a regular bus service requires a good maintenance of road infrastructures and specific places for bus stops. A bus lane would also make this public transport more efficient and attractive.

Finally, the development of new housing projects might increase the shortage of public transport investment. Faced with a housing shortage that brought hundreds of thousands Israeli in the street in 2011, the government implemented a housing plan to comply with the immediate need. As the easiest option is to build on state-owned land, most often in peri-urban fringe, and where the prices of lands are the lowest, more and more people might be located in areas where access to public transport is not guaranteed (see the discussion in Chapter 3).

4.5.3. Adopting accessibility-based planning and investment frameworks

In order to build a sustainable transport sector, the focus behind policy decisions and investment should be shifted from following mobility demand (passenger and tonne-kilometres) and increasing speed to improving accessibility (OECD, 2019[1]), i.e. the ease of reaching destinations for goods, services, jobs and other activities (Litman, 2019[2]). Target 11.2[29] of the UN Sustainable Development goals explicitly calls for better accessibility, with a particular focus on public transport.

There are important opportunities for generating two-way alignment between climate change mitigation action, and broader well-being and sustainable development objectives in the transport sector, if focusing on accessibility instead of mobility. The link between enhanced access to opportunities and well-being outcomes (including climate) is much stronger than that of physical movement. Focusing on accessibility makes the role of public and active modes, which have high social and environmental value, more central. This in turn increases feasibility and effectiveness of policies focused on better pricing car use externalities, including by improving road management and allocation. An accessibility-based approach also makes more evident the centrality of enhancing proximity through better land-use and housing policy (see chapter 2) – which is a key enabler for moving towards sustainable transport systems (OECD, 2019[1]).

In order to unlock these opportunities, Israel would need to mainstream accessibility into policy, planning and investment decision-making. Using accessibility indicators to set criteria is central to making this happen. Certain principles are necessary to ensure that accessibility-based frameworks effectively promote policies supporting sustainable development. Among these are using accessibility indicators that can: a) track accessibility needs for different transport users; b) reflect multiple modes of transport and their relative performance (specifically including sustainable modes like cycling, walking and public transport); and c) account for territorial differences (e.g. urban vs. non-urban territories), particularly acknowledging the neighbourhood scale (ITF-OECD, 2019[51]).

Analysis using accessibility indicators are available for Israel but now they need to be used to set specific objectives for policies and to identify accessibility gaps so that expansion and upgrades to the system can bridge them. (Suhoy and Sofer, 2019[3]), for instance assessed employees' commuting patterns and jobs' accessibility, providing precise information on the capacity of people to access to public transport and, more broadly to goods, services, and opportunities, using their localisation. In London, for instance the Public Transport Accessibility Level (PTAL) indicator is used for planning the system, as well as to implement mechanisms that explicitly link land-use and housing decision with transport accessibility criteria (see previous chapter).

Other useful indicators can be vulnerability indexes that incorporate income criteria to an accessibility index, in order to account for the cost burden imposed by current transport conditions on populations according to their level of income, as well as adaptive capacity in case a certain mode (e.g. cars) becomes more expensive. Such analysis could help identify areas where populations both suffer from a poor access to public transports and a level of income that makes the accession to private vehicles difficult. Monitoring changes and climate policies with these types of indicators would help to avoid potential trade-offs when implementing certain policies (e.g. carbon or congestion pricing) (ITF-OECD, 2018[45]) (see Section 4.4.3).

Accessibility needs also to be mainstreamed into appraisal methodologies to ensure that this is the rationale behind investment (see next subsection). This will allow shifting away from a "predict-and-provide" approach, which predicts demand and plans road expansion, ultimately creating additional traffic and not solving for congestion, pollution or GHG emissions. Instead, appraisal methodologies that can incorporate accessibility criteria can make a stronger case for channelling investment towards sustainable transport modes.

Steering investment for public transport and active modes

Promoting accessibility and well-being in investment choices

As discussed above, **Israel's public investment in transport is very low compared to international standards**. Moreover the strong demographic growth increases pressures on the transport system, especially since the current model, predominantly based in private vehicle ownership does not provide access to goods, services and opportunities to all the population. This results in negative environmental and health externalities, which will be exacerbated as cities grow. Thus in order to meet climate and other well-being objectives there is an urgent need to invest in significantly upgrading and expanding the public transport system as well as the facilities for active modes.

Investment needs to be optimised in order to address the numerous shortcomings of the Israeli transport system. An important and urgent first step is to allocate the whole of funds designated to the government's *Strategic Plan for the Development of Public Transportation in Israel,* based on methodologies that make climate and other well-being a central criteria for decision-making. The implementation of the plan should be accelerated and optimised in order to prevent people and cities from locking-in mobility systems into car dependency.

Accessibility should be a major driver for investment. As discussed before, in order to build a sustainable transport sector, the focus behind policy decisions and investment should be shifted from following mobility demand (passenger and tonne-kilometres) and increasing speed to improving accessibility.

Enhancing budget for public transport and active modes is therefore crucial, as it would enhance accessibility, contributing to climate stability and wider well-being. Shifting commutes from private cars to walking, cycling and public transport would decrease GHG emissions from the transport sector and improve air quality. The mainstreaming or these low space intensive modes would also significantly reduce congestion issues in Israel. Finally, active modes have beneficial effects on health for people who use them and reduce the risk of obesity: high level of obesity rates observed are the result of unhealthy diets and a lack of physical activity (Graf and Cecchini, 2017[52]). Moreover, studies show that cycling, as a moderate activity, reduces the risk of Type-2 diabetes, cardiovascular diseases, and certain forms of cancer, osteoporosis and depression (ITF, 2013[53]).

As the share of public transport and active modes is low and has been declining for decades in Israel, their access should be facilitated by more and better infrastructure. Due partly to an increase of the share of workers performing outside their residential area, the share of people going to work by walking or cycling has been declining for decades: from 19% in 1983, it has reached 10% in 2016 (Bleikh, 2018[6]).

The quality and comfort of public transport and lanes for active modes should be a major driver for investments. Investment should be focused on providing reliable, accessible, comfortable and frequent public transport, in order to both improve direct well-being and the share of commute with public transport. In effect, it appears that the poor quality of public transport is the main barrier to its mainstreaming in people's daily travels (Suhoy and Sofer, 2019[3]). It is essential that the new train and bus lines created in the big cities in Israel offer comfort, reliability and extended hours to make people shift away from private cars. Similarly, safety for active modes should be enhanced to increase use: the deployment of cycling lanes and safety policies in parallel has allowed bicycle travels to increase by 20% in Copenhagen between 1996 and 2010 (ITF, 2013[53]).

Prioritising public transport and road maintenance over road construction

Considering the general costs and benefits of a project leads to reconsider the "predict and provide" approach implemented in many cases that consists in predicting the demand for transport and providing additional roads accordingly, without taking into account dynamics and other well-being criteria. More particularly, this leads to consider the induced demand, which is the increased demand due to additional transport capacity, which is particularly strong for investment in additional road capacity.

Taking into consideration the benefits from different types of infrastructure, it appears that public transport should be prioritised over road investment. Although there is a need for more road infrastructure, the IMF points out that, ultimately, the return rate of road investment (in terms of economic output) is below the return of investment for mass transit (IMF, 2018[38]). Road investment's return rates rapidly declines as more attractive and larger roads bring more cars, which ultimately increases congestion. Experience in the United Kingdom in the 1990s shows that road expansion actually added traffic. In contrast, investment for mass transit have a constant return rate, according to the IMF. Taking into account other well-being criteria (like the time spent in transport), many studies show that investing in additional road capacity does not solve congestion issues, as it actually facilitates and encourages car travel, which may completely offset the additional fluidity first provided by an extra lane for motorised modes (Hymel, Small and Dender, 2010[40]).

Nonetheless, road quality should not be overlooked as buses still make up a large majority of journeys by public transportation. Budget for road maintenance should not be reduced. Qualitative bus lanes should instead be built on existing road structures or by expanding them when possible.

Defining a clear appraisal methodology based on well-being and accessibility

Israel should develop and implement a sound appraisal methodology to assess the impact of projects on accessibility and gear investments that promote well-being. This methodology should integrate the criteria set out above in order to foster accessibility and well-being (climate included).

Taking an extended cost-benefit analysis is an option, as it allows to calculation the costs and benefits of different policy options while setting a broad set of criteria. It is important however that the appraisal is transparent on the criteria used to calculate the cost-benefit ratio (CBR) and includes non-monetised, and even qualitative analysis to: a) adjust the CBR and b) bring more comprehensive analysis (beyond the BCR) into the decisions. In the case of transport, benefits would include the time saved in transport due to an additional investment, but (as practice in the United Kingdom shows-see below) can also take into account wider economic and well-being benefits, which include dynamic effects (i.e. the creation of job and activity due to additional transport options) or the non-monetised effects (i.e. improved security, landscape) (ITF, 2019[54]).

A particular focus of this appraisal should be made on providing access to population with impaired mobility, as it lays as a key dimension for well-being. A first reason is that accessibility for all is a universal right, acknowledged by the UN as a post-2015 Sustainable Development Goal. Moreover, it can bring economic benefits to the region and the country by providing people access to opportunities. Finally, there is a large scope of beneficiaries, and everyone can be benefited at a certain time. Impaired mobility includes passengers with disabilities, but also encumbered passengers (with small children, heavy luggage). Facilitating public transport for mobility impairment would reduce the need for private car for a large share of the population, which also includes elderly people (12% of the population of Israel are 65 years old and over)[30] and families (ITF, 2016[55]).

Such methodology should be applied systematically to transport projects in order to provide consistent policies. In the United Kingdom, the Department for Transport (DfT) made the case for improving its Transport Investment Strategy In 2017 in order to streamline accessibility by setting an appraisal methodology for promoters. Scheme promoters have access to a Web-based Transport Analysis Guidance (WebTAG) to inform the value for money of their projects, taking into account multiple criteria, monetised (which include GHG emissions) and non-monetised (e.g. movement to more or less productive jobs, dynamic clustering, and landscape). This tool presents the impact of projects on the economy, the environment and society and is used to drive investment decisions. In order to mainstream the approach, DfT staff systematically checks the compatibility of projects with WebTAG guidance (ITF, 2019[54]).

4.5.4. Widening financial capacity to ensure sustainable transport budgets

Setting optimal fares

An extended and improved public transport network will probably increase operational costs, which raises the question of financial stability. Introducing competition into the public transport market (which has been the case in Israel since 2000) is key to prevent high fares reflecting operation inefficiencies and providing regulators with transparency on operation costs. International comparisons show that fares can cover a large part of public transport operational costs (but not the maintenance, expansion and regulatory costs). Increasing fares in Israel might be an option, as they are now relatively low (inter-urban fee in Tel-Aviv was ILS 5.90 in 2019, which amounts to EUR 1.5) and many studies have showed that keeping prices low is not as efficient as improved capacity to increase the demand for public transport.

In addition to allowing recuperating a high share of operational costs, public transport pricing can also be used to optimise frequentation during peak hours. As a high density of people in public transport might bring discomfort to users, but also slow the pace of vehicles and therefore be detrimental to the performance of public transport. Differentiating on-peak and off-peak hours is an efficient way to avoid crowding during peak hours by applying an increased fare during these periods. This would optimise the distribution of public transport demand through the day and incentivise modal shift from private car to public transport by limiting the crowd during rush hours.

However, increasing public transport fares can have detrimental distributive outcome, as surveys show that lower-income households spend more than others in public transport. In Israel, households from the lowest decile (10% of households who have the lowest disposable income) spend an average of 2.87% of their income in public transport, whereas this share is 0.93% for the whole population and 0.24% for the 10th decile (10% of households who have the highest income).[31] It is important that low-income households are not priced out from public transport and have thus ensured access to opportunities and jobs, allowing to avoid poverty traps.

Overall, a balance can be found between financial equilibrium and affordable transport if keeping fares close to levels where operational costs are recouped and fares optimise usage if targeted subsidies are then applied (ITF, 2018[15]) Targeted subsidies based on income criteria are the most efficient tool to offset these distributional impacts. In contrast, providing free public transport is expensive for public budget and does not generate the desired outcome on modal shift. Experience in cities that have tested free public transport shows that while generating some modal shift from cars to public transport, the larger effect is an undesired modal shift from walking and cycling (ITF/OECD, 2017). The regions of Paris, London or Barcelona provide subsidies for public transport based on statutory criteria (for students, unemployed people, elderly, etc.) (ITF, 2018[15]); this method has the advantage of limiting administrative costs because the paperwork is simpler for households than having to report all yearly incomes. However, status criteria fail to cover all people who have difficulties paying for public transport. While implementing its integrated transport system, the city of Bogota created specific subsidies for low-income households (a "pro-poor" public transport). In order to properly target recipients, the city used the national targeting system, a dataset with precise information on household built to design the social safety net programs, Evaluation showed that this subsidy had beneficial impact both for public transport uptake (increased resort to public transport was 56% higher among subsidy recipients than other car users) and job productivity of informal workers (ITF, 2018[15]). This example shows that subsidies for low-income households have many benefits, but requires strong coordination between transport and other authorities so that information from other welfare programs is shared. Israel could look into establishing a similar system.

Finding additional funding and using new financing mechanisms

International experience shows that transport fares can only cover a part of operational costs of transport systems and generally fail to cover expansion, maintenance and regulatory cost. As discussed in the next Section 4.5.5, it is key to create planning and regulatory capacity inside the government (which could be done through dedicated staff in a Metropolitan Transport Authority). Covering all these costs, means new stable sources of income will be needed.

The need for investment in public transport is important and accepted by the government, which has already allocated ILS 250 billion (EUR 62 Bn) to public transport over the next 25 years. However, given the limited extent of the public transport system and expected growth in population, additional funding and possibly new financing mechanisms should be considered to accelerate the pace of expansion and improvement of transport infrastructure.

Increasing the participation of the private sector in financing infrastructure is an option, as employers and businesses benefit from a performant transport system (by providing access to the productive workforce and limiting commuting hours, for instance). The *Versement Transport* (Transport Tax), which is a payroll tax applied to firms with more than 9 employees, is levied under this rationale and amounted to 50% of the budget of Ile de France Mobilité, in the Paris Region (ITF, 2018[15]). Similarly, the local authorities of the United Kingdom have had the opportunity since 2009 to levy a tax of 2% of the rateable value to existing commercial development with a rateable value above a certain threshold. This modality allowed the Great London Authority to levy GBP 4.1 billion for a 14.5 billion project (ITF, 2018[15]).

International experience has also showed that charges on private vehicles (parking charges, fines and congestion charges) are also an option to raise funds. In the Paris Region, half of fines and offences go to the metropolitan transport authority. The congestion charge and penalty charge notice fees (driving offences and parking fines) accounted for 5% of TfL's 2013 budget (ITF, 2018[15]).

Land Value Capture (LVC) mechanisms can help cover the cost of new public transport infrastructure by leveraging on future land value increases that are due to new infrastructure. This is often done on the basis of a land value tax. In London, LVCs contributes to a large part of many projects. Private developers contributed through the Community Infrastructure Levy to the redevelopment of the Vauxhall, Nine Elms and Battersea Opportunity Area that consisted in a massive increase of public transport capacity in the area. Tax Increment Finance was also used. An accessibility index was taken as base for negotiations on private actors' contributions to the cost of the infrastructure that the new development will rely upon (ITF-OECD, 2017[56]) (see previous chapter).

Israel's fiscal and debt positions and solid governance frameworks also provide for an expansion of investment through PPPs or indeed through public borrowing. Public-Private Partnerships (PPP) have been used to finance the toll roads, the light rail system in Jerusalem[32] [1] the Tel Aviv Jerusalem railway and the Tel Aviv metro. The institutional capacity and finance expertise available in Israel has resulted in relatively problem-free PPPs in the transport sector. There have been failures in the light rail PPPs in Israel as a result of selecting before resolution of key issues (European Investment Bank, 2011[57]). Contracting procedures can be improved but PPPs in this sector will always increase the overall cost of investment. Moreover, provision for contingent liabilities in case of revenue shortfall and project failure are explicitly covered and even if PPPs are not included in headline balance sheets the liabilities inescapably revert to the government and should be included in long term public debt (Araújo and Sutherland, 2010[44]).

4.5.5. Adapting governance: building metropolitan transport authorities and developing a national policy for metropolitan and urban transport

In Israel regulation and planning of public transport services is done by the central government, through the Public Transport Division of the Ministry of Transport (MOT). Past reforms have allowed progressive improvements in the the governance of public transport. For instance, a reform in 2000 opened bus services (which represented 18% of total trips in 2016 (Bleikh, 2018[6])) to a competitive tendering process, allowing to increase competitiveness in the sector. By 2012 35% of bus services (bus-kilometres) were operated by eight new actors. This was an important change, since before the reform activities were mostly concentrated in only two bus cooperatives. On the one hand, the lack of a competitive process provided little information for the authority to benchmark services and incentivise competitiveness. On the other hand, it created high dependence of the system in the two main companies, which limited the authorities' regulatory capacity (Ida and Talit, 2017[58]). The reform resulted in quality improvements in parallel to cost (and in some cases fare) reductions (Ida and Talit, 2017[58]).

While these improvements are relevant, two particular features of the public transport governance structure in Israel are worthy of revision: the regulation of services by the central rather than the local level of government, and the central role of the private sector in the regulation of services. As said before, the regulation of public transport in Israel is led by the central government. This presents shortcomings as local level governments tend to better placed to address local particular transport needs (ITF, 2018[15]). Israel also developed a New Public Management approach, in which private consulting companies (chosen through tendering) perform a number of regulatory, planning and supervisory activities (Ida and Talit, 2017[58]). An important shortcoming of this arrangement is that as these activities are outsourced, the development of technical expertise within the government is limited.

The development of metropolitan transport authorities (MTAs) would be a good way of shifting towards local level regulation and planning, while building high level in-house technical expertise. As shown by their success in other countries, these authorities could also help Israel and the sector to advance in pending issues, which are key for transport to meet climate and other well-being goals, such as strategic level and integrated planning (ITF, 2018[15]). These entities are not only valuable in the case of large metropolis. Rather, they are a good framework for supporting a variety of other urban areas (e.g. small urban areas and regions where several small cities and rural areas form a single economic unit). In some countries (e.g. France) forming MTAs has been a requisite for municipalities to be able to leverage funding (e.g. the *Versement Transport* tax discussed in the previous section), with the aim of fostering coordinated decisions and investment.

Presently, metropolitan planning bodies exist in the case of large metropolitan areas in Israel. This is the case of the JTMT (Jerusalem Transportation Masterplan Team) in Jerusalem, which is a body supported by both MOT and the city of Jerusalem that is involved in all public transport planning activities. In Tel Aviv, *Ayalon Highways* is a planning governmental body that manages planning for most of the large infrastructure projects. Projects involving this type of entities are also coordinated with municipalities. In smaller cities and other areas, cooperation also exists but depends on the local authority's ability or willingness to promote public transport. While, the creation of these bodies shows an improvement in getting local governments involved in the provision of transport, these are far from being fully functional MTAs. The creation of such entities would ensure local entities have a prominent and balanced role in the decision-making process, while maintaining cohesion and coherence at metropolitan level (ITF, 2018[15]).

Box 4.2 describes the elements that are necessary for an institution to be qualified as a fully functional MTA.

Being the existence of dedicated and highly skilled staff one of the necessary elements for these institutions to be fully functional, MTAs can also be an important vehicle to build planning and regulatory capacity within the public sector in Israel. In addition international experience suggests that *assigning power and responsibilities to these institutions that go well beyond public transport* (e.g. to include active modes, road-safety, traffic and parking management) is an asset. This should be taken into account if the decision is to develop such entities. Finally, while being public these institutions need to be technical bodies, independent of the political cycle.

Box 4.2. Conditions for a functional Metropolitan Transport Authority

Based on international experience, the following elements are necessary for a metropolitan authority dedicated to transport to be qualified as a fully functional MTA:

- Formal authority with legal backing over a specified territory, with clearly defined responsibilities
- Dedicated funding and decision-making authority over use of the transport budget
- Dedicated and highly skilled staff
- Authority over strategic-level planning and responsibility for integrated land-use and transport planning
- Regulatory capacity
- Predominant role of sub-national authorities in the decision-making process (e.g. through predominant role in the governing board).

Source: (ITF, 2018[15]).

Given the centralised nature of Israel, the development of MTAs would need to be embedded in a process of decentralisation (also see precedent chapter), where responsibility over transport service delivery (among others), along with financial and decision capacity would progressively be transferred to local entities. As highlighted in Box 4.2, transfer of responsibilities needs to be accompanied by the transfer of funding and/or fiscal authority at local level. In this context, the new framework could be designed to allow MTAs to concentrate some of the new responsibilities and funds, avoiding excessive fragmentation of responsibilities and decision-making that could lead to a lack of coordination between local entities that are part of the same metropolitan area. MTAs can also facilitate coordination between central and local governments. All of this is relevant as already now (before a decentralisation process) the lack of coordination between different authorities has hampered transport projects, such as the reorganisation of the Tel Aviv bus network in 2009 (Oecd, 2018[59]). Different types of governance structures, i.e. voting and representation rules, can be chosen for MTAs, but as highlighted in Box 4.2, sub-national authorities need to have a predominant role in the decision making process.

Specific challenges that MTAs could address

Among the most important issues that MTAs could help improve are: strategic level and integrated planning, and regulation (including by improving data collection, analysis and management). The capacity of MTAs to build this planning and regulatory experience, is of course subject to the provision of adequate permanent technical staff, and thus having a budget that takes into account these costs (see Section 4.5.3 dedicated to enlarging financial capacity for transport investment).

Strategic level and integrated planning

International cases of successful MTAs like those in Barcelona, London and Paris have shown that these entities can play a crucial role in integrating spatial and transport planning and guiding both towards environmental and well-being outcomes.

In the three cases, the MTAs are the body in charge of developing the long-term plan for transport, which covers all transport modes and is explicitly linked to the corresponding spatial plan. The plans guide all investment decisions, as only projects that are in line with the plan are eligible for financing. Mobility Master Plans in all three cases are also developed integrating public consultation procedures and taking contributions from all actors sitting in the MTA governing body (which has representation from all local authorities in the area), making them an important tool to ensure coordination among stakeholders. In the case of Paris, the Plan de Déplacements Urbains (PDU) is part of a national framework (established in 1982) that makes these tools a requirement. The Grenelle laws influenced further requirements that Mobility Master Plans need to include, among these are precise targets related to mitigation of CO_2 emissions, which need to be aligned to national objectives.

In Israel, a large part of the population does not have access to public transport in peripheral areas. Carrying out strategic planning at metropolitan and regional levels (thus including small cities and rural areas that are part of the economic unit around a larger city) would allow to plan for connecting such areas, for instance by creating new bus services. A particular focus should be made for localities where Arab citizens make up the majority of the population, since they still suffer from a lower level of service than other localities, in spite of recent efforts from government to narrow the gap. An adequate design of the government structure of the MTAs should allow having representation from these areas and could foster dialogue between all localities, making enhancement of these areas (e.g. through improvement of existing road infrastructures, bus services) part of the mobility master plan for their corresponding region.

As Israel is implementing its housing plan, building projects in peripheral areas should however be carefully assessed and regulated in order to avoid locking-in people to car dependency. For instance, a certain level of access to and through public transport can be required for housing projects (see previous chapter) and an environmental impact assessment can be made mandatory. The development of on-demand collective transport services could also help to bridge public transport gaps where certain housing development are already poorly connected. Nonetheless, regulations need to allow the development of this type of services, while at the same time ensure they contribute to climate and other well-being goals.

MTAs in Israel could also lead the development of multi-modal transfer centres, as these need to be included in Mobility Master Plans. Multi-modal transfer centres have to be integrated in cities and peripheries in order to promote multi-modal mobility, since they have the potential to enhance resort to public transport. Ile-de-France Mobilités defines these as a place of interface between rail and other modes, including cars and active modes (cycling and pedestrian); taking ideally impaired mobility needs into account (ITF, 2018[15])If provided with the adequate technical capacity MTAs are well placed to develop the standards that can ensure the economic, environmental and social sustainability of these infrastructure (ITF, 2018[15]).

Transport regulation

As discussed above, reforms in the transport sector have helped enhanced services. Nonetheless, there is still a big margin for making further improvements. MTAs could strengthen regulation in the sector by exploring best practice to further improve contracts. Introducing quality incentive contracts with bonus and penalty payments (like those used in London and Barcelona) could be a good option, instead of the current system of fines. In addition, MTAs could widen monitoring capacity, which is still a challenge in Israel (Ida and Talit, 2017[58]).For instance, TfL in London, uses monitoring surveys, mystery travel surveys, and customer satisfaction surveys, in addition to the regular checks performed by independent contractors commissioned by the MTA. A separate survey is used for assessing operators´ driving skills, grading drivers according to measures such as speed, braking and road position. On top of this, regular contract compliance audits ensure that "on-bus" revenue is accurately accounted for and lost mileage reported correctly. TfL also has important data requirements for operators regarding accidents (ITF, 2018[15]).

More stringent environmental sustainability standards could also be progressively introduced into contracts. Launched in 2016, the Clean Car Revolution includes the subsidising of hybrid taxis by a total amounts of ILS 30 million and financial incentives to bus companies for the purchase of electric buses. Besides, the electric car ride-share programme provides support to local authorities for the establishment of car-sharing programmes. A more efficient, and cheaper way for the government to improve the environmental performance of the public transport fleet (more particularly buses and trains) would be to condition tenders for public transport concessions on environmental standards (green vehicles, construction work with limited climate and environmental impact, biodiversity preservation, etc.). Some additional incentives could also be maintained but their effectiveness should be carefully assessed.

Finally, regulatory frameworks have to be adapted to facilitate the adoption of a Mobility-as-a-service (Maas) approach. Especially with new modes of transport being developed (shared-bicycles, micro-mobility, on-demand collective services) through a growing number of start-ups (a sector that is particularly thriving in Israel), transport regulation needs to be regularly updated and adjusted. On the one hand, regulatory barriers need to be lifted, on the other regulation needs to ensure that new services are effectively bringing environmental and social benefits (rather than creating negative externalities). In this context progressively building and expanding regulatory capacity is particularly important. MTAs could be well positioned to improve data collection, analysis and management, facilitating the tailoring of better regulation and better planning. Transitioning to improved regulatory frameworks would nonetheless require changes at the national level (see below).

Developing a national policy for urban and metropolitan transport and setting the frame for progressive regulation

Even when engaging in a decentralisation process and developing MTAs, the central government would still have a relevant role in the successful delivery of public transport, which could be ensured by developing a national policy for urban and metropolitan mobility. The government could in this way guide local policy decision and investment towards climate and other well-being goals, standardise local planning tools to make sure they follows good practice, and bridge technical capacity gaps across cities. Three main elements of national urban and mobility policies that international practice has shown to be especially effective are the following: 1) developing specific sectoral objectives, targets and guidelines that can translate the general principle of developing sustainable and inclusive mobility into operational goals; 2) constructing planning frameworks that promote the development of urban mobility master plans (preferably making them compulsory and making MTAs responsible for them in the case these are created); and 3) advancing specific programmes that strengthen the capacity of urban authorities to fund projects through the assignment of national specialised funds (ideally making urban mobility master plans a requirement for eligibility) (OECD, 2016[60]).

The central government can also set the basis for flexible, yet active regulation that can unlock the potential of new emerging modes to contribute to mitigation and other well-being goals, and foster the adoption of MaaS. In this respect, the central government can build on international experience such as that of Finland, where the New Act of Transport Services has allowed removing barriers that impeded the development of more flexible services (more tailored to the populations needs). At the same time the new legislation introduced relevant open data requirements from all transport providers, which can allow regulators to better monitor activity, take action when and where negative externalities arise and facilitate the expansion of benefits (ITF, 2018[15]).

References

Bank of Israel (2019), *Press Releases - Supply of bus services to Arab localities*, https://www.boi.org.il/en/NewsAndPublications/PressReleases/Pages/New-research-Supply-of-bus-services-to-Arab-localities.aspx (accessed on 13 November 2019). [49]

Bleikh, H. (2018), *Back and Forth Commuting for Work in Israel*, http://www.taubcenter.org.il (accessed on 12 November 2019). [6]

Börjesson, M. and I. Kristoffersson (2017), *The Swedish Congestion Charges: Ten Years On- And effects of increasing charging levels*, http://www.cts.kth.se (accessed on 15 November 2019). [42]

Casullo, L. et al. (2019), *Assessing incentives to reduce traffic congestion in Israel*. [39]

Cornago, E., A. Dimitropoulos and W. Oueslati (2019), "Evaluating the Impact of Urban Road Pricing on the Use of Green Transport Modes: The Case of Milan", *OECD Environment Working Papers*, No. 143, OECD Publishing, Paris, https://dx.doi.org/10.1787/ddaa6b25-en. [37]

Crozet, Y. and A. Mercier (2018), "Urban Toll: Rethinking Acceptability through Accessibility", *International Transport Forum Discussion Papers*, http://www.itf-oecd.org (accessed on 13 March 2020). [26]

D'haultfoeuille, X., P. Givord and X. Boutin (2013), *The Environmental Effect of Green Taxation: The Case of the French "Bonus/Malus"*. [19]

EcoTraders (2019), *The Electricity Sector: Main policies, barriers and opportunities*. [21]

EcoTraders (2019), *The Tranport Sector - Main policies, barriers and opportunities*. [36]

Eliasson, J. (2014), *The Stockholm congestion charges: an overview*, http://www.cts.kth.se (accessed on 14 November 2019). [41]

ELTIS (2014), "Complete overhaul of Lisbon's parking policy (Portugal)". [32]

Environment and Health Fund and Ministry of Health (2017), *Environmental Health in Israel | 2017*. [7]

European Commission (2019), *Handbook on the external costs of transport*, http://dx.doi.org/10.2832/27212. [10]

European Investment Bank (2011), *Study on PPP Legal & Financial Frameworks in the Mediterranean Partner Countries*. [57]

Fulton, L. et al. (2017), *TRANSPORTATION Three Revolutions in Urban*, https://itdpdotorg.wpengine.com/wp-content/uploads/2017/04/UCD-ITDP-3R-Report-FINAL.pdf (accessed on 30 June 2019). [23]

Gal, J., S. Madhala and H. Bleikh (2017), *Social Service Budgeting in Local Authorities A chapter from The State of the Nation*, http://www.taubcenter.org.il (accessed on 14 November 2019). [50]

Goetz, M. (2017), *Policy Brief Electric Vehicle Charging Considerations for Shared, Automated Fleets Introduction and Background*. [22]

Graf, S. and M. Cecchini (2017), "Diet, physical activity and sedentary behaviours: Analysis of trends, inequalities and clustering in selected oecd countries", *OECD Health Working Papers*, No. 100, OECD Publishing, Paris, http://dx.doi.org/10.1787/54464f80-en. [52]

Hymel, K., K. Small and K. Dender (2010), "Induced demand and rebound effects in road transport", *Transportation Research Part B: Methodological*, Vol. 44/10, pp. 1220-1241, http://dx.doi.org/10.1016/j.trb.2010.02.007. [40]

Ida, Y. and G. Talit (2017), "Reforms in the regulation of public bus service in Israel", *Case Studies on Transport Policy*, Vol. 5/1, pp. 80-86, http://dx.doi.org/10.1016/j.cstp.2016.12.002. [58]

IEA (2019), *Tracking Clean Energy Progress*, https://www.iea.org/tcep/ (accessed on 4 November 2019). [18]

IMF (2018), *Israel : Selected Issues (country report No. 18/112)*, https://www.imf.org/en/Publications/CR/Issues/2018/05/01/Israel-Selected-Issues-45828 (accessed on 5 November 2019). [38]

International Energy Agency, I. (2019), *Energy, Prices and Taxes - 1Q2019*, http://www.iea.org/t&c/ (accessed on 21 October 2019). [13]

Israeli Tax Authority et al. (2008), *Green Tax Report-Report of the inter-ministerial commission for Green Taxation.* [8]

ITDP (2016), *Street Design and Management Policy.* [27]

ITF (2019), "Improving Transport Planning and Investment Through the Use of Accessibility", *International Transport Forum Policy Papers*, Vol. 66. [54]

ITF (2019), *The Social Impacts of Road Pricing Summary and Conclusions*, http://www.itf-oecd.org (accessed on 19 August 2019). [43]

ITF (2018), *Policy Directions for Establishing a Metropolitan Transport Authority for Korea's Capital Region*, http://www.itf-oecd.org (accessed on 15 November 2019). [15]

ITF (2016), *Economic Benefits of Improving Transport Accessibility Roundtable Report Airport Demand Forecasting for Long-Term Planning Economic Benefits of Improving Transport Accessibility.* [55]

ITF (2013), *Cycling, Health and Safety*, ITF Research Reports, OECD Publishing, Paris, https://dx.doi.org/10.1787/9789282105955-en. [53]

ITF-OECD (2019), "Improving Transport Planning and Investment Through the Use of Accessibility Indicators", http://www.itf-oecd.org (accessed on 23 January 2020). [51]

ITF-OECD (2018), *The Social Impacts of Road Pricing Summary and Conclusions*, http://www.itf-oecd.org (accessed on 3 July 2019). [45]

ITF-OECD (2017), *Income Inequality, Social Inclusion and Mobility Roundtable Report 2017 - Income Inequality, Social Inclusion and Mobility.* [56]

ITF-OECD (2017), "Strategies for mitigating air pollution in Mexico City". [16]

Kodransky, M. and G. Hermann (2011), *Europe's Parking U-Turn: From Accommodation to Regulation.* [33]

Lisboa, C. (2018), “Sítio da Câmara Municipal de Lisboa: Estacionamento”. [31]

Litman, T. (2019), *Evaluating Accessibility for Transport Planning- Measuring People’s Ability to Reach Desired Goods and Activities*, http://www.vtpi.orgInfo@vtpi.org (accessed on 17 October 2019). [2]

Litman, T. (2018), *Evaluating Accessibility for Transport Planning Evaluating Accessibility for Transportation Planning.*. [30]

Litman, T. (2015), *Evaluating Complete Streets The Value of Designing Roads For Diverse Modes, Users and Activities Evaluating Complete Streets: The Value of Designing Roads For Diverse Modes, Users and Activities Evaluating Complete Streets: The Value of Designing Roads For Diverse Modes, Users and Activities*, http://www.vtpi.orgInfo@vtpi.org (accessed on 19 August 2019). [28]

Lockard, J. et al. (2018), *Sustainable and Safe- A Vision and Guidance for Zero Road Deaths*. [29]

Marten, M. and K. van Dender (2019), “The use of revenues from carbon pricing”, *OECD Taxation Working Papers*, No. 43, OECD Publishing, Paris, https://dx.doi.org/10.1787/3cb265e4-en. [47]

Mattioli, G. et al. (2017), *Developing an index of vulnerability to motor fuel price increases in England.* [46]

OECD (2019), *Accelerating Climate Action: Refocusing Policies through a Well-being Lens*, OECD Publishing, Paris, https://dx.doi.org/10.1787/2f4c8c9a-en. [1]

OECD (2019), *Taxing Energy Use 2019: Using Taxes for Climate Action*, OECD Publishing, Paris, https://dx.doi.org/10.1787/058ca239-en. [11]

OECD (2018), *OECD Companion to the Inventory of Support Measures for Fossil Fuels 2018 - en - OECD*, https://www.oecd.org/tax/oecd-companion-to-the-inventory-of-support-measures-for-fossil-fuels-2018-9789264286061-en.htm (accessed on 16 July 2018). [14]

OECD (2016), *Car Purchase Tax: Green Tax Refrom in Israel.* [4]

OECD (2016), *Multi-dimensional Review of Peru: Volume 2. In-depth Analysis and Recommendations*, OECD Development Pathways, OECD Publishing, Paris, https://dx.doi.org/10.1787/9789264264670-en. [60]

OECD (2015), *Environment at a Glance 2015: OECD Indicators*, OECD Publishing, Paris, https://dx.doi.org/10.1787/9789264235199-en. [35]

Oecd (2018), *OECD Economic Surveys: Israel 2018.* [59]

OECD/ITF (2019), *Assessing incentives to reduce congestion in Israel*, OECD. [44]

Paul-Dubois-Taine, O. (2013), “Rapport du groupe de travail présidé par Pour une politique du stationnement au service des usagers”. [34]

Ryan, L. et al. (2018), “An Assessment of the Social Costs and Benefits of Vehicle Tax Reform in Ireland”, *OECD.* [17]

Suhoy, T. and Y. Sofer (2019), *Getting to Work in Israel: Locality and Individual effects*, http://www.boi.org.il (accessed on 8 November 2019). [3]

Tamir, O. et al. (2015), *Assessment Of Greenhouse Gas Emission Reduction Potential And Recommended National Target For Israel*. [5]

Timmers, V. and P. Achten (2016), "Non-exhaust PM emissions from electric vehicles", *Atmospheric Environment*, Vol. 134, pp. 10-17, http://dx.doi.org/10.1016/j.atmosenv.2016.03.017. [20]

Trajtenberg, M. et al. (2018), "Undoing the "Gordian Knot": a transportation roadmap for the short run", https://www.neaman.org.il/EN/Undoing-the-Gordian-Knot-a-transportation-roadmap-for-the-short-run (accessed on 16 October 2019). [9]

Transport for London (2004), *Congestion charging Central London Impacts monitoring Second Annual Report*. [48]

van Dender, K. (2019), "Taxing vehicles, fuels, and road use: Opportunities for improving transport tax practice", *OECD Taxation Working Papers*, No. 44, OECD Publishing, Paris, https://dx.doi.org/10.1787/e7f1d771-en. [24]

van Essen, H. et al. (2019), "Handbook on the external costs of transport", *EUROPEAN COMMISSION*, http://dx.doi.org/10.2832/27212. [25]

Vermeulen, R. (2019), *Emissions testing of a Euro VI LNG-diesel dual fuel truck in the Netherlands*. [12]

Notes

[1] Source: OECD.stat.

[2] The BAU scenario includes a steady growth of the car fleet (+2.38 % per year for passenger cars, with an annual population growth of 1.8%), the plan would consist in a small increase of car mileage in 2030 relative to 2016 (44.4 million vehicle-km against 43.9 million vehicle-km in 2016).

[3] More precisely, for around 60 percent of employees, the number of job localities accessible by public transportation is less than half than those accessible via private vehicle.

[4] Source : OECD.stat.

[5] As a comparison, in 2015, as Israel was ranked 22nd in terms of GDP per capita, it was 35th among OECD countries as regard to car ownership.

[6] In comparison, the average number in OECD countries increased by 4.7% in this same period.

[7] The use of cars in Israel amounts to 17,700vehicle-km per vehicle in 2015 according to OECD statistics. It is the second highest number after the United States, compared to an average of 9.4 million vehicle-km in other countries.

[8] Source: OECD.stat.

[9] In contrast, this number amounts to around 1% in the European Union.

[10] Taking a 1 ILS= 0.22541 EUR.

[11] Ministry of Environment Protection, 2019.

[12]https://consultations.tfl.gov.uk/environment/ultra-low-emission-zone/user_uploads/ulez-iia-report_final.pdf

[13] Source: Statistical Yearbook of Jerusalem, Chapter II.

[14] Source: Jerusalem Statistical Yearbook of Jerusalem.

[15] Source: EcoTraders, 2019.

[16] Even though the number of imported vehicles increased by 7.6% between 2008 and 2012 (before the formula update), total revenues dropped by 13% (OECD, 2016[4]).

[17] As a reminder, the average car purchase tax amounted to 60.6% in 2014, for all private vehicles.

[18]https://www.timesofisrael.com/we-have-sinned-against-israels-land-water-and-air-yom-kippur-food-for-thought/?utm_source=The+Daily+Edition&utm_campaign=daily-edition-2019-10-08&utm_medium=email

[19] ILO data.

[20] This scenario does not exactly match the one estimated in 2015 by the Ministry of Environmental Protection, who chose to keep the measures which social benefits exceeded costs, and notably excluded the deployment of electric vehicles on this ground. As the purpose of our estimation is to assess the effect of different fleet compositions and since the costs of measures may have evolved since 2015, the mitigation scenario here includes all potential mitigation measures, whatever their cost.

[21] This hypothesis stands on the fact that the increase of car ownership considered in the BAU scenario (+2.38% per year) is already very low, relatively to observed data in recent area (around +5% per year).

[22] As a comparison, population density amounts to 410 people per km square in Israel and to 35.8 people per km square in the United States.

[23] With an average of cost of ILS 5.7 for GBP 1 in 2010, this would account for ILS 0.057 to ILS 3.94 per vehicle km in 2010.

[24] Source: Transport Analysis Guidance (TAG) Data Book, November 2018.

[25] This household survey accounts for yearly income and therefore does not consider inter-annual variation of income nor household's wealth.

[26] Earmarked spendings have many disadvantages as they constraint in the long-term the available income and do not reflect exactly the need for funding.

[27] Source: Statistical Yearbook for Israel, 2018, Number 169.

[28] Defined as the percent of population that can arrive with transit to the destination within 45 and 60 minutes from each metropolitan ring. The compounded average for all rings was set as 60%.

[29] Provide access to safe, affordable, accessible and sustainable transport systems for all, improving road safety, notably by expanding public transport, with special attention to the needs of those in vulnerable situations, women, children, persons with disabilities and older persons.

[30] Source : World Factbook, CIA.

[31] Source : Israel Census 2016.

[32] Source : https://mof.gov.il/en/InternationalAffairs/InfrastructuresAndProjects

Annex A. Public investment in Israel

Israel suffers from a sizeable infrastructure deficit, stemming from chronic underinvestment that has been lingering for more than two decades (the orange line in FigureA A.1) (OECD, 2018[1]). Public investment in Israel only amounted to about 2% of GDP in 2016 while the OECD average tends to be around 3.5% to 4% (the blue line in FigureA A.1) (OECD, 2018[1]). As noted in the OECD's Economic Survey of Israel (2018[1]), "Spending on public infrastructure, which recovered after 2007, was then cut again between 2013 and 2015 to bring the public deficit back under control." Israel's vulnerability and ability to adapt to climate change, as well as its mitigation capacity, depend on its choices about the nature and location of infrastructure today FigureA A.1. Achieving a low-emission, climate-resilient development pathway requires a radical shift in Israel's energy, transport and buildings infrastructure (addressed in the main chapters of this document). Israel's underinvestment in infrastructure could have long lasting effects on Israel's emissions profile in the future potentially jeopardising its ability to reach net-zero by 2050.

FigureA A.1. Public investment in terms of % of GDP[1]

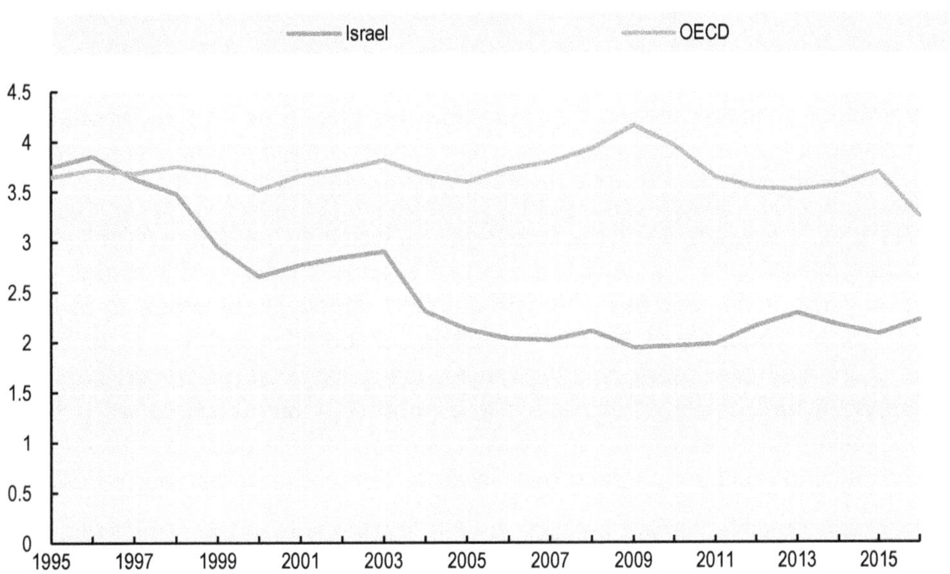

Note: [1]Excluding capital transfers to state-owned enterprises for infrastructure development, which have been significant in Israel.
Source: (OECD, 2018[1]) (From: UN Department of Economic and Social Affairs, Population Division (2017). World Population Prospects: The 2017 Revision; OECD, Economic Outlook Database).

StatLink https://doi.org/10.1787/888934156276

In particular, the lack of investment in public transport infrastructure forces Israelis to rely heavily on the use of private vehicles. This, together with robust demographic growth, leads to ever-increasing emissions, pollution and congestion, amongst others. Israel's road congestion is far higher than the OECD average (OECD, 2018[1]). Despite a relatively low vehicle ownership, Israel presents high mileage per vehicle, and thus, dense road traffic and congestion. In 2014, road traffic in Israel was 2730 vehicles per 1000 km, with 1998 passenger vehicles per 1000 km. In the same year, the OECD average was 774 and 576 total and passenger vehicles per 1000 km respectively (OECD, 2018[1]). Road congestion is very costly, equalling approximately 2% of GDP, far above the level observed in other developed countries (around 1% in the EU and the United States) (Casullo et al., 2019[2]). These costs include the cost of extra gasoline lost in traffic jams and the value of time lost due to congestion. In addition to air pollution from PM, which is responsible for the deaths of more than 2,000 people on Israel per year, according to the Global Burden of Disease database, and the number of people exposed to this pollution have been increasing (Environment and Health Fund and Ministry of Health, 2017[3]). Finally, transport infrastructure is poorly integrated with housing developments, catalysing urban sprawl (OECD, 2017[4]) and thus contributing to car dependency and congestion (see Chapter 4).

Large natural gas reserves means Israel is investing in switching from coal to natural gas. Public spending on natural gas amounted to approximately NIS 500 million, equivalent to 0.04% of GDP in 2017 (OECD, 2018[5]). Such investments lock in emission-intensive infrastructure. The major part of this producer support is due to a long-term gas agreement at guaranteed prices between the Israel Electric Company and investors in the Tamar gas field (see chapter 2).

Constrained local budgets restrict municipalities' ability to develop any kind of infrastructure, whether it is housing, transport, or electricity. The largest share of municipalities' budgets in Israel comes from property taxes, typically about 46% (S&P Global Rating, 2019[6]). Israel uses the "arnona" system, instead of taxing the value of the land or property; municipalities tax the *use of buildings* since 93% of the land is state-owned. State-owned land, however, is primarily rural, while urban cores tend to be privately owned. Tax rates change between municipalities, but the national government restricts the upper bound of taxes on the use of residential properties. This promotes the development of commercial properties (rather than residential ones), since this is more profitable for local authorities. Municipalities are chronically in debt, in absolute terms, even though, there is a decreasing debt burden as a percentage of municipalities' operating revenues (from 40% in 2006 to 25% forecasted in 2019) (S&P Global Rating, 2019[6]). This precarious but perpetual condition means that municipalities often rely on the national government for investment in infrastructure. As it is often the case, centralisation makes it difficult to tailor investment to local conditions and needs, and often leads to inefficient infrastructure.

For example, in Netanya (a city located on the coast), the municipality needed upfront financing to develop housing infrastructure (OECD, 2017[4]). Land in the city core tends to be privately owned, and the city lacks the funds to adapt sewage, water, and basic infrastructures to densify these areas. In contrast, developing state-owned land – in the periphery of the city – enables collaboration with the national government for large-scale projects, for example, developments with a capacity of 5000 residential dwellings. The Israeli Land Authority provided funding for infrastructure and public facilities for Netanya (OECD, 2017[4]). In Netanya, these incentives have resulted in an urban core rampant with plots of undeveloped private land in the centre of the city and rapid peripheral growth in areas that are underserved (OECD, 2017[4]).

Israel needs strong and credible climate policies to shift investments in the right direction. In the short-term, the Israel government can correct price signals across the economy to reflect the true social costs of emissions, pollution and congestion. This can be done by using taxation and other pricing mechanisms (see recommendations of chapters 2, 3 and 4). Moreover, Israel needs to ensure that public funds are invested in sustainable infrastructure, to avoid locking in emissions until the end of the century. This can also help to mobilise private investment towards low (and preferably zero or positive) emissions infrastructure.

Annex. Green Finance for low-emissions development: some key issues

Staying well-below 2°C entails new low-carbon infrastructure projects and important retrofitting measures, which need substantial investment. Even though there are different estimates of the exact amount of global investment needed, all point to a magnitude that is within the trillions. According to the OECD, the needs for investment in infrastructure globally amounts to USD 6.9 trillion per year, until 2030 at least, to be compatible with climate objectives, and a probability of keeping temperatures under 2°C to 66% (OECD, 2017[7]) Public funds on their own will be insufficient because of the constraint put on government budgets, even including public finance (e.g., institutional investors on public pensions funds) will fall short of reaching the goal of 6.9 trillion annually (OECD, 2017[7]). Therefore, mobilising private finance is critical to create the low-carbon resilient infrastructure of the future, in addition to retrofitting or even decommissioning of existing infrastructure to be compatible with mitigation. Governments can mobilise investment in low-emissions infrastructure by fostering: (1) an enabling policy environment to catalyse investment – such as strong and credible climate policies that signal long-term policy stability to investors as discussed in the previous chapters and discussed further in *Investing in Climate, Investing in Growth* (OECD, 2017[7]); (2) Strategic use of public finance to mobilise private finance for sustainable infrastructure; (3) co-ordinated cross-government development of pipelines of bankable projects; and (4) the development of green taxonomies and instruments to ensure that private investors can find the right combination of risk-return profiles in sustainable projects. The following paragraphs briefly address issues 2-4 in the Israeli context. Further detail of specific green finance issues are dealt with in the appropriate sectoral chapters.

Strategic use of public finance to mitigate risks and enable transactions

Public actors in Israel can use a variety of instruments to mobilise institutional investment in sustainable infrastructure. Institutional investors manage up to USD 54 trillion of assets (e.g., pension funds as well as insurance companies) in the OECD countries alone (Röttgers, Tandon and Kaminker, 2018[8]). A recent analysis presents findings from an updated database of institutional investments on 152 projects in G20 countries between 2010 and 2018. This work identifies a variety of ways public finance can mitigate risks using public finance, or enabling transactions without assuming liability on public funds (Röttgers, Tandon and Kaminker, 2018[8]). Risk mitigants are instruments that direct use of public funds in a project or backing of a project with public funds. Options include, for example, co-investment when a public actor (national and subnational governments, MDBs, DBs, etc.) invests alongside private, or cornerstone stake, which is when there is investment by a public actor in a fund or project to reach a majority of equity stake, in order to attract private investors, amongst others (Röttgers, Tandon and Kaminker, 2018[8]). Israel could use other instruments, as transaction enablers, that would not require using public funds, but facilitate investment. For example, warehousing and pooling is when smaller projects are bundled together to achieve commercial scale that is attractive and viable for institutional investors (Röttgers, Tandon and Kaminker, 2018[8]).The *OECD Progress Update on Approaches to Mobilising Institutional Investment for Sustainable Infrastructure* provides a typology of de-risking instruments and techniques available to public actors to crowd-in private capital including institutional investment for infrastructure (Röttgers, Tandon and Kaminker, 2018[8]).

One option moving forward could include introducing or strengthening a green finance mandate of existing national development banks or even establishing a dedicated public financial institution like a green investment bank. Green investment banks are the critical actor missing from the landscape of financial institutions; they facilitate development by educating consumers, centralising administration for originators and lenders, and connecting capital supply to financer demand. These banks are capitalised from a diverse mix of public and private funds, and can reduce risk to private investors. A number of such institutions already exist in other jurisdictions- Clean Energy Finance Corporation (Australia), Connecticut Green Bank (USA), Green Finance Organisation (Japan), Green Investment Group (UK), NRDC Green Bank Development in India, Mexico and Chile; Coalition for Green Capital (South Africa, Colombia, Rwanda, Indonesia and the USA).

Pipelines of bankable projects to signal where private actors should invest

The gap between the need for sustainable infrastructure and current investment – the 6.9 trillion needed each year globally until 2030 - is not due to a shortage of capital available in financial markets. The problem can be partly be explained by a lack of bankable projects (OECD, 2018[9]). Countries often lack detailed infrastructure investment plans, therefore, it is unclear where project investments are needed, when they should be built, how to finance them, or if they are sufficient to meet long-term objectives. Essentially, inhibiting the flow of sustainable infrastructure investment (OECD, 2018[9]).

In contrast, well-defined infrastructure planning can facilitate investment flows; Israel should consider developing robust infrastructure project pipelines. Investors can then identify and source investment opportunities that match their needs from the available options (OECD, 2018[9]). This will scale up investment in "suitable" projects across sectors; accommodate the requirements of investors; and allocate preparatory support to certain projects (OECD, 2018[9]). This could help Israel achieve its mitigation objectives while investing in projects that are not yet bankable. The report, *Developing Project Pipelines for Low-carbon Infrastructure*, provides best practices on how to do this (OECD, 2018[9]).

Carrying out strategic and integrated long-term planning is identified as an important need in this report. As discussed (chapters 3 and 4), generating a strong planning framework that aligns actions from different levels of government with climate and wider well-being goals will be crucial. The development of master plans, which include pipelines of projects that need to be prioritised for different territories to contribute to national goals are key to constructing this framework. Israel could consider engaging in a decentralisation process that can shift responsibilities and funds to the local level (which is generally better positioned to respond to local needs). In this case, local institutions e.g. metropolitan bodies could be assigned the development of such master plans. The central government could guide and support this by: a) making master plans compulsory; b) developing guidelines for ensuring best practice (including for analysis underlying the development of pipelines as part of these planning tools); and c) creating incentives through national programmes that can provide additional funds for the development of infrastructure projects, but which are only granted when master plans are developed and for projects that are part of the pipeline included.

Sustainable finance taxonomies and instruments

There are efforts worldwide that grapple with how to determine whether investments are in line or not with the Paris Agreement and broader environmental and sustainability goals. Making finance flows consistent with climate targets, as called for in Article 2.1c of the 2015 Paris Climate Agreement (UNFCCC, 2015[10]), means shifting investments and finance away from activities that undermine these objectives. A number of frameworks are being developed to ensure investments are consistent with low-emissions development pathways – perhaps, the most highly anticipated is the EU Sustainable Finance Taxonomy, recently adopted by the European Council[1], which not only assesses an activities to climate objectives but also whether or not it causes significant harm to other environmental objectives. Israel could consider building on these frameworks to classify its own investments.

The EU taxonomy for sustainable activities is a framework to identify which economic activities – not financial products - are sustainable, and therefore, qualify for a future voluntary EC Ecolabel (Finance, 2019[11]). After implementation of the taxonomy, every financial product subject to the NRFD[2] regulation and marketed in the EU will need to make reference to it. The current draft EU taxonomy[3] provides criteria for defining activities that are beneficial but not for defining those that are detrimental to climate objectives or that may play a role in the interim. The EU Taxonomy evaluates six environmental areas – mitigation, adaptation, water, circular economy, pollution and ecosystems. In order to be classified as environmentally sustainable, an activity must demonstrate that it makes a substantial contribution to one of the six environmental areas, while it does *no significant harm to the other five.* So far, the draft taxonomy covers agriculture and forestry; manufacturing; electricity, gas, steam and air conditioning supply; water, sewage, waste and remediation; transport; information and communication technologies; and buildings, classified by NAEC codes for industrial activities. The criteria developed to date only cover certain production processes. Activities and products that are not covered by the EU taxonomy will be ineligible as taxonomy compliant, regardless of level of emission intensity.

There is a proliferation of other sustainable finance taxonomies that Israel could also draw on. The Climate Bonds Initiative aims at classifying green bonds. Other taxonomies evaluate whether the multilateral development banks are sustainable and offer a climate finance tracking methodology. Other countries have created national level methodologies – China Green Taxonomy, Japan Green Bonds definition, France Label GreenFin, others.

Climate risks and financial stability

The then Governor of the Bank of England, Mark Carney, highlighted three major financial risks stemming from climate change: physical risks from climate impacts, transition risks from the potential for stranded assets during the transition to low-emissions economy, and the liability risks facing those responsible for activities contributing to climate change. Since the publication of the recommendations of The Task Force on Climate Related Financial Disclosures (2017), 50 central banks and regulators have joined (42 members and 8 observers), the Network for Greening the Financial System (NGFS). The Bank of Israel is not part of it as of yet. In early 2019, the NGFS made a call to action: to integrate climate-related risks into financial stability monitoring and micro-supervision, taking into account sustainability factors to their own portfolio management.[4] An increasing number of Central Banks have been approaching the subject of climate change for the last few years. For example, Netherland's Central Bank (De Nederlandsche Bank) is stress testing the financial system to energy transition risks, while the Bank of England is starting to stress test climate resilience (De Nederlandsche Bank, 2018[12]). The new head of the European Central Bank, Christine Lagarde, stated that European Central Bank will start including climate change into the Bank's economic forecasts, and argues that rating agencies, such as Moody's, should start to consider climate change when evaluating credit.[5]

References

Casullo, L. et al. (2019), *Assessing incentives to reduce traffic congestion in Israel.* [2]

De Nederlandsche Bank (2018), *An energy transition risk stress test for the financial system of the Netherlands*, De Nederlandsche Bank, https://www.dnb.nl/binaries/OS_Transition%20risk%20stress%20test%20versie_web_tcm46-379397.pdf. [12]

Environment and Health Fund and Ministry of Health (2017), *Environmental Health in Israel | 2017.* [3]

Finance, T. (2019), *EU taxonomy technical report by the TEG.* [11]

OECD (2018), *Developing Robust Project Pipelines for Low-Carbon Infrastructure*, Green Finance and Investment, OECD Publishing, Paris, https://dx.doi.org/10.1787/9789264307827-en. [9]

OECD (2018), *OECD Companion to the Inventory of Support Measures for Fossil Fuels 2018*, OECD Publishing, Paris, https://dx.doi.org/10.1787/9789264286061-en. [5]

OECD (2018), *OECD Economic Surveys: Israel 2018*, OECD Publishing, Paris, https://dx.doi.org/10.1787/eco_surveys-isr-2018-en. [1]

OECD (2017), *Investing in Climate, Investing in Growth*, OECD Publishing, http://www.oecd-ilibrary.org/docserver/download/9717061e.pdf?expires=1511263658&id=id&accname=guest&checksum=1A7E03B32D7079B807ECEF0BCAC610E9 (accessed on 21 November 2017). [7]

OECD (2017), *Spatial Planning and Policy in Israel: The Cases of Netanya and Umm al-Fahm*, OECD Publishing, Paris, https://dx.doi.org/10.1787/9789264277366-en. [4]

Röttgers, D., A. Tandon and C. Kaminker (2018), "OECD Progress Update on Approaches to Mobilising Institutional Investment for Sustainable Infrastructure", *OECD Environment Working Papers*, No. 138, OECD Publishing, Paris, https://dx.doi.org/10.1787/45426991-en. [8]

S&P Global Rating (2019), *Public System Finance Review: Israeli Municipalities*, S&P Ratings Direct, https://www.maalot.co.il/Publications/SR20190123152558.pdf. [6]

UNFCCC (2015), *The Paris Agreement*, https://unfccc.int/process-and-meetings/the-paris-agreement/the-paris-agreement (accessed on 8 June 2018). [10]

Notes

[1] https://www.consilium.europa.eu/en/press/press-releases/2020/04/15/sustainable-finance-council-adopts-a-unified-eu-classification-system/

[2] The Non-financial reporting directive of the EU, that requires large public-interest companies with more than 500 employees to disclose certain information on how they operate and manage social and environmental challenges.

[3] On the data of the 18th December 2019.

[4] https://www.ecb.europa.eu/press/key/date/2019/html/ecb.sp191121_1~af63c4de7d.en.html

[5] https://www.theguardian.com/world/2019/dec/02/christine-lagarde-ecb-should-do-more-to-tackle-climate-emergency

www.ingramcontent.com/pod-product-compliance
Ingram Content Group UK Ltd.
Pitfield, Milton Keynes, MK11 3LW, UK
UKHW051504290926
15471UKWH00008B/1417

9 789264 682511